strangers to the city

Urban Man in Jos, Nigeria

LEONARD PLOTNICOV

Strangers to the City

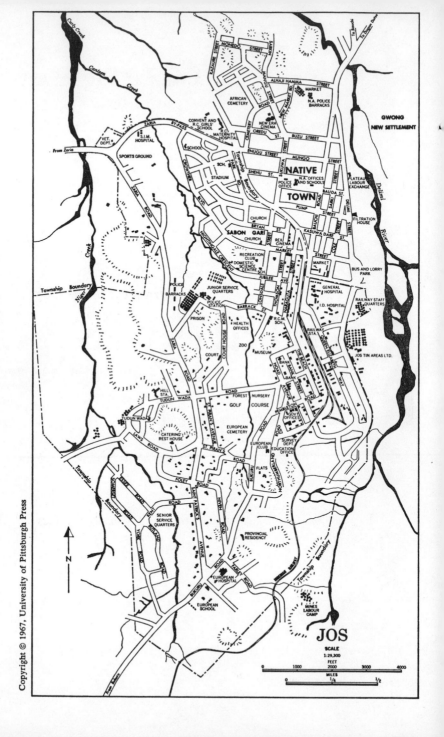

JOS

SCALE
1:29,300

FEET
0   1000   2000   3000   4000

MILES
0   1/4   1/2

N

Leonard Plotnicov

Strangers to the City

Urban Man in Jos, Nigeria

University of Pittsburgh Press

Library of Congress Card Catalog Number: 67-13928

ISBN 0-8229-5135-5

Copyright © 1967, *University of Pittsburgh Press*

Manufactured in the United States of America

Second printing, 1969

Third printing, 1971

TO

Isaac Olu Oyewumi
Isaac Cookey-Jaja
Gande Ikowe
Peter Adam Ekong
Musa Ibrahim Dan Zaria
David Aba Kagoro
David Njoku
Pam Choji Kwol

ACKNOWLEDGMENTS

In this, my first book, I take the opportunity to express thanks to the many fine teachers who helped shape my understanding of anthropology. Among those who made a particular impression on me, Edward Norbeck stressed the virtues of critical questioning and lucid communication, and Lloyd Fallers tried to impart to his students a penetrating appreciation of the domain and multiple dimensions of anthropology. Walter Dyk first introduced me to the "study of man," a discipline that he felt should not neglect the significance of concrete men. I would be pleased to believe that these influences are present in my work.

The present investigation was carried out from November 1960 to August 1962 on a pre-doctoral research fellowship from the National Institutes of Health, United States Public Health Service, for which thanks for financial support is gratefully extended. I am also grateful to Professors William Bascom and Robert Murphy, whose advice and encouragement throughout the research and initial writing of this study have played no small part in whatever success may have been achieved. Lack of space precludes mentioning by name all the persons to whom I feel obliged and am thankful for their aid; however, for their meticulous care in the editing and preparation of the manuscript I must acknowledge my appreciation to Mr. Frederick Hetzel and Miss Bonnie Harrington. And for his excellent drawing of the maps of Jos and Nigeria, I wish to mention Mr. Howard Ziegler, a cartographer with the Department of Geography, University of Pittsburgh.

Two of the illustrations—the interior yard of a Native Town dwelling and the apprentice motor mechanics—were first reproduced in *Trans-Action* magazine (published by the Community Leadership Project at Washington University, St. Louis, Missouri), which kindly gave permission to use them here.

In Jos, Nigeria, Miss Audrey Smedley helped me settle into the community and provided useful advice during the course of research. Members of various government departments in Nigeria were most hospitable, and many of them went generously beyond the call of official duty in their courteous cooperation. To these persons, and to the government they represent, I am particularly grateful for assistance and for the free use of research facilities. Especial indebtedness is extended to Professor K. Onwuka Dike and his Senior Archivist, Mr. S. S. Waniko, of the Nigerian National Archives, and to Messrs. B. E. B. Fagg and Hamo Sassoon, of the Department of Antiquities, Jos. I also wish to thank the administrative authorities and staff of Plateau Province, Jos Division, and the Jos Native Administration and Local Authority for access to files, records, and books. The Local Council, Nigerian Chamber of Mines, Jos, allowed me to see and use valuable historical material pertaining to Jos.

To the Nigerians and non-Nigerians of Jos who befriended me I have many reasons to be deeply grateful. They gave encouragement, insights, and the nurturance one sometimes needs when alone in unfamiliar places. My interpreters, particularly Tani Olu and Julius Bell, were more than my ears and tongue. The aid of my principal assistant, Evarist Obi, far exceeded the demands of formal employment. I sincerely thank them as I do my informants, without whom this study would not have been possible. Most of my informants were also friends and teachers, patient and willing to help in every possible way. Some of them gave more than I can ever hope to repay—a complete trust in a stranger. They are the study and to them it is dedicated; I pray that I have in no way done them any injustice. For all errors of fact and interpretation I alone am responsible.

The names used for the informants are fictitious; any resemblance to names of actual persons is coincidental.

CONTENTS

ILLUSTRATIONS

Following page 80

Men of a Yoruba tribal union, meeting on a Sunday afternoon in the Jos Recreation Club.

Tennis at the Jos Recreation Club.

Ibo tribal sections at the celebration of the Ibo State Union during the Ibo National Day in Jos Stadium.

A carpenter, his apprentices, and some of his wares.

Workers constructing a wood body for a new lorry chassis.

Apprentice motor mechanics.

A Tiv naming ceremony.

The baptism of new members of the Assemblies of God Mission Church.

The interior yard of one of the poorer Native Town dwellings.

A mother and baby sunning themselves in the doorway of their home, a typical dwelling for a laborer's family.

A woman of one of the indigenous Plateau tribes, refreshing herself with a calabash of native beer after a day in the market.

A traditional settlement of one of the Plateau tribes, several miles west of Jos.

Modern elite women of various southern tribes at a Christmas party.

Young masqueraders (Yoruba and Ibo) at Christmastime.

MAPS

xi

TABLES AND CHARTS

Strangers to the City

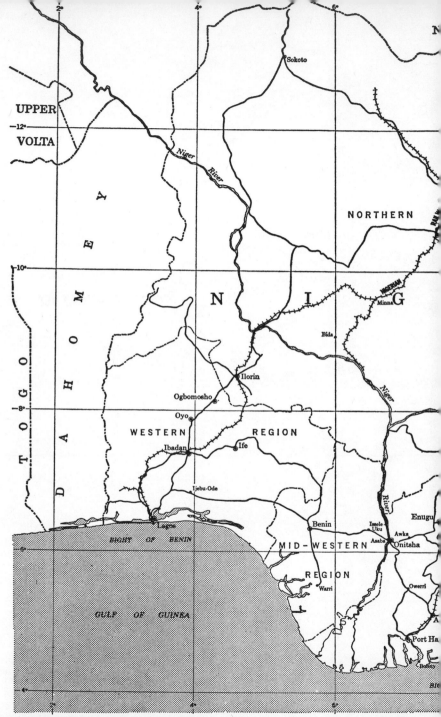

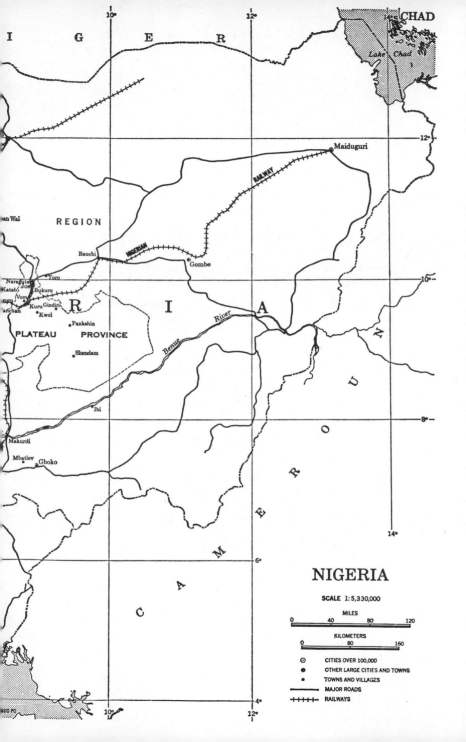

NIGERIA

SCALE 1:5,330,000

MILES

KILOMETERS

⊙   CITIES OVER 100,000
●   OTHER LARGE CITIES AND TOWNS
·   TOWNS AND VILLAGES
—— MAJOR ROADS
+++++ RAILWAYS

INTRODUCTION

T HE object of this study is to describe and analyze the adjustments individuals make to modern conditions of urban development in a West African community. For most parts of tropical
Africa, cities were not part of the traditional cultures, and did not
exist until they emerged during colonial times in response to economic stimuli or administrative needs. Thus developed the towns
of the Copper Belt in Zambia, the cities along the coast that began
as sea ports, and the towns of the interior that served as transportation hubs linking land, river, and rail routes. It was within this
general pattern that Jos, the setting for the present study, came into
being. This city is in northern Nigeria, and at the time of my research had approximately 60,000 inhabitants. Since Jos is a relatively young city, most of the residents were born and raised elsewhere; the cultural milieu of Jos is different from their traditional
way of life—whether that was in the semi-isolation of the African
bush country or in the cosmopolitan traditional urban centers of
the Hausa in the north or the Yoruba in the southwest of Nigeria.
The people feel alien to that city in two ways: geographically and
culturally. By their own admission they say that they reside in a
foreign land and that "home" is elsewhere, often several hundred
miles distant. Even the tribal peoples native to the area around Jos,

who are honorifically referred to as the "owners of the land," regard their Jos residences in the same way and look upon their native villages in the vicinity as their true homes. To them, as to most of the people living in Jos, a modern city is a strange cultural organism. Geographically and culturally, almost everyone is a stranger to Jos.

The reactions of these immigrants to the unfamiliar setting and tensions of modern city life raise many questions for scholars interested in processes of modern urbanism or in the conditions of contemporary African social change. For example, in adjusting to modern urban existence, how important is an individual's exposure to such Western institutions as Christian churches, schools, army life, and wage employment? To what extent does prior exposure to urban life—whether traditional or modern—ease the adjustment? Will persons of different traditional African cultures respond differently to modern urban life? How committed to maintaining an urban existence are the immigrants to the city? And, above all, what consistent patterns in urban adjustments are discernible in the experience of these residents of Jos?

Prior to the late 1950's, social science literature commonly asserted that the non-Western world was rapidly acculturating on the models provided by Western society. A prime object of attention were the cities. Theorists believed that urban development was too rapid and disorderly to provide a basis for healthy community life, and they frequently described social conditions resulting from the technological growth of underdeveloped areas as chaotic, anomic, or unsettled. Many studies provided examples of the breakdown of traditional moral codes, the disintegration of the family, the upsurge of crime, and other indicators of social strain or malaise. The French-speaking sociologists were prone to use the most alarming terms in regard to these developments—"socio-pathology," "states of crisis," "spiritual confusion," and "social disorder"—and even the English-speaking anthropologists could not avoid the same type of value judgments. Busia, for example, concluded from his study of Sekondi-Takoradi that it was a "maladjusted community." Among the symptoms of maladjustment he listed the breakdown of the extended family system, destitution and unemployment, conflict of cultural values, and the ineffectiveness of moral and legal sanctions against crime, prostitution, and juvenile delinquency (Busia 1950).[1]

It is not without significance that a concern with rapid social change in Africa has increasingly drawn the attention of social scientists since the end of World War II. For the present purpose we can point to two major reasons—one academic, the other practical. Between scholars and those responsible for colonial administration there has been a convergence of interest to understand and deal with the powerful historic and social forces that are manifest in the efforts of Africans to achieve political independence and the conditions of modernization that would provide African countries with a position of equality among all nations. Pre-industrial cities existed in Africa for hundreds of years and many African peoples had direct or indirect commercial, political, and cultural transactions with Europeans and Asians (including Chinese and Indonesians) since before the time of Christ, but it was World War II that abruptly thrust most of the people of the continent into the modern commercial world. By the end of the war, an African tribesman untouched by European influences did not exist. During the war young Africans were recruited to fight alongside British, French, and American soldiers in North Africa, Ethiopia, and Burma, and some saw duty in India and Europe. Contingents of American and British military men were stationed in many parts of Negro Africa where they functioned as an informal wartime "peace corps." The production of peasant cash crops, plantation crops, and sylvan and mineral raw materials was initiated or vastly increased to meet emergency demands. Large numbers of men were mobilized to provide the labor for these efforts and, concurrently, cities mushroomed

1. To explain adequately why social scientists have focused their attention on the ills of rapid social change and why they have been especially liberal in characterizing emerging urban Africa as chaotic would require an extended excursion into the sociology of knowledge (see Gluckman 1960), and is outside the concern of this study.

from small settlements. Military bases were located in towns and, to speed international communications, deep-water harbors and airports were constructed. Money, while not abundant, increased many fold and its flow was quickened with the introduction of and demand for manufactured goods. Wage work and individual entre-preneurship became the accepted pattern of adult economic life, and men moved to and fro between areas of employment and their natal homes. Many responded to economic opportunities by living either for long periods or permanently in urban centers. In short, the industrial revolution had at last come to Africa.

Any economic and technological revolution carries with it radical social and cultural changes, and it was this process that attracted the interest of many social scientists to Africa. Their academic or theoretical pursuits centered on Africa's change from a kinship based society to one in which impersonal or contractual relations became the dominant factor. A similar change had taken place in Europe and America during the past two centuries: Would developments in Africa be closely parallel? Would an application of the understanding derived from Euro-American history throw light on current changes in Africa? Conversely, could intense ob-servation and analysis of the processual changes taking place in Africa provide insights for understanding the dynamics of Western history? These and related questions captured the imagination of social scientists.

In addition to the academic stimulation such problems inspired, the troublesome social conditions concomitant with the development of industrialization and urbanization in modern Africa disturbed sensitive men and impelled them to demonstrate their concern. Per-haps an element of guilt about the previous role of Europeans in the development of Africa contributed to the conviction of social scientists that a posture of insulation in an ivory tower could no longer be maintained with honor or dignity. At any rate, they began to ask themselves what others had been asking them for a long time: "What practical good is your study and knowledge?" Thus many anthropologists and sociologists welcomed administrative invitations to make urban studies and to offer recommendations for reform. This involvement gave them a chance to express a genuine humanitarian concern; it was also an opportunity to test and refine their theories through the application of their knowledge and skills.

Recently we have come to understand that the development of urban African society is exceedingly varied and complex and that the conditions formerly regarded as indications of widespread personal, social, or cultural disorganization may instead be reasonable adjustments or healthy responses to extremely dynamic conditions; they may in fact be functionally adaptive within the process of social change (Herskovits 1962; Southall 1961a). But a little over a decade ago many observers of the urban African scene regarded its extreme social diversity and complexity with dismay. The urban populations were drawn from many tribal societies and, together with Levantines, Indians, and Europeans, represented a kaleidoscope of cultural traditions. Even among the tribes, sharp contrasts existed as to the degree of formal Western education they had had and as to their acceptance of a European way of life. Religious affiliations varied from Christian and Muslim sects to traditional African cults. The situation seemed even more complicated by the fact that Africans, in their day-to-day lives, showed little inclination to maintain any role consistently. For example, a well-educated African, who might be acknowledged as a pillar of his local Christian congregation, might also have several wives, worship his ancestral spirits, employ traditional medicines and talismans for himself and his family, and successfully run a transport business using modern organizational methods. Thus one of the foremost questions of the student of contemporary urban African society became: Why do these towns and cities exhibit so great a diversity of norms and institutions and so many contrasts and apparent contradictions in culture and behavior? The answers formerly proposed often lay in such general and highly abstract concepts as "pluralism" and "acculturation."

It is now felt that, despite the superficial malintegration of urban social organization, African cities and towns have their own unique organizational and cultural expressions. It has also become more apparent that similar underlying structural conditions in modern, cosmopolitan urban centers, composed of heterogeneous and/or stratified populations, occur all over the world:

It is . . . necessary to take account of the new social forces which are engendered in the town and tend to promote similar behavior on the part of people of very different origins. Urban life the world over presents problems of a similar character and calls for the organisations of much the same kind to deal with these problems [CCTA/CSA 1961:20].

Anthropologists who have turned their attention to the phenomena of industrialization and modern urbanization in Asia, Africa, and Latin America have been faced with the problem of choosing a theoretical framework of description and analysis adequate to the non-European cultural context and the recent non-tribal social context. Most anthropologists are accustomed to studying tribal communities that are relatively self-contained and within which social relationships for religious, economic, political, and recreational activities consist of the same and intimately known people. In Africa they are challenged with devising new research techniques to describe the novel conditions of the new towns and cities where people of vastly different tribal backgrounds are thrown together. In the urban context the social relations and activities of residents tend to be discrete: a man's recreational companions, neighbors, relatives, fellow-workmen, church members, and tribesmen living in the town may all constitute separate and distinct categories of social relationships. A man must choose the proper role identity as frequently as the social context changes. Furthermore, new social categories based on occupation, wealth or income, religious affiliation, degree of Western education, and other emerging bases of personal identification cross-cut traditional groupings and add still greater complexity to the urban scene. To the anthropologists approaching urban research there was, and still remains, the problem of how to deal with these complex social and cultural phenomena that partake of both traditional and modern worlds without losing the unique tone (spirit or essence, if you will) of the concrete situation, and yet doing this without inhibiting the possibility of developing wider comparisons and deductive generalizations. Thus one cannot quarrel with the dictum that anthropologists must approach the research tasks of modern urban Africa without grand theories and catch-all concepts that fail to account for the particularly African expressions of modern social change. Further, they must appropriately adapt traditional research methods to the dimensions and scale of urban and national societies, and thereby sharpen their concepts of social and cultural dynamics at several levels of analysis. Such advice is always more easily given than implemented, as is attested to by the various approaches anthropologists have taken so far.

Some anthropologists have carried out research in urban areas just as they had in tribal communities. They chose for concentrated study a ward or small section of a town or city, conducted their investigation in the native language by participant observation and intensive interviewing among selected informants, and were thus able to satisfy their bent for empiricism and an empathetic appreciation of the situation. Although the population is arbitrarily isolated and small enough to be manageable with techniques employed for traditional rural communities, town wards are closely interdependent with the wider community. Unlike a rural village, the city subsection by itself is not a viable community. Consequently, by their focus on such urban units, anthropologists were not able to obtain wide-scale data or to relate their sample community to the wider urban and national contexts.

Other anthropologists doubted the utility of employing conventional techniques of investigation and instead borrowed the methods developed by sociologists studying Euro-American urban areas. But this approach also had its disadvantages:

Recourse was had to extensive questionnaire techniques and statistical treatment with their obviously impersonal flavour, to the employment of numbers of field assistants who, despite their real worth, intruded between anthropologist and people in a way to which he [the anthropologist] was unaccustomed. Facts and figures which could be collected and quantified began to take precedence over attempts to assess qualitatively more critical, but less readily observable, phenomena: the number of people per house and their formal links, if any, rather than the actual state of relations between co-residents of a house, and the norms of behaviour they followed; the number of times a man shifts his residence, rather than the nature of relations between neighbours or the possible persistence of friendly relations with former neighbours; what a man says he does, or did, or would do (in reply to a questionnaire) rather than what he actually does or did in respect of, say, his kinship obligations or the trade union [Gulliver 1965:97].

A third approach, and one that has strongly influenced my own research, attempts to outline the significant areas of social interaction —ethnic, kinship, neighborly, political, occupational, recreational, religious—and then to isolate these analytically for intensive observation in order to discern the developing standards of behavior considered appropriate to the particular context. This method (if it can be considered that) is closely associated with the work of Gluckman, Mitchell, and Epstein, and has come to be known as "situational analysis" or the analysis of "situational selectivity." It has the advantage of delimiting the urban field of enquiry—the totality of which can appear as an incomprehensible jumble of contrasts and contradictions—in order to concentrate on, and thereby to abstract, the normative patterns of behavior that associate with role and group identification. It closely parallels the approach known as "reference group theory" developed by American sociologists (Merton 1957: chaps. 8–10), which seeks the determinants of behavior in the recognized fact that the groups to which one belongs provide the framework of beliefs, attitudes, and modes of conduct. The approach of situational analysis extends the value of reference group theory from the directives of normative behavior provided by membership in social groups and social categories of persons to include the normative frameworks of social institutions— the component units of which are statuses and roles.

In the new African cities, among the most important groups that provide the basis for self-reference (the cues for proper and appropriate behavior) are those consisting of kinsmen, friends, fellow tribesmen, and fellow workmen. Also, there are always many social categories of persons or groups which the individual is not a member of, or with whom he does not maintain sustained social relations, but which still are used as points of reference for determining his behavior, ideals, and evaluations of situations. This is one of the ways in which individuals come to alter their customary behavior and thus play a part in cultural changes. For example, an African might be strongly influenced by his church congregation or by its eminent members, by the status and "civilized" behavior of the modern African elite who hold valued occupational positions, or by political ideologies (such as the African Personality, Pan-Africanism, or African Socialism). Just as groups and institutions may serve as positive points of value and behavioral orientation, they may also take on negative value as a kind of anti-referent. An African who has unsuccessfully aspired to social acceptance among Europeans may react by rejecting Christianity for Islam, Western political ideologies for Communism, or Western modes of dress for traditional garb.

Finally, both situational analysis and reference group theory provide a dynamic dimension to an understanding of behavior that could otherwise appear paradoxical. Western observers have been puzzled by the social actions of many modern Africans who assume contrasting and even contradictory behavior on different occasions. But behavior based on cultural and social points of reference is not static, because social contexts are constantly changing and individuals must alter their roles and actions appropriately. We may expect the variation in a person's behavior to increase in relation to the complexity of his social matrix. In an open, stratified society, a person who is socially mobile with respect to class status may successively participate in class-distinct styles of life. In modern Africa, where social and cultural change has been rapid, where persons of diverse cultural traditions now live in close proximity, and where ethnic and class differences cross-cut communities, we find many individuals adjusting their roles to reconcile the multiple areas of social life in which they participate. At different times they are traditionalists and modernists, parochialists and nationalists, particularists and universalists, in accordance with their personal needs and the dictates of the social contexts in which they find themselves.

While there is a need for some comprehensive theoretical tool, some systematic analytic framework for modern urban African research, it is doubtful that any single concept will suffice. Probably a combination of techniques will prove necessary. It is clear, however, that the assumptions of situational analysis are implicit in observations regarding the pluralistic conditions of modern African cities. This can be seen when the differences of people's behavior, cognitive patterns, ideals, religious beliefs, and values are associated with differences of class orientation, traditional versus Western cultural modes, and the variety of ethnic cultural traditions. While I acknowledge the proven utility of situational analysis and its value for and influence on my own work, I have taken as a point of departure the individual as he operates within his social milieu. This approach is, admittedly, an experimental procedure that previously has been tested only tentatively by Epstein (1961), who advocated its adoption. His call for the use of the "social network" technique and my own discovery of its analytical power in making sense of an informant's behavior by understanding the orientation of his actions represent an independent convergence of ideas based on similar research experiences. Like Epstein, I found that by tracing a person's movements through his fields of social action one can enumerate the various social groups and institutional categories that comprise his world of social contact and reference, and one can also define the degree of intensity and the quality of participation. That an individual's social network comprises multiple frames of orientation may add complexity to our understanding, but recognition of this complexity is necessary if we are to understand observed behavioral inconsistencies. It is therefore necessary to focus on the individual's real world, his social environment as *he* perceives it, and observe how he relates to it, defines his own identity by it, and—through his adjustments to it—how he seeks to gain material, social, and psychological satisfactions, and to avoid disappointments.

I would argue that the methodological approach I employed,

here termed "ego-oriented," supplies a dimension to studies of African urbanization differing from that customarily used in sociological analysis. It offers insights and knowledge of contemporary African urban social life not readily observable and obtainable through conventional survey techniques. However, my technique is not intended to serve as a substitute for traditional methods; I regard it as a supplement to them, one which adds subjective data and the type of analysis used by novelists. This is not entirely a new proposal. Epstein (1961), Lewis (1959, 1961), M. F. Smith (1954), and Winter (1959) have experimented along these lines. More recently, R. T. Smith has strongly criticized the heavy reliance on quantitative data by Caribbean researchers to interpret wide cultural variability (1963:45) and Southall has urged the intensive study of a few persons, suggesting that by doing so we would go beyond the usual quantifiable data to a more intimate knowledge of personal and family life (1961a:27).

The great variety of social categories in Jos presented a methodological dilemma. If I had interviewed too many persons, coverage would have been superficial and it would have been impossible to gain the depth of insight that was sought. On the other hand, there was the problem of selecting informants whose character or circumstances might be considered atypical; but I regarded this as a spurious problem, for in this context there will be little agreement on what constitutes "typicality." Which ethnic group, which occupational categories, which religious affiliations can be singled out as typical? What measure of wealth, what degree of Western education, what length of residence in an urban area? Given the plethora of significant variables, the observer can be concerned with the typicality of informants only to the extent that none exceeds, in his estimation, the limits of reasonable conformity. What remains of utmost significance is the attempt to include in the selection of informants the major categories and as wide a range of important variables as can possibly be achieved on the basis of people's availability and willingness to cooperate with the investigator.

If my selection of informants shows a slight bias in favor of individuals who hold or have held some prominence within their own groups, this is only partially fortuitous. Indeed, such individuals are commonly singled out to the investigator as presumably desired informants because they are well known. But such persons also tend to be more cooperative in participating in investigations of social research because of what they regard as the special obligations and duties associated with social superiority. The views and experiences of such informants do have sociological significance since the opinions of prominent members of their communities carry greater weight than those of most people. Also, supplementary evidence shows that they share with other members of their communities similar views and experiences and thereby reflect accurately the current of cultural changes.

Of the approximately sixteen informants that I attempted to work with intensively for an extended period of time, only eight completed the full series of interviews. Of these eight, four are presented with a chapter devoted to each in the body of this book. They receive detailed description and analytic treatment in order to provide the reader with sufficient illustrative material to judge the utility of the ego-oriented method. Accounts of the remaining four informants are presented in a more summary fashion in Chapter VIII. The social categories of the informants (Table 1) show that in combination they cover the significant cultural and structural variables of the Jos African population. Ethnically, they derive from peoples located over all Nigeria. They present almost the entire gamut from ultra-conservative to modern Western cultural orientation and show a similar range in their experience with formal education. Their variations in wealth are just as great, and they represent the major religious affiliations. With regard to prestige, importance, or prominence in their communities, the informants tend to cluster near the top, although several were in the process of being downwardly mobile, and these recognized that their former high prestige could no longer be taken for granted.

My primary informants are distinguished from other informants

TABLE 1

Social and Occupational Categories of the Informants

TRIBES

Northern	*Southern*
Hausa (Zaria)	Yoruba (Ogbomosho)
Birom (local to Jos)	Ibo (Western Region)
Kagoro	Ijaw (Opobo Town)
Tiv	Efik (Calabar)

OCCUPATIONS

Semi-skilled or unskilled	*Skilled*
Trader	Two artisans (electrician
Lorry driver	and motor mechanic)
Night watchman	Government administrative officer
	Civil engineer and contractor
	Teacher and education officer

RELIGIOUS AFFILIATIONS

Christian	*Syncretic*	*Other*
One Catholic	One Cherubim and	One Muslim
One Anglican	Seraphim	One Pagan
Two Baptists		
One nominal Christian		

and persons who provided me with information on the basis of the purpose of my relationship with them (research) and the amount of time devoted to the relationship. With each primary informant I attempted to gain an integrated picture of his personal and social life so that a cumulative knowledge derived from all of them might provide an understanding of Jos social life. The goal of under-standing Jos society, of course, could not be achieved only through the exploration (penetrating and detailed though this might be) of several of its inhabitants. Thus, supplementary research techniques were necessarily utilized, and among these was the use of a large number of additional informants. These latter were needed to provide data on selected topics in which they were particularly knowledgeable, and my relations with them followed in the customary patterns of anthropological field work.

The primary informants were all adult males and heads of families. I concentrated upon them partly in order to use their vantage point as a means to study the family, particularly the family as a system of interaction among component members. My efforts in this regard confirmed my belief that it is not easy to analyze Nigerian urban (or rural) domestic units as micro-social systems; such research would require so intense a focus on the family itself that the observer could undertake little else. However, repeated interviews with one adult family member brought much information about the other members and their pattern of interaction. Although information about others from a single informant is subject to some bias, and must be employed cautiously, the use of a single informant has certain advantages, particularly under a method of field research in which a relationship of mutual confidence is developed. Within this frame of mutuality the informant may volunteer deeply personal information, which he would not in other circumstances, and the field worker, on his side, can broach intimate topics, probe, cross-check informants' statements, compare overt with expressed behavior, and observe the development or resolution of personal and familial problems.

The many parallels between this intimate informant-researcher relationship and that of the client-analyst in clinical psychotherapy are clear. Less intensive work with informants would have elicited quite different data, as evidenced by information given late in the interviewing series by several informants. For example, the Ijaw informant offered various rationalizations to explain why he did not join the elite social clubs. Not until I was trusted, and at a time when he was under the influence of alcohol, did he volunteer the "true" and "real" reasons, as he phrased it. These were, of course, no more true or real than his other reasons, but they do represent important data for fuller analysis. The Tiv informant's altered explanation of how he lost his job with the Nigerian Railways came late in our acquaintance. Also, from my initial formal questions alone, I would never have learned of his other two wives. Similarly, the Yoruba informant was ashamed of his marriage to his third wife and avoided mentioning it until several months after interviews began. When he eventually felt free to discuss intimate and personal matters, he spoke of things which, by his own admission, he would not have discussed with relatives or close friends. For a long time he would not even dare mention the number of his children, in keeping with Yoruba propriety. Later, his uninhibited expression on personal matters was in marked contrast with this traditional Yoruba characteristic of secretiveness.

It is clear that certain kinds of data cannot be gained through superficial survey techniques and formal questionnaires. Questions on some topics elicit emotional responses that make people reluctant to answer honestly. Under such circumstances the subjects may rationalize or, to avoid embarrassing themselves, consciously lie. (Of course, imperfect knowledge of local custom and culture on the part of the field worker may also contribute to poor communication.) I seriously doubt whether one could have gained from the Ijaw informant the explanation of why some of his children died and how he managed to save the others from a similar fate, except through establishing confidence over a long period of informant-researcher interaction. Conclusions drawn solely from questionnaire surveys or from census data may be distorted not only because the data are inaccurate, but also from momentary atypical circumstances. If a field worker had taken only a house census at the time the Tiv informant was living with his brother-in-law, a reasonable conclusion might have been that the traditional Tiv prohibition of a man residing with his in-laws was no longer upheld under modern urban conditions. Unless such a census was complemented with depth interview information, the researcher would never have known that the Tiv deplored this breach of custom and at the first opportunity moved away. On the other hand, quantitative demographic studies could establish whether this situation represented a trend or was only an individual instance.

Through conventional methods of field research we can readily learn that a population holds cultural elements of diverse origins, but until we elicit details of their manner of integration from individual informants we cannot know precisely how the elements are combined. In Africa, where economic, political, and social relationships are often so intimately combined with religious elements, it is particularly instructive to seek the emerging patterns of integration for any understanding of modern developments. Using the Ijaw informant as an example (Chapter 5), we can see how, with the use of simple attitude surveys, a researcher might be led astray from the underlying nature of his religious affiliations, which are not radically different from those of his peers. Specifically, an attitude *survey* would have revealed him to be a religious person, a good Anglican, and a close friend of an Anglican clergyman. But while Cookey-Jaja and his wife were indeed exemplary Anglicans, he privately called white missionaries "agents and spies of the European imperialists," believed deeply in the efficacy of native magic, attributed passing his school examinations to magical aid, thought his children were the target of a malicious spirit which he then tried to placate through traditional African ritual, and spent over two hundred pounds pursuing native studies of the supernatural. From his account we see how the mystical orientation of this competent, apparently Westernized, civil engineer even determined his selection of a wife, and importantly influenced his life in other ways.

The Ijaw informant saw no contradiction between his personal religious views and those of the Anglican Church, but the Efik informant did recognize that his ambition to become a Freemason was not sanctioned by the Catholic Church. In fact, while he volunteered this information without any prompting from me, he also claimed that it was precisely because he was a devout Catholic that he felt constrained to dissolve his son's polygamous marriage. Previously he had expressed liberal ideals regarding his children's marital choices. Both he and the Yoruba informant protested that tribe and religious affiliation were not as important as other considerations in marriage, but later both demonstrated that they themselves were not convinced of this ideal, which was then being widely propagated as desirable for the new Nigeria.

Sometimes the anthropologist uncovers a situation that tests his informant's convictions by forcing him either to implement or to reject his professed ideals. The investigator should be in a position to record both the previously expressed beliefs and the results of the testing situation, for although the informant may be able to verbalize what factors determined his beliefs and choices of action, it is more likely that the researcher will have to supply this kind of information-in-depth from his intimate acquaintance with the informant and his knowledge of the social matrix.

To observe, understand, and accurately and precisely report on behavior within a patterned matrix of the social structure and culture of a modern African city requires the research skills of the social scientist and the sensitivity of a good novelist. The anthropologist observes sympathetically and arranges his observations analytically. He attempts to gain both an inside and an outside view of his informant by following his movements through his social and ideological fields and by observing his actions within his social network. He seeks to understand his cognitive and evaluative perceptions, to know his ambitions and his frustrations. The observer must also balance research on the informant with complementary research on the history, social organization, and culture of the urban milieu in which the informant is viewed.

The effort is worthwhile. Much of past urban African research has tended to assume that while particular individuals may differ in their orientations, any single individual is consistent in his cultural orientation. Thus the summary data resulting from surveys based on this assumption express differences in cultural orientation as represented by blocks of individuals. Since each block is defined by cultural and behavioral differences, it, therefore, presents a distorted picture. While there are limits to the oscillations of an individual's orientations, in the African urban context it is not realistic to view the populations as being composed of static entities. Persons not only move out of and into different social categories as a function of basic changes in their personal histories and careers during their lifetime, but, as mentioned previously, they also shift from one type of cultural orientation and behavior to another in their daily lives, generally reflecting the appropriateness of such shifts in accordance with differences of social institutions and cultural situations. Thus it is clear that although analysis of social institutions in Jos cannot be neglected, this kind of traditional investigation must be complemented with a focus on the movement of individuals between and among the different institutions of their everyday lives.

The conventional sociological approach is presumably based on the changes apparent along the continua from traditional to modern, African to Western, and rural to urban. In most cases, this approach has failed to reward observers with a straightforward nomenclature of type changes.[2] It has been assumed that immigrants who remain in the urban environment change in a unidirectional pattern parallel to the institutional changes, and that the variety of individual characteristics to be observed might also be placed on a similar continuum. But the patterned unidirectional change does not exist, and the attempt to order the existing variations serially on the assumption of unidirectional change has led to frustrating results. The data presented here clearly show that even if there is a direction to institutional and individual changes, they are not necessarily parallel. Perhaps there has been too much emphasis on the study of change in institutions per se. Unless research is deliberately focused on the social movements of individuals, we could never

2. Apparently this has elicited Southall's complaint that such attempts have been "dismissed by qualitative assessments of chaos, disorganization, or breakdown of norms, which fail to penetrate sufficiently beyond general impressions to the actions of the persons concerned" (1961a:26).

estimate the extent to which an individual may, in the normal course of his daily life, shift between tribal and modern, African and Western, institutions.

If contradictions are present, they are in the mind of the observer, not the observed. For the participant the institutions exist to be used and exploited, neglected or avoided. They are for him part of the urban scene, to be taken advantage of as long as the appropriate behavior for the relevant institutions are known. An ego-oriented approach helps us to understand the meaning to the participants of the changing and emerging institutions in modern African cities. Considering the historical, political, economic, and cultural elements that continuously play a part in the development of new African urban centers, can the social situation be anything but complex? An ego-oriented approach to urban conditions in plural societies may not hold the promise of high-level structural analysis or high-level theory, but it provides the possibility of demonstrating, through following the actions of individuals, the kinds of human regularities that do exist. In their professed beliefs and values and in their behavior, the principal informants fit previous descriptions of "typical" urban Africans, as well as demonstrate a wide range of variability. One cannot dismiss their inconsistencies and contradictions or their failure to behave according to their expressed values as dishonest responses to the ethnographer, although this always remains a possibility. Such behavior I attribute to their use of different cultural sets of references in varying social contexts, as well as honest, reasonable, and pragmatic attempts to relate to conditions in Jos.

The ego-oriented approach used alone has limitations just as does sole reliance on the broader, conventional sociological approach. They should be used to complement one another. This study is only a preliminary attempt to integrate the two approaches. Ideally, its potentiality should be tested further in urban areas that have already been studied sociologically, with more complete demographic data about them than exists for Jos. Specifically, when the results of this and similar studies are applied to the problem of the commitment of immigrants to their native homes, I believe the present dominant ideas will be altered and the myth of an inevitable unidirectional change from African to European culture dismissed.[3]

Interview Procedure

Interviews followed the same outline and general pattern for all primary informants. There were some slight variations in individual interview procedures, and these are described specifically for each informant at the beginning of his account. The variations included the total length of the interview series, the place where interviews were normally held, the use of an interpreter, whether or not payment or the presentation of gifts or refreshments was involved, etc.

When possible, all interviews were held in the familiar atmosphere of the informant's home. In this environment I had an opportunity to become familiar with members of the family and to observe their behavior and interaction. However, at the insistence of some informants meetings took place at my quarters. Here the atmosphere was not entirely foreign, for I lived in a compound with four African families in the African Reservation (Sabon Gari) of the Township,[4] under physical conditions similar to those of the surrounding African houses.

I attempted to extend the series of interviews to a year or more on the premise that in this length of time informants would gain a sense of security and confidence and would volunteer information normally withheld under more transient circumstances. The protracted informant-researcher relationship also allowed me to return to topics on which I had received inadequate or contradictory information and, more important, the extent of time gave me ample

3. For a recent discussion of how situational change is confused with progressive change, see Mitchell (1966: 44–45).

4. The administrative, physical, social, and demographic differences between the Town (or Native Town) and Township sections of Jos is described in Chapter III.

opportunity to observe the informants' behavior and to relate it to their expressed mores and norms. The long span of interviews also permitted me to develop friendships with many of the informants, and the resulting informal interaction with them and their families and friends was in itself valuable.

At the first interview I explained the purpose of the research and the possible time span of the series to each informant. If, for whatever reason, a man felt he could not continue the interviews for the entire time projected, he was either dismissed or interviewed several times in an attempt to gain information on general topics with which he was familiar. At the start of the interviews, and from time to time during them, I told the informants of my intention to question them on subjects or on specific points about which they might be reluctant to give information. I begged them to be honest about their diffidence rather than misinform me.

Each interview lasted approximately two hours, or occasionally less, but the number of interviews per informant per week varied greatly, depending largely on his availability. The language used during the interviews was English, except with the Tiv and Yoruba informants, who could not speak English. With them I used native interpreters, for, although these informants were also proficient in Hausa (which I spoke but not well enough for intensive interviewing), there was the possible advantage of their expressing themselves more freely in their native tongues. The same interpreters, a Tiv and a Yoruba, were used for almost all the interviews with both these informants, lending stability and familiarity to the interview situation.

I presented the same outline of topics to each informant. In addition to the attitudes and basic data usually included in formal questionnaires and schedules (tribe, age, occupation, degree of Western education) I explored the informants' work histories, their geographic and social mobility, wealth and property, associations and affiliations, marital histories, children, and kinship and friendship social networks. All these data are presented in detail for each informant in their respective chapters.

I employed one technique which appears to be new to ethnographic research, or rarely used. This technique, which I call the "photo network," proved quite useful. Photographs of relatives and friends are prominently displayed in Jos homes, and albums of photographs are often kept on living-room coffee tables or brought out for the inspection of visitors. From the very beginning of a new acquaintance people would show me their photographs of relatives and friends, and my interest in the pictures demonstrated my interest in the hosts and served as a means of establishing rapport. It was plain that the experience could be anthropologically profitable, for the photographs offered leads to social activities and people important to the informants. The number of pictures and the selection of the photographs most prominently displayed gave indications of the relative degree of urban or Western sophistication and of the importance to the informants of the subjects or persons represented. Asking about each photograph resulted in clues to the history of the informants, their social relations, connections within their social networks, and their affiliations and memberships in organizations and associations. In showing the style of costume or dress worn (Western or Nigerian), the richness of adornment and jewelry, occupational uniforms, and the date and place the photograph was taken (if it were not a studio), the photographs provided information on the informants' background, the relative wealth of kinsmen and friends, and their degree of familiarity with Western ways.

During the course of interviews and growing familiarity it became clear that the informants were not always to be taken at their word. I checked many of their contradictory statements through repetition of interview topics, outside observations, and the gossip of others. One very valuable source of information of this sort came from the interpreters, who developed a protective attitude toward me. Often, on the way to or from an informant we would discuss aspects of the interviews or the social situation of the informant, and my interpreters at times provided me with cultural insights or information about the informant. Sometimes the interpreter made these comments after an interview during which he had been stimulated by a particular topic or by something the informant had said. The interpreters' remarks alerted me to certain aspects of the informants' behavior that I had been unaware of, and sometimes I found it rewarding to raise these matters in the course of subsequent interviews. Occasionally, however, the interpreter became so intensely involved in the course of a particular interview that I had to caution him to restrict himself to translating and not to act as a contributor.

Selection of Informants

The informants were selected to cover the widest range of possibly significant sociological and cultural variables—different tribes, variations in age, wealth, occupation, degree of Western education, religious affiliation, and status in the community.[5] These differences were not only theoretically important; they were intended to reflect the plural social and cultural conditions of Jos. One of my primary concerns was to cover as many significant ethnic groups as possible, significant to Jos or Nigeria in the sense of being important politically, economically, or numerically.

Five of the eight informants who completed the interview series were directly or indirectly introduced to me through Social Welfare Officers, who themselves were Nigerians. One informant (Hausa) had previously assisted me in translating Hausa administrative records, and another (Ijaw) was introduced through an acquaintance. I asked a personal acquaintance, a Birom, to provide himself as a representative of an important ethnic area for which no informant had been found. Whether or not a particular individual was taken

5. The designations "traditional elite" and "modern elite" are sometimes used loosely in African studies. Here, traditional elite refers to persons holding positions of prestige within the context of native cultural institutions —chiefs, lineage heads, or persons holding high rank or native titles in traditional tribal secret societies or other native sodalities. A member of the modern elite, by contrast, holds a comparably high rank in institutions of Western origin, such as recreational or athletic clubs, political parties, international fraternities, trade unions, government agencies, modern commercial firms, professional occupations.

on as an informant ultimately depended on his availability and willingness. The length of the proposed interview procedure caused many prospective informants to reject my proposal immediately and I rejected others because they showed reluctance to give the time or to respond honestly. Three informants were "lost" for these last reasons after the interviews had started.

The problem of sampling or representativeness is familiar to ethnographers and has frequently (and critically) been remarked upon by their sociologist colleagues. How representative are the responses of cooperative informants, and how much important information is lost when it is impossible to deal with a statistically representative body of informants? There is little that ethnographers can do to compensate for such possible data lacunae and the biases of selected informants that may together serve to skew analysis and interpretation. This is the region where ethnographic field work partakes of common sense and art as much as scientific methodology. Merely to attempt a comprehensive ethnographic description of a society would require a company of researchers with unlimited time and funds. Not only is this impracticable but it is also considered theoretically unnecessary. It is often said that the researcher's theoretical interest will determine his research strategy. No anthropologist now attempts to achieve a fully comprehensive account of all aspects of the society he studies, and a restriction of interest becomes all the more necessary when one deals with complex modern urban conditions. With my attempt to understand personal social action in Jos intimately and in depth, I could not hope to make the broad coverage of informants required for a statistically representative sample of the population. While it is a major thesis of this study that intensive interviews of a small number of individuals and the ego-oriented approach can add insights and new dimensions to our understanding of urbanization, I have nevertheless attempted to reflect the social realities of Jos by selecting what I regard to be representative informants, ones who had qualities representative of important social attributes present in Jos. There can be no pretense that this small number of individuals is statistically significant and representative of the population as a whole, but, as Table 2 shows, the eight informants who completed the interview series do indicate some of the major social and cultural variables to be found in the city.

TABLE 2

Range of Variables of the Informants by Tribe

	Yoruba	Ibo	Ijaw	Efik	Hausa	Birom	Kagoro	Tiv
Age[b]	60	55	43	55	60	27	23	65
Polygamous	x	x	—	—	x	x	—	x
Total number of all marriages	3	3	1	1	4	2	1	5
Total number divorces	1	—	—	—	2	—	—	1
Total number living children	23	2	7	4	6	4	3	10
Percentage of personal life spent in urban setting	100	60	90	100	85	25	55	10
Percentage of personal life spent in Jos	65	60	35	45	25	5	5	5–10
Has kin of same or ascending generation in Jos[a]	M	F	F	0	F	0	0	0
Annual income averaged for past five years[b] (in sterling)	5,000	150	1,000	300	400	600	125	55

[a] M = many; F = few; O = none.
[b] Approximations in most cases.

Chapter II

PHYSICAL SETTING, EARLY HISTORY, AND ECONOMIC BASIS OF JOS

T HE city of Jos, situated on the Jos Plateau, is about 4,000 feet above sea level and lies close to the geographical center of the northern provinces of Nigeria. The northern provinces (formerly known as the Northern Region) are so large in comparison with the rest of Nigeria that on maps Jos appears to be at the center of the country. Nor is this impression misleading, for although Jos is not the geographical center of Nigeria, its strategic location has made it a communications center of the country. Highways connect it with most of the major cities of the North, and its airport handles flights from all over Nigeria. Prior to the recent Bornu extension of the Nigerian Railways, Jos marked the terminus of the railroad line from Port Harcourt in the eastern provinces, and through the link at Kafanchan it is connected with the rail line that extends from the port of Lagos in the south to Kano in the extreme north.

Good communications developed early in Jos because of the needs of the tin mining industry and the colonial administration. A telegraph line with Bauchi (approximately eighty miles to the east of Jos) was established before 1910, when the administration of Jos was under the Resident of Bauchi, and a narrow-gauge rail shuttle line reached eastward to Zaria, where it met the main rail line from Lagos. By 1920 a local network of motor roads was developed by the local mining companies in response to their needs.

The Northern Region of Nigeria is divided into thirteen provincial administrative units.[1] Plateau Province, which corresponds closely with the topographical plateau, consists of several administrative units called Divisions, and Jos, on the northern edge of the plateau, is the seat of its administrative headquarters, as well as the headquarters of Jos Division. The reactions of a former provincial Resident are useful in understanding the contrasts in this section of Nigeria:

There is probably no such small area in Nigeria where contrasts are so striking except in some of the larger towns. Here we have the customary progress in civilisation as represented by motor vehicles, elaborate mining machinery, tarred roads and fine buildings. The reverse of the picture is the naked pagan living in a small village in the well nigh inaccessible crags, still isolated and still suspicious of his neighbours. . . . The natural beauty of the high Plateau is often marred by the frenzied efforts of man to wrest Nature's precious minerals from below ground [Annual Report for Plateau Province, 1951].

Similarly, an Administrative Research Officer has called Jos

a curious place. . . . Its surrounds are beautiful and it is itself built on a pleasing site. . . . In spite of all this it lacks unity and coherence and seems to suggest that several people must have had a new idea and thought it would be a good one. [For example, in the center of the Township] . . . is a large open space, part being occupied by a golf course and the rest by farms [Ames 1934:428–431].

The two main seasons of the year are a wet and a dry period that roughly coincide with the summer and winter seasons of northern latitudes. The Plateau has the same seasons as the surrounding country, with modifications resulting from its higher elevation.

1. Since the military take-over in Nigeria in January of 1966 there have been changes in the structure and practices of administration and an expressed intention to review the Nigerian Constitution for the purpose of recommending revisions. Rather than speculate on what reforms these changes will take, I have left the description of Nigerian government and administration in this chapter and the next as it was at the time of my study.

Yearly temperatures range from 50° to 95° F, and the average annual rainfall is between 40 and 70 inches, which is higher than that for the surrounding country. From October to March, when there is little rainfall, the harmattan, a dry northeast wind from the Sahara Desert, carries minute particles of dust that choke the atmosphere with a thick orange-brown haze. During this period the maximum temperature variations occur; the days are hot and the night-time temperatures sometimes drop close to freezing.

The climate of the Jos Plateau can be treacherous. In its Annual Report for the year 1944 the Nigerian Department of Labour noted 880 deaths that year among the conscripted and volunteer labor force on the minesfield. One-third of the deaths were attributed to cerebro-spinal fever (meningitis); the two other chief causes were pneumonia, or bronchitis, and dysentery. "Men from the more northerly provinces, Sokoto and Bornu, where wide fluctuations of temperature are normal, were found to be much better suited to the high Plateau than men drawn from the low lying areas of Benue and Niger Provinces with an equable climate" (p. 4). Other observers have noted that "it is quite common to hear people from Southern Nigeria refer to the 'bitter climate' of the Jos Plateau," but this is attributed to the low humidity there (Buchanan and Pugh 1955:32). Many Africans who live in Jos for several years become accustomed to its coolness and are uncomfortable when they visit other parts of Nigeria.

When Europeans first set foot on the Plateau, its bracing atmosphere led to the belief that it was one of the healthiest places in West Africa. Lord Frederick D. Lugard, the first Governor of Nigeria, even considered establishing a health and rest station there for Europeans. It did not take many years and many European deaths to alter this view. The Plateau has had its fair share of diseases common both to tropical countries and to backward areas. Illnesses directly attributed to the generally cold conditions and wide fluctuations of temperature include pulmonary tuberculosis, cerebro-spinal meningitis, bronchitis, pneumonia, and rheumatism. While these diseases are still prevalent, they were much more so in the past, when health and medical facilities were not as well developed as they are today. Other common illnesses in the area are smallpox, relapsing fever, chicken pox, mumps, typhus, Hansen's disease, intestinal worms, malaria, malnutrition, filarial diseases, bilharzia, and guinea worms. In the past, when sanitary conditions were unsatisfactory, Jos was sometimes threatened with yellow fever, and even today rabies remains an occasional danger. But Lugard was not entirely mistaken in his health project for at least the tsetse fly does not live at this altitude, making Jos free of sleeping sickness.

If the Jos Plateau was not the Elysium that Lugard regarded it, health conditions have improved considerably since his tenure of office, and the scenic beauty and the comparatively pleasant climate have continued to attract Europeans. Today, church missions and foreign commercial firms maintain rest houses in and around Jos for their staff members on local leave, and Europeans prefer Jos as a permanent duty station as well as a place to spend a holiday. The West African headquarters of several missionary societies, including one large American organization, are located in Jos, and their staffs form a considerable portion of the local European residents. Because of its favorable climate, its role as an administrative center, and its mining activities, the Jos Plateau has probably had the largest concentrated resident European population in former British West Africa.[2]

Upon retirement many of the Europeans associated with the min-

2. In 1951 the European community of Lagos was 4,200. "Outside [Lagos] the largest European community is that of the Plateau Province; here, in a climatic environment unique in West Africa, mining, commerce and administration support a total of 1,200 Europeans" (Buchanan and Pugh 1955:97–98). Although this figure is given for Plateau Province as a whole, most of the Europeans of the Province are concentrated in Jos Division, and within the Division there is a further concentration in and around Jos. The percentage of Europeans among Africans in Jos Township has varied from 1.5 to 2.0, thus approaching similar percentages found in East and Central Africa. See Coleman (1960:251) for the relative proportion of Europeans to Africans resident in African countries. His Table 1 shows Nigeria as second only to Liberia in having the fewest Europeans and the most Africans in its population, proportionately.

ing industry choose to settle permanently on the Plateau, as do some of the missionaries. Government census figures do not distinguish between temporary and permanent European residents, but from the large number of homes privately owned by Europeans, and from my own observations of Europeans in long continuous residence, it may be concluded that while the total European population of the Jos Plateau is second to Lagos, the Plateau has a larger number of permanent European residents.

Initially Europeans were drawn to the Jos Plateau to exploit its rich tin ore resources. During the eighteenth and nineteenth centuries small quantities of "straw tin"[3] of unknown source reached Europeans trading at West African ports, but it was not until 1884 that English traders became aware of a native tin industry in the north of Nigeria. (With the establishment and development of modern European tin mining, the indigenous tin industry rapidly declined and was discontinued during the second decade of this century.) Through Hausa traders some of the metal reached agents of the Royal Niger Company stationed near the Benue River and interest in discovering the source of the tin ore led to European occupation of the Plateau.

At the turn of the century Sir William Wallace commanded an armed force sent to subdue the Emir of Bauchi. Sir Richard Temple, a political officer of this expeditionary force, toured and mapped the area. He is supposed to have been the very first European to set foot on the Plateau. The samples of tin ore concentrate that he found below the Plateau were submitted to the Directors of the Niger Company in London, who were impressed with the richness of this ore and correctly concluded that the trickle of almost pure tin metal, which had been filtering through to Mediterranean and West African ports, originated on the Plateau. They determined to send an exploratory expedition to pinpoint the deposits and obtain further samples for assay.

3. So-called "straw tin" because of its appearance as thick strands of wire. This was the form in which tin smelted by Africans was transported and traded. Africans used it to tin brassware.

In March 1902, G. R. Nicolaus, a mining engineer, undertook a successful expedition to the Plateau, and in 1903 he returned there with Colonel H. W. Laws, also a mining engineer, escorted by a full company of the West African Frontier Force (consisting of native African soldiers under British officers) armed with Maxim machine guns. This second expedition encountered opposition from mounted native warriors, but, with the aid of the Maxim guns, it fought its way across the Plateau and established a permanent mining camp early in 1904.[4] From this camp at Naraguta, north of Jos just off the Plateau, mining operations were begun. They did not reach full production, however, until the second decade of this century. At first more attention was paid to prospecting than production not only because it was reasonable to determine the richness and extent of the deposits but also because of difficulties incident to native hostility, lack of labor, and poor transportation. So rich were the first samples that even superficial working yielded considerable profits.

A series of military campaigns to pacify the hostile local tribes was begun in 1902, and by the middle of 1905 an administrative section was opened in Bukuru, on the road between Keffi and the tin mines at Naraguta, in order to quell the periodic uprisings of pagan tribesmen. Hausa and Yoruba contingents of the West African Frontier Force armed with Maxim guns were called in to secure the northern end of the Plateau against the periodic raids of local warriors. However, Plateau natives continued to obstruct the routes along which processed tin was transported and to harass the mining operations. The British mounted major punitive campaigns in 1906–07, and the subsequent growth of the European interests indicates their success.

It appears that in January of 1907 there were only three Euro-

4. Colonel Laws, who led the European occupation of the Plateau in 1903, claimed that a small hill village called "Guash" occupied the present location of Jos. Hausa traders, who arrived later, supposedly mispronounced Guash as Jos, and the name stuck. According to Gunn, the original native village of Guash was founded by the Afusare people of the Jarawa tribe, who are sometimes called the Afusare of Jos or Jarawan Jos (Gunn 1953:63).

peans on the Plateau (Annual Reports, Northern Provinces: 541),
but by the end of 1909 many European prospectors and mining
engineers had been attracted to the tinfields, and by the end of
March 1910 there were more than fifty syndicates with declared
aggregate capital of at least £2,500,000 registered for mining
operations on the Plateau.[5] Although mining and tin-smelting equipment had been imported in 1905, in 1906 tin ore was still being
carried to the coast by human porterage and river craft; by 1911 it
was head-carried a short way to the railway line at Zaria and thence
to Lagos by rail. After 1914 freighting was entirely by rail, and
exports increased tenfold between 1910 and 1916.

After the tin industry had experienced alternating periods of
prosperity and poverty, mainly in response to the price of tin on
the London market, an international effort was made to stabilize
production for all tin ore producing countries. With the economic
depression of the 1930's the tin ore producers of the world initiated
voluntary restrictions in order to reduce output and thereby control
prices. Annual production quotas were based on the relative production of the countries concerned, and the signatory governments
in an agreement signed in 1931 included Great Britain, Bolivia,
Malaya, and the Netherlands East Indies.

These regulations have remained in effect, and the restricting
quotas assigned to the Nigerian tin mining companies by the British
government partly accounts for the fact that few African entrepreneurs have been able to enter the industry. For a new company
to form and commence mining there is not only the need for capital
and technical skills, but mining quotas must be obtained and these
are already held by producing companies. In addition, African tin
mining entrepreneurs are few because until recently Africans were
legally kept from participating except at the levels of unskilled or
semi-skilled labor.

European commercial tin smelting, using wood for fuel, was early

5. Apparently the richness of the tin ore deposits and the Pax Britannica
took several years to be established, and not until both were confirmed could
large-scale mining operations proceed.

abandoned in favor of restricting exports solely to ore concentrate, and, for reasons mainly related to economic interests in Liverpool, local smelting was not resumed until 1961. In that year a smelter was opened by a Portuguese firm holding an international patent on electrical smelting, a very economical means of smelting since hydroelectrical energy is abundant on the Plateau, whereas fuels must be shipped in.[6] At the beginning of the following year, 1962, a British smelter (connected with operations in Liverpool) capable of smelting all locally-produced ore was established, using an oil-fueled process. Local smelting has considerably benefited the smaller mining companies (who receive payment for their ore much more rapidly than in the past), has created some additional local employment, and is a source of national prestige to independent Nigeria.

Nigeria, sixth largest world tin producer, accounts for approximately 5 per cent of world production, and the Plateau produces the greatest part of this output. In addition to tin ore (cassiterite), the Plateau minesfield produces such metallic ores as wolfram, zircon, and tantelite, but only columbite (columbium ore) has ever come close to challenging cassiterite as the chief metalliferous mineral exploited. Until recently Nigeria was almost the exclusive producer of the world's columbite, and the Plateau produces 80 per cent of Nigeria's tin and columbite and 83 per cent of the country's metalliferous output. Tin and columbite account for about 90 per cent of Nigeria's mineral production, excluding fossil fuels. Columbite, however, has an exceedingly restricted world market. Tin, therefore, remains the most important metal ore mined.

Despite its historic association with tin mining, Jos has achieved an enviable economic independence of the mining industry. While the area owes its initial development to the mining industry, it has come to derive much of its revenue and economic stability from transportation and other commercial activities so that even if the mining industry suddenly collapsed, Jos would survive, though perhaps reduced in size. Perhaps the clearest demonstration of Jos's

6. For reasons unknown to me, the Portuguese smelter had ceased operations during 1965.

present economic independence from mining activities is indicated by the fairly steady growth of the city population, despite the fluctuations of the minesfield labor population—fluctuations which were in response to the vagaries of the London tin market (see Chart I).

Although the mining industry suffered severely during the world economic depression of the 1930's, Jos Township was not badly affected. At that time the population of the Township consisted largely of southern Nigerian and other West African skilled and clerical workers for government and commercial firms, workers whose skills were still scarce. These men were hard to replace and they were retained until conditions improved. On the other hand, the majority of workers in the Native Town were unskilled and they experienced adverse conditions.

A significant portion of Jos's commercial activities remain oriented to the needs of the mining industry and to the local African and European communities connected with the minesfield. Among those enterprises of any importance not directly related to mining activities, excepting those connected with transportation, are plants for tire recapping and the bottling of carbonated beverages. In addition, there are small and medium-sized printing plants and furniture factories owned by Africans or foreigners. The remaining industries, almost entirely African-owned and serving the local market almost exclusively, include house construction, lorry-body building, tailoring, and the manufacture of native shoes, mattresses, metal boxes, and luggage.

It is hard to speculate on the economic future of Jos because it is so intimately tied with national politics. Up until about the time of Nigeria's independence in 1960, southern Nigerians and West African non-Nigerians in Jos held virtually unchallenged the favored occupational and commercial positions wherein Africans were to be found. From 1959, when the Northern Region was formed and acquired semi-autonomy, the Northern Regional government initiated a "Northernization Policy" that favored the natives of the Region and resulted in a continuous attrition of the advantages held by non-northerners (excepting Europeans). This policy not only

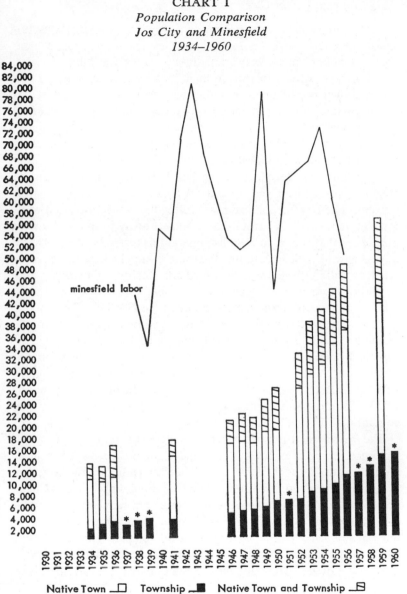

CHART I
Population Comparison
Jos City and Minesfield
1934–1960

minesfield labor

Native Town ☐   Township ■   Native Town and Township ▣
*Figures for Native Town not available

affected individual southern Nigerians (against whom it was primarily directed)—who were no longer awarded government contracts, scholarships, loans, grants-in-aid, plots for business sites, and who were often replaced in their jobs by less experienced and less qualified northerners—but through the perverse twists of Nigerian politics, it had a direct bearing on the continued commercial development of Jos itself. Because Jos had been economically dominated by southern Nigerians, and because its population (much of it southern) had continuously voted into office persons in opposition to the ruling political party of the Northern Region, the Northern Regional government and the federal Nigerian government (which was controlled by the political party ruling the North) diverted commercial, industrial, and other developments away from Jos. Foreign businesses that sought to establish operations in Jos because of their advantages to their expatriate staff were compelled by the government to settle elsewhere in the Northern Region. (Obviously, this could not occur with the location of tin smelters.) New roads were built and old roads improved elsewhere in the Northern Region, but those leading out from Jos were left untarred or received only minimal upkeep. For example, the road connecting Jos with the Regional capital, Kaduna, is mostly unpaved, and the road south from Jos is the only motor vehicle route directly linking northern Nigeria with the Eastern Region. It receives heavy traffic all the year round, yet this road remained untarred and was reputed to be in the worst condition of all major Nigerian roads.

The commercial importance of Jos depends partly on its strategic position as a nexus of lorry and train transportation routes. Until recently it was the terminus of the eastern line of the Nigerian Railway, and by both road and rail was the direct link between Chad, northeastern Nigeria, and southern Nigeria. This advantageous position of Jos may be greatly diminished by the Bornu extension of the railway, which has recently been completed. This extension, which now connects Port Harcourt with the Lake Chad area, does not emerge directly from Jos but from a point on the rail line many miles south of Jos, thus leaving Jos as a cul de sac. Southerners allege that this was done deliberately to isolate Jos.

The railway tracks cannot now be moved to Jos, but with the recent military take-over of the Nigerian government there appears to be a new ideology in the political climate of the country, and if the professed ideal of a united Nigeria becomes an actuality rather than an empty slogan, Jos may be expected to regain lost ground in its commercial growth.[7]

7. Documentation for this section on the history and economic basis of Jos may be found in the following references: Bauchi Province Reports 1902–06; Bower 1948:4–26; Buchanan and Pugh 1955:206, 230 (under fig. 150); Calvert 1910:13; Cook 1943:229–230; Gunn 1953:63; Hance 1960: 136; A. G. Hastings, cited by Bower 1948:4–5, fn. 6; Laws 1954; Mackay *et al.* 1949:19–20; Nigeria Handbook 1936:109, 112, 238; Plateau Province Annual Report 1932, 11/1932; Rowling 1946: par. 91; and Stapleton 1958: 33, 46–47.

Chapter III

URBAN CHARACTERISTICS:
CITY AND POPULATION

Administration

A LTHOUGH the colonial policy practiced by the British administration in Nigeria might have worked well for a homogeneous population with a tradition of centralized government, it was ill-suited to Jos (see Hailey 1951:61). Various commentators have described this so-called Lugardian model of colonial administration as "elastic," "expedient," and "flexible." I would suggest that, as applied to Jos, it was also paternalistic, preferential, and inconsistent—all factors which eventually led to deep grievances among the immigrant Nigerian residents.

The policy of "indirect rule," first expounded by Lord Lugard, intended that government administration be carried out through traditional native authorities who, if not immediately ready to adapt their systems of government to modern conditions, could learn to do so through education. This method was economically and politically expedient for an imperial power. For its time, with its pretense that the natives were being represented by their traditional rulers, it was also a liberal expression of the "white man's burden." It was committed to bringing the traditional political structures in line with modern times while maintaining the purity of ethnic cultural lines. James Coleman describes the program as one designed

to minimize the contact between educated masses and the illiterate masses . . . which [in the Northern Provinces] included (1) cantonment schools for educated southerners, to confine them to urban communities and isolate them from the native administration system; (2) the training of northern *mallamai* to replace Western-educated clerks; and (3) the education of chiefs' sons, which had been the main motivation for opening Nasarawa School in Kano and King's College in Lagos in 1909.
  The Lugardian policy of excluding educated elements from the native authority system and of preventing their contact with the masses was not peculiar to the north, although it was more thoroughgoing and endured much longer there than elsewhere. It was characteristic of the official attitude throughout Nigeria until the early 1930's, when signs of change began to appear [1958:162].

Jos was officially founded about 1915, but by 1912 there were enough residents to warrant the designation "Hausa Settlement, Jos." From the very beginning the colonial administration tried to keep culturally dissimilar ethnic groups separate. Thus the urban center of Jos was divided into two separate administrative units: a Native Town, subordinate to the Jos Divisional Native Authority, which was then located in Naraguta; and the Township, which was a separate entity of its own within Jos Division, where Asians and Europeans eventually settled, but in a special "reservation" apart from most of the Africans. Eight blocks, with a total of 150 house plots, were also laid out creating a separate township for non-northern African clerks and traders, who would thus not come under the jurisdiction of the native administration. The squatters who had been living at that site, mainly Hausa-speaking northerners, were removed to the present site of the Native Town. The intention —and the result—of these measures was not only to separate non-Africans from Africans but also to establish residential, administrative, and social segregation between southern and northern Nigerians, for southerners had early received Western education and training in modern occupational skills, while northerners were still backward in these respects.

The administration predicted there would be a "gradual withdrawal of the more alien elements of the Native City population into the Township Sabon Gari [the Hausa term for "new town," but referring to Native Reservation] . . . [so that there might be] no disturbance or interference with the Native Administration" (Jos Township Report for the First Quarter 1921, 208/1921). This view was later altered to consider—but to do nothing more—the possibility of ultimate amalgamation of the native reservation of the Township with the Native Town (Plateau Province, Office File 274/S.2, 1950–55). The administration also considered handing over control of the area to the indigenous population of the local native peoples, but this aim never transpired.

Townships were created elsewhere in northern Nigeria to accommodate the immigration of educated Africans who were needed to fill clerical and other positions of skill for government and business. Those who were recruited for these positions came from southern Nigerian tribes and from other English-speaking West African countries, particularly Sierra Leone. It became evident to the colonial administration that the traditional authorities of northern Nigeria could not cope with a modern cosmopolitan situation such as was created when educated Africans formed an urban population. Therefore, when the Divisional Headquarters was transferred from Naraguta to Jos, it began a series of reforms about 1920–21 in the city's administration to deal with its special problems. At that time, the governor of the Northern Provinces declared Jos officially to be a second-class township. First-class townships were allowed to elect councils, but because Jos Township was second-class, its council was determined by the administration (and today is determined by the regional administration). The geographical and jurisdictional boundaries of the Township were defined by the governor, who also authorized a Local Authority, a civil servant counseled by an advisory board, to make such by-laws and ordinances as came within the limits of the Township Ordinance of 1917. The advisory board of 1921 was composed entirely of Europeans representing government departments and European commercial interests. Except for the later inclusion of African and Levantine advisory board members, the Township administrative structure remained virtually unchanged up to the time of Nigeria's independence in 1960.

Both the Township and the Native Town have had limited powers of local government and civic administration even since the country's independence. The Township is under the jurisdiction of the Ministry for Local Government of the Northern Region, with communication and command generally channeled through the Resident (since 1962 called the Provincial Commissioner) of Plateau Province. The Native Town, however, is a Subordinate Native Authority under the partial control of the Jos Native Authority, which is coextensive with Jos Division.[1]

The efforts of the administration to maintain as distinct the separate ethnic identities of the community extended to courts of law. By 1920 or earlier there was an Alkali's Court in the Native Town, and all subsequent native courts in Jos were Alkali Courts, despite the loud protests of non-Muslims who sought to establish "Mixed" (Native) Courts in the 1950's.[2] A Supreme Court was established when the Township was founded in 1915. It was presided over by the Local Authority (then called a Station Magistrate) and had jurisdiction over "all suits and matters to which a 'non-native' is a party" (Jos Township Report for the First Quarter 1921, 208/1921; "non-native" in this context is a non-northerner). In 1934 the judicial powers of the Local Authority were considerably reduced when the Magistrate and District Courts in Jos took on most judicial functions.

1. The civic administrative functions and activities of the Township Local Authority and the Town Native Authority are similar. Further details on the formal colonial administraton of these divisions can be found in Hailey (1951, pt. III:61 ff).
2. For a description of the structure and practice of Alkali courts, see Sklar (1966:355–365).

During the time of my residence in Jos the Nigerian Federal Police had jurisdiction only in the Township, and the Native Authority Police were responsible for maintaining law and order elsewhere in the city. However there was some coordination of their activities in Jos and on the minesfield. (Further, see Hailey 1951:69.) Since January 1966, the two police forces have been combined into one.

In 1921 the office of Hausa District Head was abolished. By then the alien residents were numerous, heterogeneous, and according to the Resident "presented problems which required much thinking out" (Plateau Province Annual Report for 1921). The Resident's version of an ultimate solution was to have all communities under the administration of the local populations, in line with Lugard's policy of indirect rule. This was not possible in the foreseeable future because the indigenous Plateau peoples remained much as they had been twenty years earlier, before the occupation of their land. Even though the foundations of a plural society had been laid, the administration still considered "Hausa Settlements" as "purely alien enclaves having no sort of authority over the pagans [the native peoples of the Jos Plateau]: the policy is the other way on. . . . The land is the pagans' and their rights are jealously guarded" (Plateau Province, Annual Report for 1921). The problems of administering a heterogeneous community were recognized as early as 1926, when the Resident wrote to the District Officer in charge of Jos Division:

In Jos Division there is no Native Authority worth speaking of. . . . We are not proposing to foist any alien scheme of administration on to these natives of the Plateau; for it is quite certain that, had the British not arrived, these people would have had to evolve some such administration for themselves or be annihilated through slavery or some such disaster. . . . The alien-native so-called "Hausa" settlement must, for some time to come, be dealt with separately as an area within a Native Administration area proper [Jos Native Reorganization, Archive File 211/1920, letter dated November 20, 1926].

The persistence of using the term "Hausa Settlement" reflects colonial administrative inconsistency, for the British regarded at least the Native Town of Jos as Muslim, despite the fact that neither the traditional religion of the indigenous people nor that of most of the population of Jos itself was Muslim. In line with this concept of a Muslim area, the administration restricted the purchase of imported alcoholic beverages by all Africans and forbade their sale in the Native Town. When "the clerks [meaning southern Nigerians and other West Africans] in Jos did not abuse the privilege" of buying beer and wine, they were permitted to purchase a certain amount of liquor (Bauchi Province Annual Report for 1922). The educated Africans in Jos bitterly resented this restriction and successfully fought for its repeal, which came in the late 1930's.[3]

This type of British protectionism amounted to paternalism. In controlling liquor sales the administration was not so much concerned with morals as it was with defining and protecting a Muslim area, and similarly it persisted in keeping the native courts in the Native Town Muslim. Paternalism carried over into other areas. For example, courts were closely supervised by Residents and District Officers, who had the power to review and revise decisions of the Alkalis or to transfer to another court any case in which they felt there had been a miscarriage of justice. Consequently, petitions and appeals of all sorts bypassed institutional government channels and went directly from the African petitioners to the foreign Administrative Officers. The language of these letters of appeal often clearly expressed the dependence of the Africans on these political and social father figures.

The paternalistic attitude to Africans extended beyond the bounds of formal government and was undoubtedly strengthened in Jos by the large resident European population. Even the Local Council Nigerian Chamber of Mines (a kind of Chamber of Commerce of

3. Irritating to the non-northern African population in Jos was the clear bias of Englishmen for Muslims, especially Hausa. Non-northerners, particularly the Ibo, were considered intruders. This bias was evident in government reports and has been noticed by other observers. Banton mentions that in Freetown the "Englishman frequently has more respect for the native Muslim than for the native Christian" (1957:116). Similar references may also be found in Coleman (1958:145–153; 1960:337).

the mining industry that had always excluded African members) discussed such questions as an increase in the quota of liquor purchases to Africans. Also the Local Council Nigerian Chamber of Mines was sometimes invited by the Administration to offer its opinion on questions of policy, and members of the Chamber did not hesitate to speak out without invitation.

Although there is little direct information in the government records about the early forms of native administration in Jos Town, the patterns are suggested from various evidence. In line with the established policy of maintaining distinct ethnic lines, the administration early encouraged a system of civic participation by residential wards in the Native Town. The exact nature of popular representation in the Native Town during the 1920's is uncertain, but it appears that the various ethnic communities were informally represented by tribesmen of their own choosing, who held unofficial titles in Hausa as *Sarkin Yorubawa, Sarkin Iboawa,* etc. (translated as "Chief of the Yoruba People," "Chief of the Ibo People"). The Hausa representative was called *Sarkin Jos,* but this title, "Chief of Jos," referred to the Native Town and not to Jos Division, which it later came to be associated with. In 1929 there were six wards, each with a Ward Headman responsible for collecting taxes and settling minor disputes. He was also supposed to keep the local District Officer informed of vagrants, trouble-makers, prostitutes, habitual criminals, and other undesirables whom he wished repatriated or at least removed from Jos (Jos Division Quarterly Report, 1929). From all indications it is clear that the administration thought representative local government in terms of tribes, with traditional authority as its keystone.[4]

In 1932 an unofficial Advisory Council to the *Sarkin Jos* (of the Native Town) was formed as a result of a demand for the appointment of a *Sarkin Yorubawa* (apparently that title had previously

4. For a description of a similar situation in Northern Rhodesia and an excellent analysis of the inapplicability and incompatability of traditional ethnic authority and representation under modern urban conditions see Epstein (1953; 1958).

been withdrawn). The members of this council, composed of four ex officio ward heads and twenty-three southern representatives of various tribes, acted as advisors on matters affecting southerners and nominated African members to the Township Advisory Board. According to Perham (1937:151) the southerners were "by no means easy neighbors" with the northerners during this period. Perhaps it was partially as a means of protection that the southerners took an active interest in civic affairs. In 1934 they were asked to assist in the town revenue assessments and to sit as honorary assessors in the Court of the Alkalin Jos when he dealt with cases involving a southerner.

From local tradition as well as the records of the administration it is certain that from 1914 to 1952 the Hausa of the Native Town elected one of their members to be chief of their community with the title of *Sarkin Jos.* Ten such chiefs served in direct succession and were supposed to manage the day to day affairs of the Town. Administration records are full of the dismissals of these chiefs for inefficiency, bribery, graft, and corruption, but a tradition had been established to which the Hausa community clung tenaciously. After the Jos Town Council was formed in 1951, the leader of the Hausa community always sat as its vice-president and assumed the title of *Magajin Garin Jos* (a traditional Hausa title which can be translated as "Town Administrator"). This title was in fact a sop thrown to the Hausa community which felt (correctly) that the administration was trying to transfer power from it to the indigenous people, particularly the Birom. The Hausa protested against this and constantly petitioned to have the Native Town removed from the jurisdiction of the Birom Native Authority. This protesting led to the 1952 suspension of the Jos Town Council by the Birom Tribal Council on the grounds that there were too many political intrigues in the town council, that it was not working satisfactorily, and that the members were irresponsible and obstructive. In 1954, to ease the growing tensions between Birom and Hausa, the name of the Birom Native Authority was changed to Jos Native Authority, and the chief of the Birom became Chief of Jos. It was not until 1958 that the Chief of Jos resigned as president of the town council to allow an appointed Hausa to replace him.

When the Jos Town Council was established its elected members were proportional to tribal representation within each ward. Election to the ward councils, begun in 1950, was also based on tribal representation, and the ward councils acted as electoral colleges in the town council elections of 1951. The intent to accommodate as many ethnic groups as possible resulted in a Town Council swollen with representatives: "The elected Jos Town Council has not proved a great success. It was rather too big for its purpose and those who were put forward have spent most of the time in arguing and very little of it in creative process of thought" (Annual Report Plateau Province, 1951).

The ward councils, also unsuccessful, were abandoned in 1953. The records indicate that only the council of the Ibo ward (*Sarkin* Arab ward) had met regularly and shown any sense of civic responsibility. Subsequent town councils were also short-lived. Since the Yoruba, with the Ibo, were recognized by the administration as being more civic-minded than the Hausa, an attempt was made to restrict Hausa seats on the town council. In 1953 a District Officer expressed to the Resident his view: "In the past it was considered necessary [to allocate seats in the Council on a tribal basis] in order to prevent a Southern majority, but it is wrong in principle and when Northerners received this protection they abused it" (Provincial Office File NAC/30).

Nominations for election to the town council in 1954 were again based on wards—four members from each of the four older wards and three from one new ward were elected. This procedure still had the effect of representation by tribes, since wards were dominated by different tribal groups and would have given the Hausa a disproportionate majority if the franchise had not been limited to plot-holders or those who had paid a tax of £2 or more during 1953–54. Since 1956 the elections to the council have been based on wards, but political parties have played a more prominent part and candidates have since been identified by party affiliation as well as by tribe. However, even as late as 1956 some members of the town council held the official Hausa titles of *Wakilin Yorubawa*, *Wakilin Hausawa*, and *Wakilin Ibo*, these being the recognized representatives of these tribes in Jos Town. After 1956 several town councils were disbanded and reformed. Titles indicating tribal representatives were discontinued, and there developed a policy reversal in an attempt to discourage ethnic representation. Ward representation officially continued in the council through the appointment of ward heads as ex officio members[5] and through the number of representatives allocated to each ward on the basis of its total, not tribal, population.

Local politics were bound to be based on tribal loyalties. This feature is not limited to Jos, and one cannot hold the colonial administration entirely responsible for it since the tribesmen themselves continually clamored for tribal representation in the councils and the native courts, reflecting their belief that this was a necessary measure for the protection of their ethnic communities in an alien area. This brief review cannot do justice to the extent and occasional ferocity of inter-tribal hostilities in Jos. Skirmishes between political parties, each tribally dominated, have been reported periodically from the early 1950's to the present. There is singular absence, however, of any official record or even recognition of the bloody riot between the Ibo and Hausa that occurred in 1945, costing the lives of at least two persons. But the administration did not disregard the situation completely. In one annual report there is the admission that Jos "with its polyglot population, must always be considered a potential trouble spot" (Jos Division Annual Report for 1954).

The evidence from Jos would support Coleman's observation that "for the vast majority of Africans socialization is to the kinship, lineage, tribal, or status group, which for all practical purposes continues to be regarded as the terminal political community" (1960:332). Unquestionably, the extreme concern of tribal groups for official representation is a natural response to living as im-

5. No non-northerners are co-opted to native authority councils.

migrant aliens in a culture where tribal affiliations tend to be the primary loyalties. It is largely for this reason that voluntary associations in Jos are most frequently based on tribal affiliations and are rightly called tribal unions.

General Characteristics

Characteristics commonly associated with West African non-traditional urban centers are ones that apply to Jos: a large proportion of immigrants, ethnic diversity, and a tendency for ethnic groups to live in separate quarters and to be identified with specific occupations (Church 1959:15–28; Little 1959a:7). Like other large mining towns in tropical Africa (Church 1959:19), sections of Jos are divided by tribe or otherwise homogeneous people. As mentioned previously, the division occurred originally because of the colonial administration's decision to keep educated immigrant Africans separated from the illiterate northerners. After establishing the division, the colonial administration set higher values on building plots within the Township and enforced a building code not in keeping with the traditional Muslim practice of wife-seclusion. Since the Muslim northerners generally had smaller incomes than southerners, economic as well as cultural factors inhibited the settlement of northerners in the Township. But even northern landlords who own buildings in the Township tend to reside in the Native Town. Inertia and familiarity are additional reasons for this gross settlement division. Once the pattern had been established, immigrants gravitated toward more familiar neighbors, either because they were of the same religion, culture, family, tribe, or were friends. (This general pattern can be observed from Tables 3 and 4.) Although wards and quarters are not given official tribal designations, there is significant ethnic clustering in the Native Town. (There are no similar spatial designations, such as wards, in the native reservation of the Township.) Birom, Ibo, Yoruba, Calabar, and Urhobo clusters are particularly noticeable when one compares their tribal percentages of the total town population (Table 3, column b) with the percentage of the ward population of the town total (bottom of each ward column).

In the Native Town, women of all tribes may be found as petty traders in the market, except where restricted by the Muslim religious observance of seclusion. The unskilled male labor force consists mainly of Hausa and central Nigerian tribesmen. Wealthier Hausa are also traders and middlemen, dealing mainly in produce. In addition, Hausa hold semi-skilled and skilled jobs, and their proportion in these areas is growing as a result of the Northernization Policy and as education facilities in the North become increasingly available.

Most of the artisans, junior clerks, canteen clerks, and professionals are southern Nigerians, with a preponderance of Ibo. The Ibo also figure importantly as traders, particularly in the transport of food products in both directions between Jos and the South; many own their own fleets of lorries. Most of the civil engineering contractors are also Ibo, as are many of the landlords. The Yoruba in Jos are mainly traders, although many are also landlords and lorry owners dealing in the transportation of passengers and goods. Many are found in the skilled work associated with the Ibo. In Jos there have always been many people from Sierra Leone (mainly Freetown Creoles) and Ghana. These have largely been chief clerks or senior service office-holders in government and business; they are the nucleus of the modern Western-oriented elite among the Africans in Jos.

Church observes that European-created towns usually have a central administrative and commercial quarter, which "is in complete contrast to African towns where there is little or no functional segregation by quarters and where commerce is often carried on in or outside the compound" (1959:19–20). While Jos has a commercial and administrative section removed from the residential area, it maintains the traditional commercial activities in the ubiquitous petty trading of women who sell tinned food, cigarettes, gari (cassava flour), soap, cosmetics, and similar items from small stalls at or near the entrance to house compounds.

Jos has lacked attraction for the target worker, whose rapid or seasonal influx in other parts of Africa has resulted in an imbalance in the sex and age proportions of the population and created social problems associated with overcrowding and a lack of females (Gutkind 1960, 1962; Little 1959a:7). Although the tin mines outside Jos entice seasonal migrations of unskilled workers, with few exceptions these men do not live in Jos or stay to find employment there.

There are no census data for Jos with which to compare age ratios over time, but from the available data the totals of children and adult males and females have been graphed (see Charts II, III, and IV). The data indicate that no serious imbalance in the sex ratio has existed since the mid-1940's, and the upsurge in the number of children from the late 1940's onward would also indicate that Jos had by then become an urban community of some stability. Families have evidently regarded Jos as a place where they can raise their children. The unusually large number of schools in Jos has played an important part in this development since many parents who wish an education for their children do not have to send them elsewhere.

Over 90 per cent of the Jos school-age children attend school (Provincial Office File EDU/18, 1959, p. 121), an extraordinarily high percentage for Nigeria, which can be partially accounted for by the large number of schools. In Jos Division there are secondary and trade schools, teachers colleges, and other schools for intermediate grades at Kuru, Vom, Bukuru, and Gindiri, and outside the Province, at Toro. In Jos itself secondary schools are of recent origin, but educational facilities include a trade school for mining, a domestic science center for girls, and several commercial colleges offering instruction in typing and clerical work. The elementary and primary schools have more than 6,000 children enrolled. Adult education classes started in Jos in the fifties, but they have not been regularly maintained. The results of all these efforts are impressive:

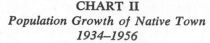

CHART II
Population Growth of Native Town
1934–1956

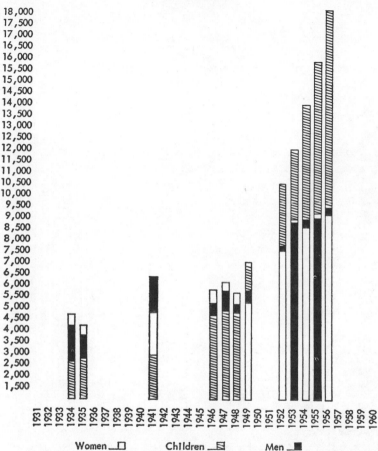

Women ⬜   Children ▨   Men ◼

EXPLANATION OF CHARTS II, III, AND IV: The columns in these charts do *not* represent the cumulative totals for men, women, and children. The top of each black, white, or striped symbol indicates the number of persons in that category resident in that year. For example, the 1941 column of Chart II reads as follows: 6,500 men, 5,000 women, and 3,000 children were resident in Native Town (total: 14,500 persons). The most numerous group appears at the top of the column, the next most numerous below that, and the least numerous at the bottom.

CHART III

Population Growth of the Township
1934–1960

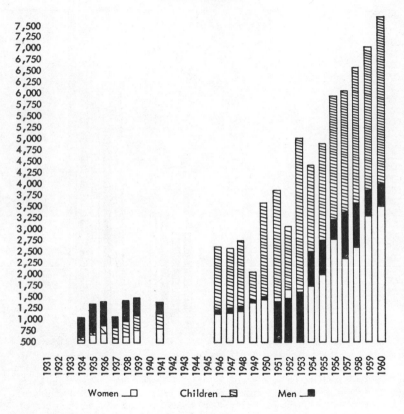

7,500
7,250
7,000
6,750
6,500
6,250
6,000
5,750
5,500
5,250
5,000
4,750
4,500
4,250
4,000
3,750
3,500
3,250
3,000
2,750
2,500
2,250
2,000
1,750
1,500
1,250
1,000
750
500

1931 1932 1933 1934 1935 1936 1937 1938 1939 1940 1941 1942 1943 1944 1945 1946 1947 1948 1949 1950 1951 1952 1953 1954 1955 1956 1957 1958 1959 1960

Women ▭   Children ▨   Men ▰

CHART IV

*Combined Population of Native Town and Township
1934–1956*

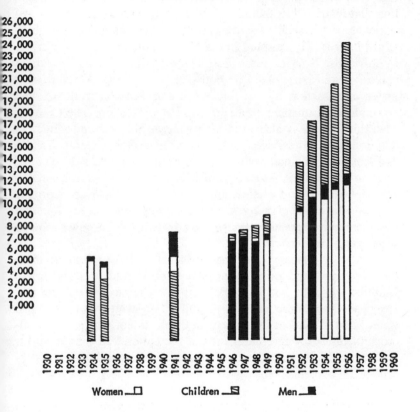

Jos has the most literates of all the northern Townships, and 47 per cent of the population has passed Elementary IV standard or higher. For the same grade the percentage of Kaduna (the capital of the Northern Region), the next highest, is 34.6.

Considering conditions in other parts of Africa, Jos has an abundance of hospitals and clinics for its population. The European Hospital, so named because of the past practice of racial segregation that restricted its facilities to whites, is open to Europeans and Africans of the senior service class and those wealthy enough to afford its fees. The hospital in the Native Town is used exclusively by Africans. Both of these hospitals also function as outpatient clinics. A third hospital, for both Europeans and Africans, was under construction by the Sudan Interior Mission in 1962, and served as an outpatient clinic prior to its completion. The Catholic Maternity Home is also used as a general hospital and clinic. In addition, medical services include the Government Child Welfare and Ante-Natal Clinic; a clinic for schoolchildren; and a third clinic, open to the general African public, run by the Seventh Day Adventist Mission; and a clinic for lepers. There have been private medical practitioners in Jos since the late twenties, not to mention the many native practitioners whose advertised skills cover a much wider range of services.

Because Europeans have resided in Jos in large numbers, there has been early and extended development of amenities and urban facilities: schools, hospitals and outpatient clinics, telephone service, paved roads, better housing and urban sanitary codes, piped water, a large number of grocery and department stores, and numerous facilities for entertainment and recreation.[6] In these respects Jos's early development had no parallel in Nigeria, with the exception of the capital, Lagos.

6. One of the significant social consequences of this early development of modern amenities in Jos is that it led to local African nationalist frustration with the "separate-but-not-equal" policy regarding access to these facilities.

In other parts of Africa, slum conditions are often cited as a regular occurrence in the towns, and there is often an absence of the services considered essential for the orderly development of an urban area. While slum conditions are not entirely absent in Jos, there are building and sanitary codes, nuisance regulations, tarred streets, sewage systems (in the form of deep, open trenches along the roadsides), street lights, police protection, a fire brigade, administrative councils, and advisory boards—all of which mark the city as one of the most progressive in Africa.

It must be noted, however, that although progressive, Jos is by no means equal to European cities of a similar size. It cannot be the case if for no other reason than the limited funds available for the development of civic amenities. For example, septic tanks are used in the Township and in the Government Residential Area, but most disposal is by bucket. Pit latrines in the Native Town are being replaced by bucket latrines, and the Local Authority of the Township and the Jos Town Native Administration maintain bucket-removal services for a small annual conservancy fee. The night soil removed is composted. Efforts are made from time to time to provide more and better health services, to acquaint the public with these new facilities, and to encourage their use. These measures are reported to be quite successful. In 1952 the Health Department initiated local radio broadcasts giving elementary hygiene and health instruction in English, Hausa, Yoruba, and Ibo. These broadcasts, it is claimed, stimulated a five-fold increase in attendance at the Child Welfare Clinic.

Except for a few short periods in its history, Jos has been free of the problems of congestion. Reports indicate that there was overcrowding, though not acute, in 1929, 1945, and again about 1951. These high years may explain why the Northern Region Census for 1952 indicates that the population density for Jos Township is by far the greatest of the northern townships (Northern Region Census 1952, Chart II b). In 1945 the houses in the Township were described as of solid construction; there were fewer slum dwellings and much less overcrowding than in Kano. The Native Town, however, was not equally praised, the center being "grossly congested" (Rowling Report 1946:par. 135).

Jos does not have to cope with the problems created by squatting, the lack of residential security of tenure, and property speculation in peri-urban fringes—conditions that are prevalent in East Africa (Gutkind 1960:129–131). However, it has not been without similar problems caused by the demand upon urban land. One effect of the Northernization Policy was the development of a black market in new plots. Since the number of plots allocated to southerners was limited to 20 per cent and a time limit imposed on the number of years a southerner could hold a plot, many resorted to buying plots from northerners at about £500 each. Even before the extension of the Northernization Policy to plot allocations, there were frequent charges of graft, bribery, and corruption in the allocation and distribution of new plots.

The government maintains a policy of rent control in the Town and Township. The maximum allowable rent depends on a combination of the materials used in the construction of the walls, roof, and ceiling of the house, and whether water in the compound is supplied by pipe or by well. If electricity is not metered, the landlord may charge an additional fixed amount, depending on the kind and number of the tenant's electrical appliances, but regardless of the extent to which they are used. Receipts for rents are an established practice, and the few observed extra-legal arrangements heavily favor the tenants. While services such as repairs are often minimal, there are many examples of landlord altruism. While in Jos, I saw tenants permitted to live rent-free for several months because they were in dire circumstances. This was especially interesting when the parties concerned were of different tribes.

Because of government control the poor housing conditions prevalent in African urban areas are not an acute problem to the people living in Jos. Physically Jos is an attractive place in which to live. Many people say they would rather live and work there than elsewhere, mainly because of the favorable climate and social conditions. The government and commercial firm clerks, skilled workers, and others holding occupations subject to periodic transfer do not hesitate to tell you that they would prefer to remain in Jos if they had their choice.

The commonly described pattern of the primary and secondary school (involuntary) drop-outs, the young men leaving the bush farms for the lure of the city, and the young women following them, is applicable to Jos. They may not find employment in Jos, but they are encouraged to remain by the certainty of free subsistence from their relatives or fellow townsmen while seeking employment. They move on to another city or they remain in Jos continuing the search for jobs because there is no employment where they came from and they are ashamed to return home empty-handed. All of them seek employment in order to help their families at home, and custom enjoins those who are successful in finding jobs to support their younger kinsmen attending school. It is the ideal of every family to have one of its members achieve a university degree and, through higher education, a professional occupation or a senior service position with government or industry. It is believed that when such a kinsman has broken the "occupation barrier" in this way, his sense of family duty will be expressed in providing economic and occupational advantages and privileges to the other kinsmen. It is impossible, of course, to completely transform this ideal into reality.

The degree to which Africans in the city are committed to an urban life is one of the prevailing issues in modern African research and an answer is attempted in the concluding chapter of this study. In Jos, the predominant attitude is that regardless of birthplace, home is the place of one's localized lineage or ancestors. Most people, except Hausa, say they plan to retire at "home" when they leave salaried employment or businesses in Jos. How many of these actually do is undetermined. Many who express this wish also state their desire to maintain their property holdings or to continue their trade or other business in Jos and to return occasionally to inspect their enterprises and to collect their profits or rents. From

Jos alone it was impossible to acquire quantitative data on the number of Africans who actually return to their home town to retire, although my impression is that these are few. As often as this ideal was voiced, regrets were expressed at the prospect of leaving the physical and social climate of Jos and the lifelong friends there. There was little charm in the prospect of going home to money-hungry relatives and age-mates, to family squabbles and land disputes, to threats of witchcraft. Several persons who intended to retire at home later returned to Jos to live out their lives. The people of Jos make up a stable urban population, and the community itself continues to develop its own viability.[7]

Ethnic Relations

In Jos, ethnic association affects almost all designations and social relations. Government reports makes generalizations based on attributed ethnic characteristics, official census figures are based on tribal categories, and tribal representatives are chosen as assessors in the Native Courts on the basis of population proportions. An applicant for a job or a loan may be overlooked due to the foreign businessman's estimate of the personal, ethical, moral, and commercial characteristics of his tribe. The Northernization Policy of 1959 was a deliberate attempt by the Northern Region government to discriminate against southern tribesmen, and this policy was forced on expatriate commercial firms by the administration so that they too hired and promoted in favor of northern tribesmen.

7. The above remarks were written before last year's clashes between Ibo and Hausa in Nigeria. The subsequent return of alien peoples to their tribal areas, particularly the mass exodus of Easterners from the North, has again proved that the conclusions of social scientists (myself in this case) regarding modern African developments are vulnerably subject to the vagaries of shifting realities. When I carried out my research, and up until 1966, Jos was a viable and stable urban environment. But it could not remain so in the face of national social, economic, and political instability. I have not altered the gist of the original text because I believe my analysis to be valid and that with a return of national stability my remarks will continue to hold true for Jos as well as similar urban areas in Nigeria.

The African himself has a strong attachment to the tribe of his birth, which determines in varying degree his political and religious affiliations, style of life, occupational and business opportunities, and directions, dress, diet, and other life habits. The Nigerians in Jos cannot conceive that one may be both black and detribalized. One is identified by name, facial scars, dress, physiognomy, etc., as belonging to a particular ethnic group.[8] This identification extends to non-Africans as well; Europeans are frequently specified as "Irishmen" or "Welshmen," etc.

The extreme heterogeneity of Jos reflects the variety of peoples in Nigeria, of whom almost all are represented. A list of the tribes of Jos citizens would be impressive, and a list of only the central Nigerian tribes represented in Jos would require dozens of designations. (The more numerous and important are listed in Tables 3 and 4.[9]) The population of the city consists almost entirely of immigrants, or "strangers to the land," as they are called. "Owners of the land," the indigenous peoples, make up less than 2 per cent of the urban population, and are also strangers to the cultural life of the city. The heterogeneous cultural influences of the Jos immigrants have historically remote and immediate origins in Asia, Europe, and the Americas, as well as in Africa. In spite of the diversity of people, Jos does not have the language problems found

8. Thus it is that Herskovits can attack the indiscriminate use and misapplication of the concept of "detribalized" (1962:290–291). He lists more than half a dozen authors who have expressed dissatisfaction with that term and suggests that tribal cohesion is strengthened rather than weakened in urban surroundings. Certainly it is so in Jos.

9. The census figures used here, although taken from government files and published sources, should be viewed with some caution. Herskovits has noted the difficulty of acquiring reliable African demographic and census data (1962:182–183). To his comprehensive survey I would add two points from personal experience. In official records two or more different figures were frequently given for the same year. When reviewing the tax rolls on which local census figures are based, I noticed that people will refer to themselves or be recorded as Hausa when they are of various other Northern tribes. Similarly, names of known persons were recorded as Ibo, for example, when they were in fact Ijaw or Edo. Unfortunately, these data are the only materials we have to work with.

TABLE 3
Native Town Population, 1950

	Garba			Galadima			Mantau			S. Arab			Native Town	
	Total	*per cent* a	b	Total	*per cent* a	b	Total	*per cent* a	b	Total	*per cent* a	b	Grand Total	%
Birom	4		2	192	3	92	10		5	2		1	208	1
Hausa	2,122	46	21	4,631	70	45	2,875	65	28	562	13	6	10,190	51
Nupe	100	2	44	60	1	26	65	1	28	4		2	229	1
Ibo	180	4	4	990	15	22	243	6	5	3,175	76	69	4,588	23
Yoruba	2,137	46	53	648	10	16	1,080	25	27	170	4	4	4,035	20
Benin	25		20	52	1	42	30	1	24	17		14	124	1
Itsekri	20		20	25		25	25	1	25	30	1	30	100	1
Calabar	4		9	8		17	10		21	25	1	53	47	*
Urhobo	8		3	54	1	19	50	1	17	175	4	61	287	1
Cameroon	6		30	3		15	5		25	6		30	20	*
Total pop:	4,606			6,663			4,393			4,166			19,828	
% ward pop. of Native Town total:	23			33			22			21				

Column "a" indicates percentage within the ward.
Column "b" indicates percentage of the tribe within the ward to its total in the Town.
* Less than 1%.

TABLE 4

Township African Population, 1952

Northern			Southern		
Birom	125	1.8%	Edo	128	1.8%
Fulani	164	2.3	Ibibio	144	2.0
Hausa	436	6.2	Ibo	3,794	53.8
Nupe	27	.4	Other	752	10.6
Tiv	44	.6	Yoruba	835	11.8
Kanuri	23	.3		5,653	
Other	384	5.4	Non-Nigerians	214	3.0
	1,230	17.0%		5,867	83.0%

Total pop. 7,070

Source: Table 6, Northern Region Census, 1952.

in other parts of Africa (Gutkind 1960:30), for many of its residents can communicate in the lingua francas of English, Pidgin English, and Hausa, the last being easily learned by both Europeans and Africans. Cleavages in the population, ethnocentrism, and parochialism may be found at all levels, from the general allegiance to pan-Africanism or the wider concept of Negritude, to a more limited Nigerian nationalism, or to tribal loyalties, down to the ultimate in parochialism—the unquestioning support of one's natal townsmen against one's fellow tribesmen.

Strong tribal loyalty is fundamental to most residents of Jos, but this allegiance is somewhat cross-cut by political and religious differences. Tribal loyalty tends to be life-long, but it is uncertain whether individuals acquire the other institutional loyalties before or after emigrating from their natal communities. The result of expanded loyalties is some restructuring of the urban community: tribesmen are divided and members of different ethnic groups are united on the basis of church membership or political affiliation. For example, in 1945 a religious split among the Yoruba in Jos occasionally led to physical brawls between members and non-members of the United African Church, and in 1958 the Ogbomosho Yoruba members of the Faith Tabernacle Church clashed with the rest of the Ogbomosho community in Jos, including both Baptists and Muslims. In 1963 the Yoruba community was again divided over the political differences resulting from the split in the Action Group Party, though I heard of no resulting violence. (In spite of these examples, intra-tribal factionalism is not limited only to religious and political differences or to the Yoruba.)

Nonetheless, loyalties are still primarily directed toward one's tribe and kinship group. Rearing and educating the children of relatives and friends in one's tribe, for example, is a common practice, consciously regarded not merely as an obligation, but as a possible future reciprocal investment. Another not uncommon practice is to provide a home for the children of a friend or relative by employing them as servants. Unfortunately kinship does not necessarily assure harmony between apprenticed children and their related masters. The files of the Social Welfare Office bulge with cases of Jos students, runaway apprentices, and young relatives who were exploited as household servants.

What has been labeled "tribalism" finds many expressions in Jos, often ones of hostility. In 1961 the Kanuri complained to the District Officer that they were being discriminated against in favor of Hausa and Fulani in the allocation of building plots. Conflict between Hausa and Birom over political control in Jos has already been mentioned, and their mutual hostility is expressed often and in many ways. Also mentioned earlier was the 1945 riot between Hausa and Ibo. Administrative records abound in complaints of all sorts made by Africans against specific tribes. Expressions of tribal pride are just as common. Solidarity is evinced in tribal union membership and in the non-northerner's avoidance of inter-tribal marriage. Persons will not only laud their own tribal traditions but, often in the same breath, will seek to demonstrate their ethnic group's superiority by denigrating the customs of another group. For instance, a man from Calabar said to me, "The Ibo buy their women [implying that people from Calabar have greater respect for the sanctity of marriage]. We Calabar were the first to be educated in the Eastern Region and all the great Ibo men of today have received their primary education from Calabar men. We had the first batch of doctors and barristers in the Eastern Region but now we are few [proportionately, not absolutely]. We used to lead in all fields of sports but now we are swamped and eclipsed by Ibo."

The Northernization Policy, which is the outgrowth of a phenomenon common to colonial territories approaching or having just achieved self-government, has "in many instances tended to activate latent particularistic interests and to sharpen status, racial, and tribal cleavages" (Coleman 1960:318). In northern Nigeria the implementers of this policy progressively removed educated southern Nigerians from government and commercial posts and replaced them with previously disadvantaged northerners. Extension of this policy favored northerners and denied southerners in matters of scholarships, loans, grants-in-aid, contracts, and building plots (see Coleman 1960:282, 317–318). The consequences of this policy have been very discouraging to a large part of the population of Jos. In some cases it has resulted in substantial losses of wealth and financial hardship, as well as widespread anxiety and bitterness. What the future holds, now that the Northernization Policy has been officially repealed, no one knows, but perhaps the remarks of an expatriate civil servant, written on February 19, 1959, indicate what we may expect:

I am of the opinion that the vast majority [of southerners] want only to be allowed to trade without interference, to live in peace, and to be allowed, if possible, to settle here permanently. They are perhaps only too well aware that if they allowed themselves to meddle in politics they would run the risk of antagonizing the northerners, and being in a very small minority they are naturally very cautious. [Letter from the Jos Local Authority to the Resident, Plateau Province, Township File TOW/3].

Although inter-tribal antagonisms are recorded at least as far back as the time of the Great Depression, when it was rumored that the Europeans would leave, the Hausa would take over, and the Birom would drive out the Hausa, there are many friendly inter-ethnic relations. In rare instances southern tribesmen have been converted to Islam and have become "Hausa" in speech, dress, and custom. More common than this type of conversion is the expression of friendship between persons of different tribes. The "Young Juju Society," which performs Ibo masker-plays during Christmas and Easter, is made up of young Ibo and Yoruba boys. Men of different tribes who work together aid one another by mutually offering hospitality, loaning money, and finding employment. The prominent figures of the community, who may be either traditional or westernized, Muslim, Catholic, or Protestant, and of conflicting political affiliations, are found on the Board of Governors of the Roman Catholic Mission secondary schools in Jos. Inter-tribal harmony occurs most often in the fringe strata of society. At two extremes, the modern westernized elite feel themselves above tribalism, and the criminals of Jos gang together regardless of tribal affiliation.

Alongside parochialism there is a conscious effort in Jos to express a cosmopolitan liberalism. For example, when the tribal unions stage public ballroom dances to raise funds, and play host to the wider community, the master of ceremonies usually shares his duties with a prominent local personality of another tribe, or these duties are assumed in toto by a person of a different tribe. These ballroom dances are always inter-tribal affairs. Members of other tribes who have personal connections with members of the hosting tribal union thus have an opportunity to express sentiments of personal attachment, to make contacts of friendship or business, and to express non-parochial sentiments generally. A similarly functioning affair, even more widely attended, is the annual church bazaar. These festivities are held at harvest-time and, while the sponsoring church may be dominated by one tribe, people of different tribes and churches participate in the gay, carnival-like atmosphere.

Tribal Unions and Voluntary Associations

African voluntary associations comprise a host of friendly societies, mutual benefit groups, social clubs, church groups, sports and recreation association, marketing organizations, amateur traditional singing and dancing groups, tribal unions, and other groups.

These are mainly to be found in the new cities, among immigrants, for whom they serve functions traditionally performed by kinship, community, and other primary groups. Most remarkable is the flexibility of these organizations in adapting to modern urban conditions and assuming responsibilities and actions to meet a wide variety of needs.

Under conditions of traditional society, kinship and community institutions provided individuals with economic, social, and psychological security. A person could depend on aid should misfortune strike him, and if bad conditions were widespread he knew that his lot would not be worse than that of his kinsmen and neighbors. Emigration out of the traditional community upset these assurances, so that throughout Africa voluntary associations (and in Jos, tribal unions particularly) have arisen to meet the needs formerly satisfied by traditional institutions, and which colonial or independent governments could not provide for.

While immigrants may view themselves as living in an alien community, they do not regard themselves as existing in a social and cultural limbo—a state of suspended animation that requires for revitalization a return to the natal home. On the contrary, they are committed to living in an alien area, and wish their existence under these circumstances to be as meaningful and satisfactory as possible. For most people in Jos it is largely through membership in their tribal unions that these satisfactions are realized. Southall's observation on these unions applies remarkably well to Jos: "Where towns are closely associated with a locally dominant tribe . . . specifically tribal associations are not found among its members because the tribal structure is sufficiently elaborate and adaptable to provide alternative channels for social relationships" (1961a:38). Thus, in general, the greater the distance of the homeland from Jos, and especially if it is in the South, the stronger the tribal union is. Consequently, the strongest unions are those of the Ibo and Yoruba. The structure of the Ibo tribal union is particularly elaborate, including a hierarchy of command, and seems to be a model for other tribal unions. (For further discussion see Hailey 1951, pt. III: 19–20; Little 1957, 1959a:5–13).

Tribal unions are ubiquitous in Jos, as they are throughout Nigeria. When enough persons of an ethnic area are present in an alien community (Hausa and other Muslim northerners largely excepted) they form a tribal union, and when these associations are already present in the city newcomers are fitted in quite readily. Tribal unions not only provide the positive satisfactions of comradeship and moral and economic support; they are also designed to ease the immigrants' entrance into the alien community and aid members of long residence in various ways. Four of the informants who completed their interviews for this study were prominent members of tribal unions. Their union membership was very important to them, as will be shown in later chapters, and in this aspect they were representative of the immigrant population of Jos. An Ibibio from Itu explained the importance of the unions to the immigrants:

At home you are concerned only with your immediate family. There isn't much of unions. But whenever we live away from home we always wish to live with our own stock. We are friendlier to each other when we are away from home. We unite. We form societies when we are abroad. We say to each other, "We will not neglect you. We will suffer with you if you suffer." We are more strongly united when we are away from home and so we form unions to share our difficulties and joys. At home only your close relatives will rally round you in your difficulty, but here distant relatives and countrymen will help you once they know you are in trouble.

Tribal unions—sometimes called Family, Clan, Town, or Improvement Unions—are generally recognized as syncretistic institutions, in the sense that they combine traditional African ideas and practices with Western or European forms. For example, tribal union meetings usually open and close with Christian prayers and are conducted on the model of parliamentary procedure, but the meetings may also include entertainment in the traditional forms of drumming, singing, and dancing. The formal organizational structure of tribal unions follows a Western model, with offices such as chairman, secretary, treasurer, etc. (although there may be a proliferation of offices to include patrons, first and second vice-presidents, publicity and entertainment secretaries), and there are usually a fair number of standing and ad hoc committees. No two unions have precisely the same formal organization, and there is also variation in function and activities from group to group.

In terms of expressive functions, the emphasis of tribal union activities is on sociability and fraternity. Instrumentally, the unions provide assistance and care for the unemployed, sick, and bereaved. In line with traditional African values, one of their most important instrumental functions is to provide a proper funeral for deceased members, which should include a large turnout of mourners and sympathizers. Sometimes a union will return home for burial the body of a member who has died in the city (for comments on such Ibo practices, see Uchendu 1965:65). One of the main functions of some of the tribal associations, as the name "Improvement Union" implies, is uplifting the home community, particularly through the establishment of modern amenities. Money collected from branch unions in various cities is sent home to be used in building or improving roads, sinking wells, and constructing schools, hospitals, and churches. Most of their activities, however, are designed to benefit members living in the immediate alien areas.

Tribal unions usually provide a formal welcome for newcomers to Jos. If the new arrivals have already settled in their living quarters, the union members will turn out in force to visit them on the first free Sunday afternoon. Otherwise, a delegation from the union will meet new arrivals at the lorry park or railway station, and have temporary accommodations for their use if they are needed. The Ogbomosho Union even has rent-free flats to accommodate families for an extended period of several months if necessary.

Members are often given loans in the event of some unhappy circumstance such as business failure or litigation costs, but loans can be given for other purposes as well. Tribal unions always seek jobs for their unemployed members, and will often repatriate a deceased member's family if they are unable to pay for their own transportation. In some cases the union will also bear the expense of sending someone home who is ill when it is thought that only a traditional cure would be effective.

As instruments of social control, tribal unions in Jos are extremely important. They dispense informal justice through their courts, and the sanctions they apply can be severe from the point of view of an immigrant tribesman in a foreign and unfriendly community. Penalties are often light, but may be illegal from the government's point of view, such as the monetary fines imposed on delinquent members. More severe sanctions include heavier fines or expulsion, with the subsequent loss of the social and material benefits accruing to members. Physical violence is sometimes, though rarely, threatened, and pressures are occasionally applied to the individual's homeland family. The ultimate penalty, complete ostracism, is reversed only when the tribesman has complied with his union's commands, humbled himself, and tendered profuse apologies.

Tribal unions are a link with the homeland in two general ways. They provide a means of communication of persons, information, and commands between the home area and the various branches, and they attempt to carry on the home culture and traditions in alien communities. Aside from festivities and ceremonies, the unions aspire in various ways to reproduce the benefits of the traditional environment. For example, as far as possible, they settle disputes among tribesmen within the familiar cultural and social setting of the union, using, within the limitations imposed by government, traditional procedure and substantive law. This avoids the expense of court costs and the "shame" of public exposure, and allows the expression of traditional concepts of justice, which may be at variance with Western concepts. Most important, they insist on the re-establishment of harmonious relations between the parties in a dispute. At any and all costs, tribal unions wish to avoid reporting their fellow tribesmen to the police or to have them involved in embarrassing court cases. The exception to this rule occurs when the tribes are faced with maintaining their dignity in the community.

Southern Nigerians in Jos, especially the Ibo, are acutely sensitive about their public image. Consequently, unions warn their members against behavior that would bring their ethnic group into disrepute; but unfortunately those who do just that—the criminals, prostitutes, rowdies—are not members of their tribal unions. The unions claim they are successful in repatriating undesirables or driving them out of town, but this seems more imagined than real since they frequently petition the local government authorities to repatriate such persons.

The unions claim also that they repatriate girls or wives who have run away from their rural homes and who, presumably, would turn to prostitution were they allowed to remain in the cities, and that they search for and return the runaway wives of men living in the cities. One union in Jos returned a blind man home because he persisted, after repeated warnings to cease, in begging alms—disgraceful behavior in the union's view—and other unions sent home unmarried pregnant girls who had been living in Jos with careless guardians. In one case, a union repatriated a man who had come to Jos, on contract, ostensibly to perform sorcery against one of the union's members. He was not taken to the police, but was put on a train bound for the homeland. A telegram was sent to the Chief at home informing him of what had occurred.

A specific concern of tribal unions is to establish a strong and permanent link between the members living in the alien community and the mother community. Consequently, the ideal of each union branch is to build its own assembly hall, regarded as a concrete expression of the principle that, while members may come and go, while tribesmen in the city may be transient, the mother union (that kinship term is the referent used) remains ever present to succor all her children.

In seeking to establish a secure position for its ethnic group in Jos, a tribal union works to gain some voice or power in local government administrative decisions that affect the tribe's urban community. Government files are filled with petitions and demands from tribal unions for court assessors, council representation, a fair tribal share in the allocation of plots, the right to elect a tribal chief for their community in Jos, etc. Although it does not happen often, some strong tribal unions have even shown a concern for the general public welfare and not just for their own group's parochial interests. They have petitioned and criticized local government authorities and offered concrete proposals and recommendations on community affairs such as town development and taxation. Sometimes tribal unions demonstrate civic-mindedness when they offer the administration the voluntary services of their members, or when they allow their meeting halls to be used free of charge for public functions and local community meetings. Often they rent their hall to other ethnic groups, social, business, or political organizations, usually for a public dance.

Tribal unions are publicly projected as "cultural" groups, but they frequently affiliate with national political parties and largely determine how their members will vote in elections. Sometimes a political party creates a short-lived ad hoc tribal union, as when the Northern Peoples' Congress in Jos formed the Hausa Tribal Union, to express ethnic sentiments or to make demands inappropriate to a national political party.

Ethnic groups express pride in their traditions through public performances of plays, masquerades, and native dances to which the public at large is invited, but for which a small entrance fee is usually charged. These are occasions for the group to make money, if possible, as well as for the members to participate and enjoy traditional festivities. But such performances require a considerable outlay of funds for masks and costumes and at times for importing professional performers from the tribal areas. The group would lose money if it did not have public support wider than its own tribesmen. (Even so, an elaborate affair can be a losing proposition.) These groups also invariably give something of a free show to the community when they parade and perform around the town on their way to the designated arena, usually the football stadium. Such performances are always sponsored by tribal associations.

Ibo and Yoruba unions are the most successful in recruiting tribal members, but the officers of even these unions express disappointment at not achieving total enrollment of potential members living in Jos. It is fair to say that all tribal unions in Jos desire to have every eligible person as a member. Some unions, particularly those of the Ibo, are extremely militant and use every pressure and sanction at their command in pursuing recalcitrants who delay joining. Thus, for those tribesmen who should be members of a union but are not, their tribal association may become for them a negative reference group (see Merton 1957:291–294), and they may become alienated or estranged from their fellow tribesmen. If there are many individuals who expressedly reject membership, the officers of the union become distressed because this incompleteness of membership signifies the relative weakness of the group and a rejection of the group's norms and values. (The reader will find this view particularly relevant in understanding the social isolation of the Efik informant described in Chapter VII.)

The number of tribal unions in Jos is almost equalled by that of non-tribal voluntary associations: guilds, trade unions, political parties, secret societies, professional associations, youth societies, international fraternities, literary and debating societies, social clubs, amateur athletic associations, and the like. The functions and importance of these groups in modern African cities have been dealt with by many authors. They provide a sense of identification and belonging, a platform for expression or exhibitionism, and a medium of achieving a sense of importance through holding office or of achieving higher status in the community. Many of these organizations, to varying degrees, operate like tribal unions and offer similar benefits to their members (see Acquah 1958; Balandier 1955; Banton 1957; Busia 1950; Little 1957, 1959a, 1962; Mayer 1962; Southall and Gutkind 1957).

Many loosely organized associations in Jos demonstrate solidarity and unity of purpose and action. Some of these are best described as quasi-guilds because their membership most often consists of northern drummers, craftsmen, butchers, beggars, lepers, or the lame and blind. They elect their own chiefs and mainly direct their activities toward problems of internal organization and external relations between their members and the public. Sometimes they seek the support of the local authorities through petitions. They may react to unmet demands by exerting considerable pressure on the community, as when Hausa butchers went on strike in April 1962 and the Jos market was meatless for several days.

Modern African Elite

Modern or westernized elite groups, as opposed to tribal elites, were important to the informants in this study specifically and are significant to Jos generally. The term "elite" is ambiguous and has been employed flexibly (see Herskovits 1962:289–291). Its use here follows that of Little (1959a:10), who points out that

the modern town being mainly the product of Colonialism, social status and prestige are largely evaluated in European terms. This results in stratification of the urban population according to criteria of political power, occupation, education, and wealth.

These criteria hold good mainly for the top ranks of the political and social hierarchy, which may include men who are important in either local or national politics or who hold considerable posts in the mercantile firms; the senior civil service; and the headmasters of local secondary schools, as well as the professional classes. . . . Male and female members of the *elite* meet regularly at public functions and clubs and visit each others' homes occasionally for cocktails or dinner. To the extent to which they observe a common way of life and share a common set of business, professional and other interests, this group constitutes a separate social class and even a community on its own.

Current consensus among scholars appears to be that while a clearcut prestige system based on a model of Western culture exists in urban Africa, there is no single prestige scale which can be applied to any modern African urban situation as a whole, and that marked class distinctions among Africans are not yet clearly present. In Jos there is a clear distinction between the modern or westernized elite and the traditional or tribal elite. The Ijaw informant is an example of the former and the Tiv and Yoruba informants examples of the latter. (For a more detailed analysis of the modern African elite in Jos see Plotnicov 1967b.)

The modern African elite in Jos show a distinct preference for social interaction with persons following the same style of life, but they are not "detribalized." They take pride in their tribal histories and traditions, cite achievements of their countrymen, and participate actively in their tribal unions. Nonetheless, their modern cos-

mopolitan character contrasts sharply with the prevailing parochialism of most of the Jos population. The Royal Free Masons, the
International Order of Oddfellows, the Reformed Ogboni Fraternity,
the elite social clubs and modern secret fraternities in Jos, are mainly
composed of educated Africans, many who consider themselves as
belonging to ethnic groups that are minorities in Jos or Nigeria.
It is appropriate for them to express ideals of universal brotherhood
and other anti-parochial sentiments. Almost every man from Sierra
Leone or Ghana whom I knew, members of clearly distinct minority
groups in Nigeria, were active in elite social organizations. Members
of the elite societies and clubs carry into their extramural social
relations the principles of basing social relations on non-particu-
laristic criteria. They count among their acquaintances and friends
Europeans, Indians, Levantines, West Indians, West Africans, and
members of all Nigerian tribes whose way of life is similar to
their own. The influence of Jos elite members is out of proportion
to their small numbers, as evidenced by the respect in which they
are held by the community and the emulation of their behavior.
Since acceptance as social equals by members of the elite is a key
to higher social status, the modern elite must also be considered
as holding a measure of social control. The elite define the rules of
polite behavior for their clubs and societies and demand appropriate decorum from candidates.

Religious Groups

According to the regional Census for 1952, Jos Township has
the highest percentage of Christians in the Northern Region among
its African population. The Census gives these figures: Christians,
84.5 per cent; Muslims, 12, and animists, 3.5. The fact that there
are three major Christian missions headquartered in the Township
(Sudan Interior, Sudan United, Roman Catholic) and that there are
also several minor missions reflects the variety of Christian affiliation among the population. In addition to the more orthodox Christian churches, one will find pentecostal groups like the Jehovah's

Witnesses, African syncretic churches like the Eternal Sacred Order of Cherubim and Seraphim, and an organization of Rosicrucians. The popular attitudes toward Christianity in Jos are often syncretistic, as others have observed elsewhere in Africa. Many good church-goers, including members of the orthodox Christian churches, carry on traditional religious practices in ancestor worship and the like, solicit diviners, make sacrifices, and believe in spirits and witches (see Little 1959a:11–12).

In contrast to the Township, Muslims outnumber Christians in the Native Town. Their group is so dominant that in the late forties the Muslim community repeatedly asked the government for financial aid in building a new mosque. However, the Jos Native Authority felt that such funds would be discriminatory against a substantial minority of non-Muslims resident in the Native Town; to support its argument the Authority compiled the following table (Table 5).

TABLE 5

Ethnic-Religious Affiliation in Jos Native Town, 1950

Muslims		Non-Muslims	
Hausa-speaking	10,281	Ibo	3,100
Kanuri	925	Yoruba	2,160
Shuwa Arab	265	Warri*	160
Nupe	563	Plateau tribes	207
Fulani	305	Ghana and Sierra Leone	125
		Unclassified	1,364
Muslim total	12,339	Non-Muslim total	7,116
Total residents in Jos Town		19,455	

* Urhobo and Itsekri.
Source: Jos Native Authority, Administration File 274/S.1, 1950.

While the figures provide some comparison with those given above for the Township, they must be employed with some caution and some modifications. The compiler of the table worked from crude data that did not include religious affiliation or beliefs as an independent variable. Thus the table presents an unqualified one-to-one association between an ethnic group and its major religious association while neglecting some exceptions to the general tendencies. For example, there are some Hausa and Nupe who are Christians, and there are quite a few Hausa-speaking persons who are neither Christian nor Muslim, but clearly pagan or animist. Among the ethnic groups listed in the non-Muslim column each has varying proportions of Muslims, from almost none among the Ibo and Plateau tribes to small proportions among people from Sierra Leone and a substantial proportion among the Yoruba. While the latter are arbitrarily designated Christian, actually Muslim and Christian each comprise about 40 per cent of the Yoruba population in Jos, with the remainder animist.

The membership of most Muslim sects indicates a tribal or parochial recruitment. The two major Yoruba Muslim sects, whose tenets and prayers differ slightly, are Nur-ud-Deen, dominated by Ogbomosho Yoruba, and Ansar-ud-Deen, identified with Yoruba from Lagos. The Ansar-ud-Deen sect carries greater prestige, having more learned members with a knowledge of Arabic and the Koran, and appears to be more successful in gaining new adherents, even recruiting Ogbomosho members.

Membership in most Christian congregations also coincides with tribal affiliation. The Ebenezer African Church, the United Native African Church, the Baptist Church, and the Faith Tabernacle Church are dominated by Yoruba. Those of the Faith Tabernacle congregation are almost entirely from Ogbomosho. There are two Baptist congregations, one having a mixed African membership, the other consisting almost exclusively of Ogbomosho Yoruba. Anglicans have two church buildings and three congregations. The St. Paul congregation is entirely Ibo, while St. Luke's has one Yoruba congregation and another congregation of mixed southern Nigerians,

TABLE 6

Ethnic Representation in Jos Schools, 1962

SCHOOLS	ETHNIC GROUPS →	Hausa	Fulani	Kanuri	Nupe	Birom	Plateau	Other
Roman Catholic	Students	16	3	1		21		56*
	Student %	1.05	0.20	.07		1.36		3.67*
	Teachers							
St. Luke Anglican	Students	43	2	?	14		39*	:
	Student %	542	0.25	?	1.76		3.91*	6.(
	Teachers				1	1		
St. Paul Anglican	Students	Tribal composition of students is over 90% Ibo; no other information given.						
	Student %							
	Teachers							
Baptist	Students	All northern					67	
	Student %						7.71	
	Teachers	1						
Township	Students	10			7	1		
	Student %	2.96			2.07	0.30		2.(
	Teachers	1						
Native Authority	Students	99	23	6	3	98	32	
	Student %	35.36	8.21	2.14	1.07	35	11.43	5.
	Teachers	4	1			3	1	
Islamiya Post Literacy	Students	85	48	7	12	2	3	
	Student %	50.90	28.74	4.19	7.19	1.20	1.80	1.
	Teachers	1	2			1	2	
Ansar-ud-Deen	Students	34			1	5	9	17*
	Student %	8.71			0.26	1.29	2.31	4.37*
	Teachers							
Nur-ud-Deen	Students	6	1			1	4	
	Student %	1.76	0.29			0.29	1.18	1.
	Teachers						1	

* Data breakdown unavailable; the tribes of "Plateau" and "Other North columns are grouped together where indicated.

	Urhobo-Itsekri	Yoruba	Ijaw	Ibo	Ibibio-Efik	Other Southern	Ghana	Sierra Leone	Other	Totals
0	55	28	12	1,266	28	2	7	1	1	1,527
7	3.60	1.83	.79	81.91	1.83	0.13	0.46	0.07	0.07	99.01
1	1	7		43	7	1	1			61
4	120	249	28	167	16	25	5	7	12	794
6	15.11	31.36	3.53	21.03	2.02	3.15	0.63	0.88	1.51	99
	4	7	3	8						24
	3	2		31						36
		788		14						869
		90.68		1.61						100
		22		1			1			25
3	8	50	27	209	5		6	3	2	338
9	2.37	14.79	6.99	61.83	1.48		1.78	0.89	0.59	99.01
		2		7						10
		4								280
		1.43								100
	1			1						11
		5					1		2	167
		2.99					0.60		1.20	100.1
		1					1			9
2	19	118	2	153	9	1	5		4	389
8	4.88	30.33	0.51	39.33	2.31	0.26	1.29		1.03	99.99
		8		1	1					11
4	4	302*		12	1				1	340
8	1.18	88.82		3.53	0.29				0.29	99.99
		11		1						13

6 of this figure are from Ogbomosho comprising 78.08% of the Yoruba repre-
nted and 69.41% of the total school enrollment.

West Africans from Ghana and Sierra Leone, and a few Christian Hausa. The Methodist and Roman Catholic congregations consist mainly of southern Nigerians. The latter church acquired the early and unique distinction of instituting an integrated European-African congregation.

The present association of ethnic and parochial ties with church membership has roots in the past. When church mission societies were allocating spheres of influence, entire villages or towns were proselytised by one mission exclusively. For example, the Assemblies of God Church of Jos has 47 male members, 43 of whom are Ibo; of these 43, 22 come from Umuahia and 6 from Asaba. There are also 47 female members of whom 44 are Ibo. Seventeen of these 44 women come from Umuahia, and the next largest group, 14, comes from Asaba. It is of additional significance that of the total membership, 36 males and 37 females joined the church in Jos, not in their home community. Members of this church, like those of the Faith Tabernacle, are enjoined from becoming members of tribal unions (described earlier in this chapter), ostensibly because the latter enjoy drinking, smoking, and dancing as part of their recreational and entertainment activities while church members are prohibited from these activities.

Most of the members of the smaller congregations are ones who have moved away from their home communities, and the smaller church, like the tribal union, provides social and economic security for immigrants. For example, the pastor and members of the Assembly of God Church visit the sick and bereaved, give them financial assistance, and help in assuming burial expenses. The church, besides being a force for social control through moral exhortations and sanctions, settles disputes between members and offers counseling and advice through its pastor and other officials. This church group is tightknit, with a high degree of solidarity; members prefer to trade among themselves. One told me, "We love all men, but we love our brothers [fellow members] best."[10]

10. Fiawoo has given similar and additional examples of these church functions for eastern Ghana (1959:83–98).

top: *Men of a Yoruba tribal union, meeting on a Sunday afternoon in the Jos Recreation Club.* bottom: *Tennis at the Jos Recreation Club.*

top, bottom, and top right: *Ibo tribal sections at the celebration of the Ibo State Union during the Ibo National Day in Jos Stadium.*

bottom: *A carpenter, his apprentices, and some of his wares.*

top: *Workers constructing a wood body for a new lorry chassis.* bottom: *Apprentice motor mechanics.*

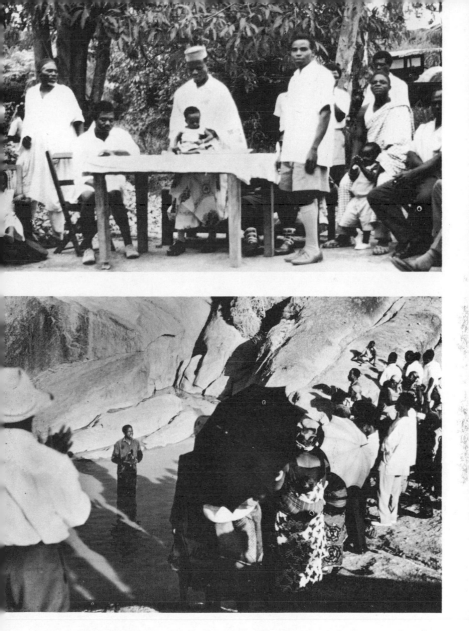

top: *A Tiv naming ceremony.* bottom: *The baptism of new members of the Assemblies of God Mission Church.*

top: *The interior yard of one of the poorer Native town dwellings.*

bottom: *A mother and baby sunning themselves in the doorway of their home, a typical dwelling for a laborer's family.*

top: *A woman of one of the indigenous Plateau tribes, refreshing her-*
    self with a calabash of native beer after a day in the market.
bottom: *A traditional settlement of one of the Plateau tribes, several*
    miles west of Jos.

top: *Modern elite women of various southern tribes at a Christmas party.*
bottom: *Young masqueraders (Yoruba and Ibo) at Christmastime.*

Congregation members try to send their children to the denominations' mission-sponsored schools in Jos. These schools follow the church pattern in showing dominant ethnic clusters, as Table 6 demonstrates. The significance of the disproportion of certain tribes in school may be seen when the tribal percentages within a particular school are compared with the tribal percentages of Jos (Tables 3 and 4). It is worth noting, in connection with the Northernization Policy, that no southerners attend the Native Authority School, the Yoruba in attendance being from the north (mainly Ilorin). Similarly, the Township School (formerly called the Government School) has less than 8 per cent northern students because it is supported by Township taxes and limits enrollment to children of Township residents.[11]

European-African Personal Relations

Europeans and European culture in Jos have provided ample models of modern society and behavior for Africans.[12] The large

---

11. These two schools are not mission-directed. About 1925 government schools were founded in Kaduna and Jos to provide education for the children of resident clerks and other educated alien Africans for whom the nearest educational facilities were outside the Northern Region. Government schools, staffed with southern Nigerian or other West African teachers, offered curricula similar to those of the South. These English-language schools were highly successful in Jos but were of no help to the non-English-speaking Muslim Hausa, whose children had to be educated in Bauchi or elsewhere. In 1938 the Native Town Hausa community petitioned for and was granted a Muslim Elementary School, which later became the Native Authority School when its enrollment was extended to children of all Northern groups. Both community leaders and parents were so pleased with the success of this school that in 1940 they requested English be taught there.

12. Mitchell and Epstein state that Europeans fulfilled Nadel's (1956) criteria for elite emulation (1959:33–34).

The Levantines and Indians who came to Jos in the 1930's and in increasing numbers after World War II also modeled their behavior on Europeans. Although these two groups are regarded by African merchants as business competitors, these ubiquitous traders are proportionately few in Jos, and their social relations with Africans have not been marked with the hostility and bitterness so prevalent in European-African relations.

European population residing in the city and on the Plateau has been unique in West Africa, for, while expatriates living elsewhere in Nigeria during colonialism were subject to periodic transfers (with the exception of some missionaries), the large European mining community in Jos was stable. Also, women began accompanying their mining husbands to Jos around 1910 and brought with them European social amenities. By 1921, less than ten years after the founding of Jos, a European social life of clubs, churches, and dancing parties had been established. Horse races, polo, tennis, and specialized shopping facilities followed soon after. Small wonder then that in 1925 the modern African elite in Jos established the African Sports Club, and in 1937 the Plateau Troop of Boy Scouts. Although there was no social mixing between modern elite Africans and Europeans, many Europeans took on a kind of personal mission to teach Africans European social graces. In 1938 the wife of the Resident achieved "considerable success" (according to the Annual Provincial Report) with her Women's League of Health and Beauty, which had classes attended by the wives and daughters of the elite Africans.

From the time they first set foot on the Plateau until the time of Nigeria's independence, Europeans made every effort to inhibit social contact with Africans. With separate housing estates, specialized shopping facilities, segregated churches, clubs, and movie theatres, they evolved an insulated European colonial way of life that was bound to raise African resentment. Those few Europeans who did treat Africans as equals, those who were not clandestine about their relations with their African mistresses, and those who in other ways did not maintain an attitude of aloofness and superiority toward Africans were rejected by the more strongly established elements of the European community. Such behavior went against the colonial model. Complaints are still heard from English residents against American and British servicemen stationed in or near Jos during World War II for their fraternization with Africans.

Nevertheless, many Europeans befriended Africans and were

considerate of and loyal to their African employees. When the sale of liquor to Africans was prohibited in Jos, Europeans were instrumental in acquiring liquor for their elite African friends. Many financed the education of Africans, and some sent Africans to universities in England. One independent European mining operator bequeathed his entire property—a mining operation and residence worth several hundred thousand pounds—to his faithful African assistant. But such evidences of European altruism are far outnumbered by less compassionate actions.

Nigerian independence has brought major social changes. Residential areas formerly exclusively European are now shared by Europeans, Levantines, and wealthy or senior-service-class Africans. Similarly, all other facilities and institutions that formerly were racially segregated are now integrated, and the Europeans themselves have changed their attitude with regard to socializing with Africans. Most, but by no means all, Africans also seem to hold the attitude of forgetting past inequities and act in accordance with their expressed view that it is possible for Europeans and Africans to be friends.

In Chapter I, I pointed out that the view of modern African urban ethnic heterogeneity and socio-cultural pluralism as being responsible for conditions of social normlessness and personal demoralization had been more recently replaced with one maintaining that institutional variety and flexibility were necessary concomitants of rapid social change and eufunctional in that context. In Chapters II and III, I tried to show that Jos was a suitable urban area for testing these assumptions and theories. It is a relatively new city, of European creation, having a highly heterogeneous population—but no one dominant ethnic group—and being about equally divided between Christians and Muslims. The cultural variations among the populace are great: some tribesmen have a tradition of city living, others do not; still others have been accustomed to modern urban conditions since childhood, while many have come to Jos with only a rural background. There is a similar range of differences in the extent of formal education, occupation skills, and wealth. We may now turn to the informants themselves to see how they exemplify these conditions and how they structure their lives accordingly. We shall also see to what extent the conditions of pluralism and modern urban life result in personal anomie, and to what extent the community as a whole holds the capacity for a viable social integration.

Chapter IV

ISAAC OLU OYEWUMI: YORUBA

Isaac Olu Oyewumi was a man of about 60, a traditionalist whose orientation was toward Yoruba values and moral codes. An ambitious man, he knew he could not achieve the prestige he sought in the world of modern Nigeria, for he had had little formal education and spoke no English. Instead, he had taken traditional Yoruba avenues to acquire a position defined as elite by traditional cultural criteria. He was a conservative, fully committed to being a dignified leader of his family and community in terms of past traditions. At the same time, he was aware that the Nigerian world of tomorrow would differ from his parents' worlds; he recognized the plural and changing social conditions in Jos and Nigeria, and tried to adjust to them. Realizing also that the way of life he valued so dearly would soon pass, he did not handicap his children by trying to foist his way of life upon them, but prepared them for the future as best he could by sending them to school. Still, he felt there were worthwhile elements in Yoruba beliefs, moral codes, and values, and that it was his duty to hand them on to his children. He could not reject tradition completely.

Olu was born in Ogbomosho, in the Western Region, in 1900 or 1901, and had never left the town of his birth until he came to Jos in 1921. When I knew him, Olu was tall, well-built, and in excellent health. His facial scars readily identified him as an Ogbomosho. In keeping with his strongly-held traditional values, he wore nothing but Yoruba dress. He spoke Hausa as well as he spoke Yoruba, and understood a bit of Arabic; but his English was extremely poor, even worse than pidgin English.

I had more difficulty in establishing confidence with Olu than with any other informant. But, in contrast to the others, who often evaded by misinforming, he was forthright when he could not (or would not) answer a particular question. Also, many inconsistencies and contradictions in Olu's statements were attributable to the short-comings of using an interpreter during interviews. In the beginning, it was difficult even to establish a regular pattern of interviews. After the close of an interview I would ask for another appointment, mentioning a specific date, but Olu would merely suggest a call at his shop some time the following week, at which time he would let me know when we could speak at length. His vagueness was not deliberate avoidance, as it appeared to be; as a socially prominent elder among his people, he was so committed to various groups that he was left with little free time. I later learned that he had sometimes given up formal group meetings in order to keep our appointments. He also faced possible criticism because of our rela-tionship. He once told me, "People are suspicious. They see me enter your car every Friday and leave with you. When they see me again, they ask me what we discussed. Should I tell them, they would have no respect for me at all."

The interview series extended from May 1961 until my departure from Nigeria in August 1962. Our interviews averaged about one a week, lasted from one-and-a-half to two hours, and were invariably held on Friday evenings after Olu had closed his shop. The same interpreter served at almost all the interviews, and we three estab-lished a cordial relationship, even though the interpreter often ex-pressed surprise at my audacity in asking highly personal questions of Olu, a Yoruba man of an older generation, and at Olu's readiness to answer them in detail, even when the answers were uncompli-mentary to himself. Olu rarely gave simple answers to questions; his was a holistic approach. He thought of questions as personal challenges to be answered with discourse and many illustrations. He frequently enlivened his points with Yoruba proverbs and occasionally, Biblical references. His prolixity and holistic approach were analytic stimuli for me, for many of his ideas were seminal and many filled gaps in information given previously.

The first few interviews were held in Olu's home. Because he was reluctant to meet there, where we were likely to be disturbed by children or visitors, subsequent interviews were held at my residence. After the interview locale shifted, I had little opportunity to become acquainted with members of his family or to observe family interaction. As a Yoruba traditionalist, he was reluctant to answer specific questions about his family, such as names, birthdates, and the number of living and dead children born to each of his wives. He explained: "The only time a man's children are counted is during his funeral oration, but even then a man sometimes begs not to have this done when he dies." Later, he did provide information about his children, but it was often contradictory. There were other topics which Olu could not discuss without being self-conscious or shy. For instance, he never revealed the amount of his and his wives' financial contributions to the church. He was not prevented from divulging this information by Yoruba tradition or superstition, but by religious ethics.

Olu learned his craft from his father, a weaver of native cloth in Ogbomosho. His father also traded in cloth, and gave Olu his first lessons in trading. Olu had always carefully considered his future. When all his age mates were marrying, Olu resisted his father's pressure to follow suit, protesting that his income from cloth weaving was insufficient to support a wife and family. His desire to seek his fortune before marrying angered his father, but Olu's elder sister and her husband sided with him and arranged for his apprenticeship in Jos, where his native skills were augmented by his being trained in tailoring. Olu's apprenticeship of about three years ended before his first visit home.

Olu described his period of apprenticeship as one of great suffering which brought him little reward. He worked hard for his master and made much money for him, selling clothes and gowns as an itinerant peddler in the mining communities of the Plateau. When he realized how easily profits could be made, he struck out for himself and eventually employed the apprentices of his former master as well as those of other tailors.

Olu was overwhelmed with his early success in trading. When he had left Ogbomosho, his father had given him £10 with which to travel and get a start in trading. After three years his father insisted that the now-prosperous Olu return to Ogbomosho to marry. Olu described his homecoming this way:

My greatest assets then were four boxes full of expensive clothes, a sleeping mattress, a mosquito net, and £35 cash. On reaching home I presented my father with a gift of £30 and he was highly impressed with all my belongings. I had more than twelve pairs of shoes. My success was a glory to him and he took great pride in the way in which I would make frequent changes of costume. People of importance came to see me.

Full of joy and pride, Olu's father gave him a bride, expressing the wish that his son would soon acquire a second wife. Olu decided against such a move; he wanted first to see his father and family living in a better house, one with an iron corrugated roof, which was then a rare luxury.

By now, Olu was fully committed to trading and the accumulation of wealth. When he returned to Ogbomosho a second time, accompanied by his pregnant wife, he took with him the savings of £250 intended for his parents' house. However, a friend inveigled him into investing the money in a get-rich-quick scheme in kola nut trading; the scheme failed and Olu lost his money, much to his distress.

I became greatly depressed. I was so anxious to get my money back that I couldn't sleep. Whenever I tried to sleep, I became covered with sweat. The strain ruined my health. Then I swore never to deal in kola nuts. Ever since I have never eaten kola nuts on any occasion. To this very day I have absolutely abstained from smoking tobacco and never accepted kola nuts as a gift because they almost ruined my life.

After this misadventure, Olu borrowed money to start trading again, and was successful in his ventures. After three years, he was able to build his parents' house in Ogbomosho. "Despite my achievements," he said, "I didn't let up in my trading. I never rested on my laurels."

During his forty years in Jos, Olu had built up an enviable trade with various ethnic groups, and was well known in the city. When I knew him, he operated out of a small shop where he sold cloth. He had once had a much larger shop, but was forced to cut back his business as a result of building a large house in the European commercial district of Jos. Before I left Nigeria, Olu was again in a position to acquire a larger shop.

From the beginning of our acquaintance, Olu let it be known that he was a wealthy man, but he always added that he was not presently able to enjoy his wealth fully. He looked forward to a time when his debts would be cleared and he could start living in the manner to which he aspired. Even though he said he was economizing temporarily, thrift appeared to be one of his basic traits. He mentioned, for example, that when he saw how much money it took to maintain his Chevrolet, he had reverted to his old bicycle for transportation. Similarly, he had sold a refrigerator after receiving the electricity bill for its first month's operation. He explained his thrift this way:

When my children grow up and are no longer a burden to me and all my debts are paid, I'll get myself all the amenities, such as electric cookers and things like that, because I'm somebody who admires utility and beauty. I'm always shocked whenever I think of my debts because I'm not used to it. This cloth I'm wearing is more than thirty years old. These shoes are over three years old. When the soles wore out, I resoled them.

Such stringency must have pained him, for he was something of a dandy and often mentioned his expensive tastes in traditional clothing.

In addition, Olu viewed himself as a man of substance and dignity who felt obliged to behave according to traditional concepts befitting a man of his age, family position, and status in the community. He was not high-born, but was elite by the traditional criteria of the Yoruba community in Jos, and was recognized as such and accorded respect even by non-Yoruba. His position made him self-reliant, pragmatic, and confident that he could achieve whatever he set out to do. He once mentioned submitting an application for a driver's license, and I asked if he meant a learner's permit. Olu said no, that he had driven for three years without any license at all. He added that a learner's permit or adequate driving skill was irrelevant, since the important thing was to be able to take care of the examining officer, which he said he had already done. Olu knew his way around Jos. In addition to his thrift and sophistication, Olu obviously had great capacities for self-discipline and self-denial.

Since one of his major life goals was to retire in splendor in Ogbomosho, many of his material and social investments were a means to that end. The amount and kind of real estate he owned was the ambition of most Nigerians: three houses in Jos, two in Ogbomosho, one in Gombe, and building sites in Ogbomosho. He had applied for additional plots in three different districts of Jos, and was confident that at least one would be allocated to him. He could not estimate the building cost of any of these houses except a European-style house he had erected in the European commercial district of Jos; that figure he knew to the penny, for building the house had brought unexpected financial difficulties.

The section of the Native Town in which Olu himself lived has a preponderance of Yoruba, who call it *Issele Ife*—"the descendents of Ife" (a traditional and historical center for the Yoruba). Olu's was a one-story mud house with an iron corrugated roof and with the kitchen, latrine, and bathroom located in the yard behind. He owned a smaller, adjacent eight-room house, of the same construction and appearance, which rented for £10 a month. Three Yoruba families lived in it: two from Oyo and one from Ijebu.

The house in which Olu intended to live when he finally retired to Ogbomosho was similar to the house he had built nearby for his father, but was unfinished and unoccupied. Still, it was not a forgotten project. He told me: "We never forget home no matter where we are or how long we remain away from home. If you visit my house here in Jos, you will see that it is furnished fully and properly with easy chairs, carpets, electric lights, and so on. Now if you went to my home town and found that my house there was not adequately furnished, would that not be shameful? Therefore, we cater to our homes both at home and away."

Olu was quite proud of the fine house he had built for his father. "Other relatives came to live in it. It has eighteen rooms and four parlors and sitting rooms. They were so happy, they prayed and wished me good luck. I saved them from strain." Olu built one other house for his relatives, in the northern boom town of Gombe. "My house in Gombe contains six rooms occupied by my 'brothers' free of charge. I set them up in business. I don't make any profit from them whatsoever."

Although a successful and prosperous builder, Olu remained rankled by the difficulties he had encountered in building his European house in Jos. Early in our interviews he confessed that it had cost him much more than he anticipated, over £13,000, and that as a result he was in debt. This house was a brick two-story, sixteen-room structure with a cement roof. The downstairs had rooms for shops and the upstairs European-style accommodations for two families. His detailed description of his suffering while this house was being built was strongly reminiscent of the recital of his woes over the kola nut fiasco. He had been forced to take bank overdrafts and to borrow money. Because he had almost no remaining capital and, consequently, curtailed credit, he had to reduce his trading activities. At the same time, his house in Ogbomosho was also being built; thus his resources were further strained.

Olu's saga of house-building sorrows can be traced briefly. Under pressure from the Local Authority, which threatened to revoke his right to the plot unless the house was completed immediately, he sought desperately for loans with which to finance the construction he had begun (apparently) with insufficient capital. He finally accepted a Syrian's offer to exchange £2000 worth of building materials for five years' occupancy of the house. When the house was finished, Olu applied for a mortgage on it from a bank in order to raise capital for his business. The European bank manager, with whom Olu had dealt for years, made the loan conditional on Olu's leasing the house to the bank for the use of its expatriate employees. The agreement with the Syrian precluded meeting this condition; therefore, the mortgage could not be granted. Olu was bitter, the more so when he learned that the Syrian, after occupying the house for one year, had sublet it for £800 a year, thereby doubling his money. To add to his distress, Olu was threatened at this time with a lawsuit by a friend for nonpayment of a loan on the due date. Just before my departure from Jos, however, the five-year agreement with the Syrian came to an end, and Olu was able to assume full ownership of the house.

His constant anxiety at not owning the European house unconditionally seems disproportionate to its worth, particularly as he was in no doubt that he would own it eventually. But to Olu, complete ownership of property was very important. It symbolized his role as a man of importance within his traditional system of values. Furthermore, no Yoruba community leader should ever be in debt. He should be a man of substance, able to demonstrate his prosperity in various ways, among the most important of which is in the area of kinship relations. This attitude is indicated in his account of his responsibilities as head of his family:

One of my sons' wives is now with me. The husband isn't here, but I take care of her as if he were. She and her children eat with us and in all respects there is no difference between them and other members of my household. If the husband sends her any money, I'm not going to ask her for some. That's their business, not mine. It's only my duty to take care of her, that's all.

During last Christmas I bought clothes for everybody in the house. We also feasted. We slaughtered a ram, invited people, and had a nice Christmas party. Somebody who calls himself a husband and is reluctant to do these things isn't fit to be a man.

When I asked Olu to show me the photographs of his family and friends that were not displayed in his house, he apologized for their small number, explaining that his children always kept their favorite pictures. The dearth of pictures was amply offset by the uncommonly large framed photographs hanging on his parlor walls, in themselves further indication of Olu's wealth. There were three different portraits of Olu himself, one showing him posed in a Yoruba cap and gown, holding a hymn book in his right hand. A heavy gold finger-ring was on each hand, and about his neck hung a gold chain which, he said, "touches the ground when I wear it." He remarked that the gowns cost him as much as £100, and that he could no longer afford such imposing self-portraits, since he needed the money to send his children through school. The rest of the pictures showed his family and Yoruba friends. In one group photograph of a voluntary association to which he belonged, all the men wore the same Yoruba dress, to indicate, as Olu put it, "that within our club we are all equal regardless of individual differences in wealth." Another picture, taken in Ogbomosho in 1940, showed a relative of his mother's father wearing the regalia of an Ogbomosho chief.

Olu took deep pride in his family traditions, and tried to uphold them. His father was born in Ogbomosho in about 1867. He died there in 1937 at the age of 70 and was, as tradition dictated, buried beneath the floor of his favorite room. Olu spoke lovingly of this tradition of burying a man in his own compound on his lineage land. He mused sadly that, as a Christian, he could not be buried in the same manner. Indeed, when speaking to me of a promise he had made to a friend, that he would bury him in his "mansion" (a large European-style house), he seemed to be expressing the wish that he too could receive such a burial. Of course, as a Christian and law-abiding man (burial is now permitted in cemeteries only), he could not publicly express such traditional views. Still, his pride in the practice of compound burial remained undiminished.

Olu always spoke of his parents with pride and affection. His father had had no formal education, yet he became chief of a section of Ogbomosho and held the title of *Jagun*. He also occupied an important position in the Ogboni Society, a traditional high-status Yoruba secret society. Recalling his father, he said:

> My father was a weaver—this was our family trade—but before that he was a warrior. That was before the white man came. After they came, the time he didn't spend weaving, he spent farming. In the old days fighting in tribal wars was no hobby but a profession. People made a lot money from that, catching slaves and selling them. Like other warriors, my father was much recognized for his bravery in battle.
>
> My father had three wives, but I knew of only two. The third one was divorced before I grew up but I don't know why. Her only child died very young. My own mother was my father's first wife.

His love for his father was genuine and deep. "When he died, I was the most sorrowful man on earth. I went home for the funeral, and relatives and friends gathered round me to make me happy and forget the past. Although I showed smiles to everyone, deep in my heart I was the gloomiest man on earth, because we were great friends." Olu valued the ideal of filial devotion and cited instances when he had been called on or felt obliged to advise others to show more respect and consideration for their fathers.

Olu's mother also came from a good family; otherwise she and his father could not have married.

> Both my father and mother came from good families. When a member of their families died, there was always a great tribute paid so that everybody in the town would hear it; but if there had been any blemish we would have had no such tributes. Whenever there are quarrels in the town, we feel pride when people bring their difficulties to the families of my parents because they came from good sources [stock].

Olu's mother was born in about 1868 and had died by 1918. She lived her entire life in Ogbomosho and was by trade a cloth dyer,

famous for her skill. Like her husband, she had no formal education and never became a Christian, but through him she became
a member of the Ogboni Society and held an important position
in it. In honor of Olu's lineage she was buried in her husband's home
and not in her own lineage land. Of her many children, most of
whom died as infants, only two surviving children produced offspring—Olu and his elder sister.

Olu was very fond of this elder sister. His attitude toward her
and their relationship as full brother and sister are further examples of his allegiance to the traditional ideals of kinship responsibilities and obligations. "The second person I loved as much as
my father is my sister. She's still alive. I love her more than I love
my children and the same is true for her because we're great friends.
Love knows no faults. That sister of mine is my mother now.
If I have a daughter near home and she's to be married, I instruct
my sister to receive the dowry and she can spend it as she likes. I
trust her. Do you think I could trust her if she were of a different
mother?"

At her request, and in accordance with his values of kinship
obligations, he had sent a daughter to Ogbomosho to live with her.
He spoke thus of the arrangement:

I don't usually send money for the girl because she is [living with]
my own sister and we'll never sit down together to balance our accounts
and debts. Whenever my sister asks me for anything, it's my duty to
find such and send it to her. Recently I heard she had malaria. I immediately bought many things: beverages of all kinds, tea, cocoa, Oval-
tine, malaria pills, a thick blanket if ever she felt cold, plus £5, and
I sent it all to her.

Recently, too, there has been famine in our town because so many
people refuse to farm. A bag of yam flour, which costs £3 here in
Jos, costs £5 there. I decided to send her a bag of yam flour. A bag
weighs more than 100 pounds and the costs of lorry transport for a bag
is 10s. She won't pay me for these things. All I receive from her is
thanks.

She once told me how she spent so much money on my father's
disease before he died that she had no money left. She asked me if I
could help her with a little money. I don't usually carry much money

with me, but I gave her all I had in my pocket—£50. She had to pay for my return fare to Jos because I had given her all the money I had. To be frank, we love each other very much. If any expenses were incurred by my parents-in-law in Ogbomosho while I was here in Jos, she would take care of it.

Olu also had a younger half-brother living in Jos, but he rarely mentioned the man, perhaps because the half-brother was a Muslim and Olu was an ardent Christian. A full sister to this half-brother, also younger than Olu, lived in Ogbomosho. Both of these half-siblings had grandchildren, but Olu never indicated any affection for or closeness to these members of his wider family.

Olu's own first two wives came from "families without blemish or stain," and he spoke of them with affection and admiration. He mentioned that the parents of his first wife were famous rich traders, among the first people in Ogbomosho to roof their house with metal. He said that his marital relations with his first wife were so exemplary that the parents of the girl he was to marry as a second wife approached his family and expressed the wish that he marry their daughter. He protested that he did not have sufficient money for a second wife, but the girl's family said they wanted no money and were prepared to accept a token amount. Olu said that in the thirty or more years he had spent with these women, he had known nothing less than complete happiness. Contrary to tradition, he had complete confidence in his wives, discussing with them all matters pertaining to domestic and family affairs, although he would never let them know his financial position or the details of business affairs. The behavior of these wives permitted Olu to act the part of a dignified Yoruba gentleman.

Olu's wives no longer wished to bear children because they were grandmothers and it was unseemly, by Yoruba custom, for them to have children who would be younger than their grandchildren. His first wife openly declared she would have no more children, and although his second wife had not expressed herself so forcefully, she slept less and less frequently with him. Despite diminished sexual activity, he refused to have commerce with a harlot or prostitute, considering it improper at his age and injurious to his family's good reputation. Because he was a virile man and wished more children, the only course of action open to him as a traditional Yoruba was to take another wife, which he did even though his action was opposed by his children and the church.

Olu showed great agitation when discussing his third marriage. He summed up the bitter experience with the observation, "It was too much sexual desire that caused me to marry that girl." A chief reason for the failure of this marriage was the woman's barrenness and her jealousy of the more prolific wives. Olu sent her to doctors for examinations and treatment, and she finally bore a son, but her behavior did not change. Eventually, Olu sent her and the child to her parents in Ogbomosho. A year later the child died and, on the urging of the girl's family and his own, he allowed her to return to him. She behaved worse than before. Because she believed that he loved his other wives more than he did her, she alternated between fits of jealousy and attempts to monopolize his affections. He told her several times—and by his actions tried to convince her —that he loved all of his wives equally, and would treat each with equal affection and respect, unless behavior such as hers compelled him to do otherwise. She did not believe him, however, and he once caught her putting a native magic love potion into his bath water. Olu was angered; he told his wife she was living in a Christian home and that he would not tolerate anyone's bringing juju into it. Some time later he discovered also that she put a love potion into the food she cooked for him. He then warned her that if she persisted in doing such things she would have to face the consequences. He caught her meddling with magic a third time, when the love potion—consisting of various ingredients in a snail shell— was placed under his pillow. When Olu discovered what had been done he flew into a rage. He said that she had not heeded his repeated warnings, and that he was divorcing her right then and there, and he sent her away.

Olu said that upon his retirement to Ogbomosho he would have to leave his wives and some of his children and grandchildren in Jos. He never made clear the reasons for this decision. Since the children could have been educated equally well in Ogbomosho, I suspect that the most important reason was his wives' desire to stay close to their eldest children. Their wish to continue trading may also have been pertinent. To some extent, Olu's wives were capable of looking after his business affairs in Jos, and this reason may have influenced his decision not to press them to return with him. He was also being reasonable and considerate of his wives in allowing their schoolchildren to remain with them.

Olu was next in line for the headship of his lineage, and, in his view, it was unseemly to return alone to assume his anticipated position of high prestige; it would be undignified not to be supported by both quantity and quality of family. The sheer number of Olu's children—twenty-three—greatly enhanced his prestige; that six of his daughters and two of his sons were married and had children of their own added even more lustre to the family name.

Although he was proud of traditional customs and had married in accordance with them, he did not attempt to impose traditional ideals on his children.

Until my wife stepped into my father's house, we had never exchanged words. That was the custom of our time. The children of today can't do that. Our daughters seek their own husbands and then present their fathers with a husband-to-be. Whatever our parents decided we had to obey. The only thing a son could say was, "Father, pray for us to have a successful marriage."

Perhaps instrumental in determining Olu's outlook was an unhappy experience with his first child, the daughter he had sent to live with his elder sister. He had asked this sister to arrange a marriage, and in Ogbomosho the girl married a man chosen by her aunt. When the bride and groom returned to Jos, Olu was so appalled with his son-in-law that he wanted to annul the marriage immediately. The man was a "lazy drunkard and he talked too much." Olu's sister begged him to give the man a chance. Olu agreed to do so when he learned his daughter was pregnant, but his estimate of the man proved correct. He was incapable of holding a job, and Olu's daughter became responsible for maintaining her husband and her family, which she did by trading in cloth.

Olu looked on children as an investment for the future, since they perpetuated one's hard-earned good name. The children, in turn, were also obliged to lead good lives. To gain this end, parents were responsible for educating their children properly, both at home and in school, and for securing their material well-being. Olu's real-estate investments were made in part for this reason: "I planned for my old age by building houses suitable for rent both to Africans and Europeans, so that I might have something to fall back on. After I built the first house at home, I went home again to build a mansion of two stories for myself, and I bought land for my children."

Olu's children lived according to proper Yoruba standards. Some of his sons were clerks, some tailors, others barbers. One was stationed in Jos with the Nigeria Police. Three of his daughters were traders, two were schoolteachers, and one was a seamstress. Olu said he had tried teaching all of his sons tailoring, but the ones not inclined to this craft he apprenticed to barbers: As he said, "I've taught some of my children tailoring and some of them barbering. The reason for choosing these trades is so that they may come home with me and settle in Ogbomosho and perpetuate my name, because clerks usually stay in the big cities and don't come home. I would like as many children as possible to return home with me."

As long as it was not to his children's disadvantage, Olu employed them as instruments to cement his ties with certain kinsmen and friends. For instance, he allowed one of his daughters to live with and be raised by his mother-in-law. Olu knew that this child would help relieve his aging mother-in-law's loneliness, and as she grew up she could assume an increasing responsibility for the domestic chores. The girl remained with her grandmother until she had to return to Jos to complete her education, but the grandmother did not want to be left alone, and asked that another granddaughter be sent to her. Olu sent her two more of his daughters.

All these relationships worked out well, but the first had been the best. Of this one Olu said, "Strangers think they are mother and daughter. Indeed, this daughter of mine and her grandmother are so close that a real mother and daughter couldn't be as intimate and loving with each other," and he provided several examples of how this relationship and strong affection have continued to prevail.

When his children stayed with their grandmother, Olu paid for their school fees and occasionally sent money for their feeding and other needs. He had sent no money for these purposes to his elder sister, for it would have been inappropriate in a relationship as close as theirs. A further example of Olu's traditional allegiance to kinship and friendship was shown when he and two close friends —one an Ewe man from Togo, the other a Yoruba from Ikare— reciprocally housed and educated each other's children. In this case, however, the children's parents provided fully for the expenses of their children. Olu's son lived five years with the Ewe family in Togo. "This is a traditional custom," Olu said. "It strengthens our love."

Although Olu used his children to express love for kinsmen and friends in a traditional manner, what was expected by custom did not overrule other considerations with regard to his children. He once risked a friendship to protect one of his daughters. The situation demonstrates that his primary concern lay with the child's welfare and shows Olu's awareness of changing social conditions and the necessity of relating rationally to these changes.

I have a daughter who received a good education. She spent five years at a Teachers' Training College. When she finished successfully, a good friend of mine, a well-to-do, asked me to let him marry her. A request from this friend was difficult to refuse, but I had to be blunt about it. She's educated, and he's not the right type for her. She should marry a social equal, so I refused that man. That friend of mine had these shortcomings: first, he's as old as myself, already had two wives and as many children as myself. Second, he's not educated and doesn't understand the ways of modern educated youth.

He's rich, his capital is more than £10,000. If I should ask him to pay £200 dowry he would be only too pleased to do it, but I thought of my daughter's happiness. How could she live in such a home? All her education would be useless. She would not be allowed to teach. She would be under the subjection of her husband and his senior wives. In short, she could never be happy. I felt that if I acceded to his request it would be the greatest injustice to my daughter, so I refused. The girl would only be of value to him for a very short time, and then he would look for a new wife. He persisted, but I begged him not to spoil our friendship.

We don't show our love to our children in public; we love them privately and we love them very much, but the world won't know about it. If I'm going along the street and my son greets me, I pretend I don't see him. Once I was carrying forty cloths on my bicycle—that's a very heavy load—and my son, who is a clerk, saw me and ran out to help me with my load, but I waved him off. It would be beneath his dignity, and it would have been embarrassing to me to have him help me. I would willingly have accepted help from anyone else and would have been grateful.

Olu granted that on the whole his children had lived up to his expectations:

We Yoruba have an abuse, an insult, which reflects from the child to its father. We say, "Were you trained by your father at all? Had you ears to listen?" The father is to blame when he refuses to train his child, but the child is to be blamed when he refuses to follow the training. In this modern world of today, children will not listen to their elders. They have no respect for us. My words to them fall on deaf ears.

We place much importance on respect shown to elders. Young educated men nowadays show false pride in despising the tradition of their elders and don't prostrate themselves when they greet elders. I have children who are teachers and who have attended high schools. It would be folly for them not to prostrate themselves when they greet me or other elders, especially in the mornings. Even the married ones must do so.

Olu was concerned with his self-esteem, and this concern was reflected in his sensitivity to gossip and public opinion; but public opinion in Jos, with its plural social and cultural conditions, can and does mean many different things. For Olu, the important social controls and rewards were those which derived from his own ethnic group in Jos. The large and somewhat self-contained Ogbomosho community there provided Olu with the social means of living according to traditional ideals and values, for he and his fellow tribesmen in Jos had kept their traditional institutions alive and strong.

An example of this reliance on the Ogbomosho Yoruba community for social sanction and support is to be found in a situation involving one of Olu's sons. While married to a barren wife this young man seduced and impregnated an unmarried girl. When Olu learned what had happened and confronted his son, the latter admitted his guilt, but said that he did not intend to marry the girl. Upon hearing this, Olu became furious, and his threat of disinheritance quickly brought his son's agreement to the marriage. Although in forcing his son to marry the girl it is probable that Olu acted out of humane considerations for the girl, he must have also been concerned for his family's reputation within the Yoruba community.

Later this marriage presented a problem that Olu solved by depending on the efficacy of traditional custom within the Yoruba community. The son's first wife, jealous of the new bride (and eventually, mother), accused the interloper of witchcraft and attempted poisoning. Olu investigated the charges and discovered that they were not only untrue, but that the first wife was planting evidence designed to cast guilt on the second. When Olu's private efforts to change her behavior failed, he called a meeting of the wives' relatives, members of his own family, and prominent members of the Yoruba Ogbomosho community to give the accuser an opportunity to make her charges public. She was found to be lying, was disgraced, and was warned against any similar behavior in the future. In this case, Olu acted as the head of his family, using the means by which the community in its traditional court role reached its decision in such cases. The prominent members of the community not only lent dignity to the "court" and weight to the decision, they also served as witnesses to Olu's role as a leader, since he was "chairman" of the meeting.

Olu's success as a traditional leader once turned sour when an old and respected friend sued him without warning because of an overdue loan. Besides being a friend, this man was the leader of the Egbe Omo Oduduwa and the Reformed Ogboni Fraternity, thus Olu's peer as a prominent traditional member of the Yoruba community. It was an insult to Olu as a friend and a fellow leader that the man did not trust him to repay the loan and that he took the matter to court without first approaching him. It seemed to Olu at that time that all the values he upheld were being denigrated, and he was further distressed because his reputation as an honorable Yoruba man was in question.

Leadership, traditional or modern, community or family, is difficult, and carries with it small as well as major problems and responsibilities. Olu was aging and his patience was wearing thin. When one of Olu's daughters, who, with her children, had been staying with him at his house was about to return to her husband in Ilorin, another daughter announced that she and her children were coming from Kaduna on a visit. Olu acted against tradition when he decided they should not stay with him and said, "I don't want them to stay with us; I want her to stay alone. I don't like it when all the grandchildren stay with us. They mess up the parlor. They spill water and food and they urinate on the floor. It's annoying, and I have had to exercise much patience. I'm glad this one is going away to Ilorin now. Formerly I stayed alone with my wives and things were very pleasant. They know the kind of cleanliness I like. Then all these children came. Well, it's better to find this other daughter a place of her own before things go too far."

Olu, aware of the disparity in beliefs and behavior between his own and his children's generations, tried to accept changes graciously, but he could not without some regret and bitterness. "Our children live a different life from ours. Maybe they emulate Western ways. They don't take much interest in family matters. I talked and talked about it, but they didn't heed, so I left it. Sometimes they say annoying words such as that people on earth should not be concerned about the people who are dead. They don't consider funeral ceremonies as important. Their way of life is different. The more you try to explain to them the more they become annoyed."

Olu himself would not be dissuaded from his traditional obligations toward kinsmen. He mentioned the house and business he had given his relatives in Gombe. Of the house which his relatives occupied in Ogbomosho he said: "Now here are some economics for your consideration. My house in Ogbomosho is far larger than the one in King George Way [Jos], and yet it doesn't bring me in a penny. Still, I have to maintain it, keep it up and pay taxes. Is that economics? They are my very close relatives and it's my burning duty to help them. That's Yoruba custom."

Olu provided many examples of his roles in kinship obligations and in wider family relationships and told me how much time, energy, and money these activities consumed. His primary loyalties were to his relatives; but he also held strong commitments to the wider community of non-kin, his neighbors, friends, fellow traders, members of his church, and the Ogbomosho communities in Jos and Ogbomosho. He was a leader among his peers, a member of many voluntary associations, and held offices of high rank in several of them. We may infer that Olu was not an aggressive office-seeker, but a conscientious participant:

When it comes to a society where you collect fees and have officers, it's a bore. I try to avoid that as much as possible and only attend the essential ones. Although I say I try to keep aloof, it doesn't mean I won't help my people when the time comes. Then, I must participate and contribute. One thing about these meetings which I want you to know is that I always make my contribution. I don't just mean money, but also discussion. I always voice my opinion, even if it is not the view of the majority. I may disagree, but I never abstain from attending meetings. The more you attend these meetings, the more you will look sharp and feel yourself a part of things.

Olu's evenings were filled with a busy civic schedule: Monday, Executive Committee of the Ogbomosho Parapo, a tribal union embracing all Ogbomosho in Jos; Tuesday, a sub-committee of the

Parapo; Wednesday, the Parapo "court"; Thursday, meetings of the various quarters of Ogbomosho, sub-tribal unions of the Ogbomosho Parapo. Olu never failed to attend all these meetings. On Friday nights he attended the Bible class of the Baptist Church. Although no meetings were scheduled for Saturday, since the time was reserved for special or emergency meetings of different groups, almost invariably Olu had a meeting to attend. Sunday, after church services, the Christians of Olu's quarter of Ogbomosho held their meetings. Olu appraised his position thus:

On Sundays, which is supposed to be a holiday, we work the hardest because we must attend meetings and see relatives. At the end of the day we are more tired than at the end of any ordinary work day. Our way of life is that of a slave, but we're used to it, and if we didn't do these things, we wouldn't be comfortable. Our children feel it is non-sense and that it takes too much of their time, but we take pleasure in doing it. In every community there are irresponsible persons who will never attend meetings. The same is true with us, but those of us who feel responsible will attend the Monday meeting, which is open to all Ogbomosho men. Any Ogbomosho man can attend. However, there are those of us who must attend; for we are the pillars of the community. If we fail to attend, we are fined. We must attend because we give reports to our respective quarters on Thursdays, and to those irresponsibles who don't attend.

Olu was also an active member of the Nigerian Trader's Association, and at one time had been a member of the Jos Town Council. He had also once been a member of the Committee of Elders of the Baptist Church in Jos, which was in effect the governing body of the church, dealing with all its local affairs that were not strictly ecclesiastical. Olu said he had been deprived of his position of Elder because he was a polygynist. He was not a member of any political party, but he expressed his allegiance to whatever political affiliations the people of Ogbomosho chose.

The central theme in Olu's life was his desire to achieve traditional elite status; this suggests several pertinent questions:
1) Why was Olu a Christian rather than a Muslim? His parents

were neither; his relatives were either Christian, Muslim, or still pagan. While there may be no apparent advantages to being a Muslim in Ogbomosho, where there are approximately an equal number of Christians and Muslims and where there is no strong association between politics and religious affiliation, there is some advantage in being a Muslim in northern Nigeria. Olu's reasons for his choice are these:

> When I grew up at home I moved with Muslims, but when I came to Jos, I came among Christians, and I liked their behavior so that I became convinced of their calling. Example is often a good teacher. The Christians I met were a good example, and I copied them and became one of them.
>
> One main reason why I chose Christianity was that Muslims can injure you by calling your name aloud when they read verses from the Koran. Thus they would ruin your life and career, but I never heard of Christians reading from the Bible to ruin a fellow citizen. And so I chose Christianity. The Bible tells us never to do evil to our fellow men, but I've seen so many Muslims who sought vengeance. God said vengeance is His alone.

2) How did Olu's Christianity affect his relations with his relatives and non-kin? This question is not as directly related to his aspiration for high status as it is to the traditional Yoruba value of loyalty to one's kinsmen. There is a potential conflict between adherence to traditional values and allegiance to the church. Olu once indicated that he chose church above kinsmen.

My relatives who are Christian are nearer to me than those who are Muslim. Members of the same family do try to convert one another. If I could have my wish, I would want all my Muslim relatives and friends to become Christians. I have relatives who are Muslims, but my love for Christianity is more than the love I have for them. I have a close relative in Jos who is a pagan. If one has a pagan relative, the best thing is to desert him completely, have nothing to do with him.

Olu said that if one of his sons were converted to Islam, he would disinherit him, yet it seemed quite reasonable to him that his friends and neighbors should choose whatever faith they wished. Indeed, Olu seemed to have let Christian values enhance his traditional sense of responsibility to non-kin. For example, he had written off over a thousand pounds in unredeemable debts, and among his debtors he listed his Hausa neighbors. In illustrating how strong a friendship he had developed with some of his Hausa neighbors, Olu referred to the purdah system.

When a man becomes sexually mature, he is not permitted to see another man's wives, even his brother's. You can know that you are a Hausa man's closest friend if you are permitted into his home whether he is home or not. You are his closest friend if he allows his wives to entertain you in his absence.

I have three or four Hausa friends like that. One man and I are as close as hand and glove. I enter his house freely, and he welcomes me heartily. One time he quarreled with his wife and sent her away. I went there to intervene and settled the quarrel. After this the woman had four children for this man, and both of them will never forget me and what I did for them.

Olu cited another incident when he was called to intervene in a domestic dispute of a Hausa friend, who was also a neighbor. Olu chastised the man's son and settled the quarrel. "The father, in appreciation for what I did, burst into tears. May I remind you that this man is a native of Kano and not of Ogbomosho. I don't get any material gain from him; instead I give him my clothes. Through friendship that man and myself became as one. Remember that I'm a Christian and he's Muslim."

Olu was very sensitive about being regarded as "tribalistic." He preferred to think of himself as neither provincial nor ethnocentric. To illustrate his cosmopolitan and liberal views, he often pointed out that some of his best friends were neither Yoruba nor Christian. He sought to give the impression that he was always prepared to accept a person on the basis of merit. On the other hand, he expressed the wish that his children might marry not only Yoruba, but Ogbomosho Yoruba. Also, Olu was deeply attached to Yoruba people and culture, and in this respect he may be regarded as being ethnocentric without necessarily being at the same time provincial; and indeed, some of his behavior that might appear ethnocentric was actually merely rational and practical: "I am illiterate.

If I should need to go to an office to ask for a favor, on entering the office, I don't care who's there, I'll first greet the people in Yoruba. If there's a Yoruba man among them, I'm sure he'll reply in Yoruba. Then I'll know I have a brother there."

Again, in the sense that one feels deep and emotional responses to things that are culturally familiar, Olu leaned toward ethnocentrism: "One day I was passing casually along the street when I saw a Yoruba orchestra. That music is very sweet to me, so I stopped to listen and to watch. I didn't know the players, having never seen them before. It was beautiful music, and I liked it so much. They played so very well. Then, to my surprise, I heard my name in the music. They were calling my name and singing my praises. I dashed [gave] them 10s. 6d. [half a guinea]."

3) Was Olu a good Christian? This question is important because Olu was basically sincere and said of himself: "I am an ardent Christian. I go to church every Sunday morning and evening. That's my duty. I was baptized over thirty years ago. Of the offspring of my own father, some are Muslims, but I chose to be a Christian." Why, then, was he a polygynist, and why did he seek to acquire still another wife? Was he a hypocrite? The answer is a qualified and uncertain "yes."

Olu was well aware that polygyny is contrary to the tenets of Christianity. Further, he both recognized and verbalized the social problems and domestic difficulties that can result from polygyny, particularly in the division of inheritance. He would not allow his daughters to marry as co-wives into polygynous households, and he frequently expressed the wish that his sons might remain monogamous. In short, although Olu was basically a traditionalist, he was against polygyny, particularly because it did not suit modern times. Polygyny was part of the past to which he belonged, and he allowed himself this luxury of being old-fashioned. His polygyny may be interpreted as both traditional and expedient. He had two wives for many years before the Baptist Church barred polygynists as Elders. Olu, then an Elder, had the choice of relinquishing his position or one of his well-loved wives. He chose the Yoruba tradition of polygyny as both appropriate and expedient in order that he might have at least one wife with him when he eventually returned to his ancestral home to assume leadership.

We could speculate whether he would have chosen to marry again if one of his first two wives had died, let us say several years ago, and his status was thereby changed to that of a monogamist. Perhaps this is an idle speculation, for he was not faced with such an actual choice; but if we pursue this line of inquiry it will illuminate the hierarchy of values Olu held. I am certain that he would have liked to have resumed his position as an Elder in the church, and certainly would have been in a position to do so as a monogamist. But I would suggest that it was more important for him to live out the remainder of his life within the framework of Yoruba traditional values. It would have been a difficult choice for him to marry again, revert to polygyny, and thereby relinquish the possibility of holding an esteemed position in the church, but, in keeping with his character and the way in which he envisioned his anticipated life of retirement in Ogbomosho, I believe he would have decided to obtain another wife and a young one at that.

As things actually stood, he was planning to return to Ogbomosho with some of his children, but without any of his wives. If he acquired another wife, this marriage would enhance his prestige in Ogbomosho during his retirement years. High social status there did not depend entirely on the number of wives a man had so long as at least one helpmate was present to indicate that he was a fully mature and responsible social person, not a deviant lacking a crucial part of his social maturity. Thus, with his wives remaining in Jos, he would need to acquire a wife in Ogbomosho who would be a social asset and complete the appropriate family retinue, and insofar as she might still bear him more children, indicate that he was still in the prime of life. In simple terms, it was more important to Olu to be a traditional leader in Ogbomosho than an Elder in the Baptist Church in Jos.

Urban prestige within the bounds of his traditional orientation was something Olu had worked hard for, but more important to

him was his status in Ogbomosho, for which he had also been preparing for many years. He was next in line to become the head of
his extended family there, and, in that role, he would become a
leader of the wider community. Personal qualifications suited him
for this role: good health, intelligence, wealth, traditional orientation, and the respect gained by his high moral behavior.[1] Olu said
he had never let three years go by without paying a visit to Ogbomosho, during which he cultivated the friendship of aged and
important citizens and maintained his good standing with his relatives, neighbors, and friends. Upon the completion of his "two-
story mansion" he would be prepared to enter smoothly into his
anticipated social life in Ogbomosho: "I pray for the day when I
will live in Ogbomosho and come to Jos once in a while to collect
rent, but I would like to live out my life in my home town." All
that remained, it seemed, was to regain financial success in his trade
and to stay alive and healthy.

1. An ability to speak English would have been an advantage. He once
said of another man, "I know of somebody here in Jos who is kind and who
has all the attributes of a good leader, but he has no education. At one time
he had a chance to lead the community, but someone questioned his ability
to lead without having had an education, so he lost his chance." Perhaps
this is why Olu once expressed the intention of attending adult classes to
study English, although the reason he gave at the time was that he felt left
out of things when people around him spoke English.

Chapter V

ISAAC COOKEY–JAJA: IJAW

T HE Ijaw informant appeared superficially to be among the most Westernized of Nigerians. In public he always wore Western clothing, and his excellent English diction and grammar were evidence of his considerable formal education. However, whereas other informants with less formal education sometimes expressed a degree of skepticism toward native supernatural beliefs, Isaac manifested a syncretistic pattern of outward Christian behavior and expressions of belief that cloaked a strong faith in traditional supernaturalism.

Isaac Cookey-Jaja was introduced to me by his best friend, an Ibo man, at the latter's residence. During our first conversation, Isaac extolled American technology; he said that he had bought an American car because of its superiority to British makes. When we parted after that first meeting, he drove off in the car—a 1956 DeSoto station wagon. Later I learned that the car was usually on blocks in his yard and was used only for long-distance trips; I was thus led to suspect that he had taken it out of storage to impress me. Our interviews continued for almost a year, were carried on in English, and were always accompanied by some kind of alcoholic beverage. It was Isaac's habit to open up and speak freely once the formal interview had ended for that session. He would sit back in

his chair, sip his stout, smack his lips, and commence a long mono-
logue on a topic suggested by something mentioned earlier. Since
we were subject to numerous interruptions in Isaac's home, most
of the formal interviews took place in my quarters. We had informal,
friendly conversations at his place as well as mine, for we were
neighbors, living about two hundred yards apart. Thus I saw more
of Isaac than I did of my other informants.

Isaac, although born at his lineage home in Opobo Town in
1918, moved with his family to Aba at the age of five. He received
his boyhood education in Nigerian schools in various towns within
the Eastern Region, and following his graduation from grammar
school at 18 he entered an engineering school in Lagos for five years.
Around 1941, when he was about 23 or 24, he completed his formal
education, qualified as a licensed civil engineer, and began working
for the government in the Eastern Region before being transferred
to Jos in 1946. Isaac spoke Hausa, what he termed "trade Ibo,"
English, and his native Ijaw dialect. He also spoke Latin, an accomplishment of which he was very proud.

Isaac's father, born in Opobo Town, died there in 1951 at the age
of 72. He acquired no Ijaw titles, but was a member of the Owoko
Secret Society and Assistant President of the Owugbo Secret Society,
and at the same time held responsible lay posts in the Anglican
Church. He had received considerable Western education and became an independent middleman in palm oil trade, at one time
shipping directly to England. Isaac bitterly accused the British, and
particularly the United Africa Company, of swindling his father
and ruining his business at the beginning of the economic depression of the 1930's.

His father married two Ibo women who came from neighboring
villages near Umuahia. He and his first wife were married in 1914,
and Isaac was their first child. He married the second wife in 1922,
but pressure from the church caused him to separate from her in
1935. Isaac's mother outlived her husband and his second wife.

She was still alive and traded in Aba. Isaac said he sent her £4 monthly.

In 1943 Isaac married a woman who amply fulfilled all his expectations of a good wife. In these expectations he held two sets of values: traditional and modern elite. True to tradition, he wanted a fertile wife from his own tribe and town, who would in addition be a distant relative, since such an arrangement would facilitate social relations upon his eventual retirement to his home town. Also, his wife was to be faithful, not jealous, a good housekeeper, cook and mother; but most important, he said, she must love and care for his family. In accord with his modern elite orientation, Isaac said that his wife had sufficient Western education to assist him in his business, and that she knew how to entertain properly. Like Isaac, his wife Cecilia showed an elite orientation and held prominent positions in the Women's Guild of St. Luke's Church and Ijaw tribal unions. She was a skilled seamstress and had a shop in which she sold Akwete cloths. She showed considerable initiative in her business enterprises, and Isaac admired her industry and aggressiveness. Many of her expensive clothes, head-ties, and jewels were purchased out of her trading profits. Together they worked out their household budget, a practice not common among Nigerian couples. They consulted each other in all domestic affairs and in matters relating to their families. Except for church services and tribal union meetings they rarely visited friends or other couples, and seldom went together to social occasions such as ballroom dances (neither of them even knew how to dance).

One of Isaac's self-styled idiosyncrasies disconcerted his wife. He felt that sexual abstinence, sometimes for several months, gave him metaphysical powers. When he first began this regimen, Cecilia thought Isaac was dissatisfied with her or that he had a mistress. Neither was the case, and after inquiring among her servants and friends, she was satisfied that her husband was not having commerce with any women in Jos. After explaining his behavior to his wife, Isaac thought she trusted him almost completely; almost, because whenever she returned to Jos from a visit to her homeland she would treat the servants to cakes and other delicacies, all the while inquiring after her husband's activities during her absence, and asking them whether any ladies had paid him calls. She always received fully satisfactory reports. Her trust in her husband's fidelity may have been strengthened all the more when she was nursing one of the children and she asked him whether he strongly desired a woman; if he did and was reluctant to seek one for himself, she could try to find an appropriate person for him. He was deeply touched by her concern, yet assured her that there was no need.

Isaac claimed that he would always remain above suspicion in his wife's regard, for marital harmony was more important to him than philandering (at least where his wife could easily learn of his infidelities, for he admitted that he had Shuwa Arab girlfriends in the remote places where he sometimes had construction jobs). Although Isaac stressed marital harmony and his love for his wife as his reasons for desiring to be above suspicion, his position as president of the Opobo Clan Union in Jos undoubtedly also acted as an important constraint. As president he was often called on to settle marital disputes, many of which concerned adultery, and he could ill afford a tainted reputation in performing this role.

When Isaac spoke of his children he expressed his own values and motivations. He wanted all of them, insofar as each was capable, to receive higher education at an American university, which, he said, would give them experience in living in a different culture. Coupled with this desire was his constant criticism of British university teaching methods as outdated, indicating his Anglophobia. In addition to the obvious advantages it would give his children, education in the United States would enhance Isaac's prestige in the community.

Isaac strongly desired his children to marry only Ijaw; he even insisted on Opobo Ijaw. He also desired each child to have a Christian spouse, preferably an Anglican. If a child persisted in another choice, however, he said he would leave the final decision to him. Isaac regarded it as an honor to pay the brideprice for his sons' wives, and hoped he would be able to pay for all the wedding arrangements.

His concern for the welfare of his seven children, three of whom were in school, was based on both occult and practical considerations. He had decided, for example, that a profession in the social services would best suit his eight-year-old daughter Venicia, simply because she was born in November; but he decided to transfer her to the Township School from St. Luke's School to avoid having her walk alone through heavy street traffic. In several years she could return to St. Luke's school, which her older siblings attended. Isaac's eldest child, fourteen-year-old Constance, was about to complete her schoolwork in Jos, and he was trying to arrange for her entrance into Queen's Secondary School in Enugu in order that she might be close to her parents when they moved—as they planned to do—to Aba. This was a government school, and Isaac thought that if she did well her chances for getting a government scholarship to study medicine in a university were better than if she were to attend a private school. Isaac wished his next oldest child to study civil engineering and eventually take over his contracting business.

Isaac had initially settled in Jos because he had encountered difficulty with his European bosses while working in the Eastern Region. He explained: "I wouldn't kowtow to my European bosses. One boss particularly was a Negrophobist, and that aroused my Europhobia. Things were unpleasant, and the British director, who liked me, didn't want these people to write bad confidential reports against me, so he had me brought up to the North." He had experienced no particular difficulties in settling in Jos. At first he lived in government quarters and his financial position was good. In addition to working as a government employee, he drew building plans free-lance, and his services were in demand. In 1950 he resigned from government service in order to start his own contracting business.

Isaac established a flourishing engineering firm; he built roads, bridges, and buildings. Many of his contracts were with the Northern Region government or Northern Native Authorities. Isaac represented himself not only as a competent and creative civil engineer, but also as a Nigerian rare in his appreciation of the proper care of machinery. He would often explain how equipment should be maintained and overhauled, and stressed how Africans were generally careless in these respects and allowed their equipment to deteriorate prematurely. It is not surprising that Isaac enjoyed collecting scrap machines and motors in order to rebuild them, and that he took pride in combining parts of several machines to create a new one.

During the first few years of his business Isaac prospered and his future seemed bright, but beginning in 1958 a series of misfortunes altered the course of his career. He suffered a near-fatal attack of appendicitis, and during his illness his assistants failed to fulfill his contract obligations. Lawsuits resulted; previous contracts were cancelled. His losses ran to thousands of pounds, and Isaac withdrew all his savings and sold much of his equipment in order to make ends meet. Further, he had to secure an overdraft from the bank for £800, on which he was still paying. From that time on he had not been able to secure a major contract, and his income was almost entirely derived from odd jobs—working as a consultant or architect, renting or selling his equipment—in addition to a small revenue from a plantation he owned at Umuahia.

As a southerner, Isaac had scarcely a chance of being awarded a Northern Region government contract now, so he planned to move his business to the Eastern Region, with headquarters at Aba. Toward the end of 1961 he went there in preparation for this move, claiming when he returned to Jos that he had been in touch with friends and schoolmates who welcomed him and said they would help him obtain government contracts. To help his cause they also advised him to show his support of the political party controlling the Eastern Region, the National Council of Nigerian Citizens. Isaac felt it would be expedient to become an active member. But the prospect of a contract to build a large hotel in Kano, in the far north of Nigeria, developed early in 1962, and this job would have

delayed transferring his business to Aba. The outcome was unknown when I left Jos, but I later learned that Isaac had not obtained the contract.

His original plan to live out his working life in the North was no
longer feasible, but he felt he could prosper in Eastern Nigeria.
Aba seemed an ideal location. It is about forty miles from Port
Harcourt, a major seaport, and from Port Harcourt it is only about
forty miles further to Opobo Town. Aba is also located on the railway line linking the North with the East and on the main road to the
Eastern Region capital of Enugu. Isaac pointed out that his father
had helped open up Aba in 1918, that his family was well known
there, and that he personally knew many influential people who
would help him get started. Also very important was the fact that
his mother and other relatives lived in the city.[1]

Isaac said that if there had been no Northernization Policy and
his business had flourished, he would have planned to remain in
Jos with its congenial social life and healthy climate. Also, "there
are no immediate family troubles as you would have if you lived
close to your people. I had planned to go home eventually in semi-
retirement and delegate someone to take care of the business here,
but still carrying it on from home. The plan originally was for us
[his wife and children] to return home last year on the assumption
that the Jos station would have been well enough established to be
run by agents. I had also planned to open my business in Aba any-
way, and possibly in Port Harcourt and Enugu as well, but not in
the West [of Nigeria]. I wouldn't actually be retiring but expanding
my business while devoting my time to home affairs."

Isaac tried not to show it, but he was sorely in need of money.
He could not complete his house despite the pressure from the Local
Authority, and he would need additional money to transfer his business, particularly his heavy equipment, to Aba. Thus, he did not
know which way to turn. He considered grand schemes and petty

1. At the time of writing this chapter, 1966, Isaac was still reported to
be in Jos.

ideas, practical plans and fantasies. He thought he might make contacts through me to export Nigerian craft work to the United States and import American manufactured products for sale in Nigeria. He hoped to find employment with an American construction firm and thereby acquire a knowledge of modern American construction techniques; he saw such a position as giving him a unique standing among civil engineers in his country. Other of his schemes included establishing a hauling service; building double-hulled, fiberglas boats with shallow drafts for use in the Niger Delta creeks; and harnessing wind or tidewater power with turbines to generate electricity for towns in the Niger Delta, where power lines could not be erected. As an immediate practical measure he put a steel body on his five-ton lorry, made the truck roadworthy, licensed it for hauling goods, and hired a driver, anticipating that by hauling sand, gravel, and firewood, he would make a profit of about fifty pounds a month. At this time he also initiated two lawsuits from which he gained several hundred pounds.

When Isaac retired from government service he moved into a house he built in the Native Town. The next year, 1951, he started building in his present compound, located in the Township, and moved into it in 1952. All plots in the Township are leased from the Local Authority for ten years, with a renewal option. His plot rates were a little more than five pounds a year, but with conservancy rates the figure approached thirteen. The compound contained several sturdy buildings of fieldstone, set in concrete, and roofed with corrugated iron sheets, all designed by Isaac, who said he would be able to complete them without financial assistance. The materials and construction were expensive by Nigerian standards: but Isaac's sacrifice of economy had achieved uniqueness, durability, and attractiveness. The main building, designed as two stories, was about one-fourth complete, but because of Isaac's financial difficulties, work on it had ceased several years ago. It was meant to house the family in one part and Isaac's contracting business office in the other. In another building was a working space for his wife's cloth shop, and a garage for a large lorry. Isaac sought praise from me by producing the blueprints and pointing out the architectural re-finements that he had introduced. He stressed particularly the novel use of cantilevers as structural elements and of such materials as glass brick. He said that many people had been envious because of the design and the materials used in his house. "That year [around 1957] I was a bit prosperous. I had bought a lot of construction equipment and people thought I was getting too rich. That was when I got the big American car. It was the first of its kind here and the best in the country. After I got the car many people imitated my example and that type of car was seen more frequently. People were trying to get back at me. They were envious of my prosperity and of the different kind of house I was building myself."

While the main house was being completed, Isaac and his family lived in a makeshift house that was intended for servants' quarters. The other buildings in the compound housed machinery and equip-ment used in civil engineering construction work: electrical genera-tors, diesel engines, water pumps, electrical motors, saws and drills, chain hoists, cement-block forms, and many other tools such as picks and shovels. The compound itself was large, and served as a parking area for Isaac's DeSoto, the 1956 Canadian Dodge five-ton lorry chassis that subsequently received a body and put him in the hauling business, a 1946 half-ton lorry, and a large cement and concrete mixer which Isaac said cost more than a thousand pounds.

Five persons, unrelated to Isaac, lived in the same compound. They included an old Kanuri man and a young Ankwe tribesman, both of whom had worked for Isaac as laborers during his more prosperous years and now remained as watchmen. A Kagoro boy acted as steward for Isaac and as helper for his wife, while a younger Kagoro boy hawked bread and cakes for her. An Ibo girl from the hinterland near Aba served for a year as the children's nursemaid, freeing Isaac's wife for her trading activities. The men slept in the unfinished house or in the sheds, and the Ibo girl and Isaac's eldest daughters slept on floor mats in what the family used as a living room. Isaac paid a small salary to the four men, but none to the girl. Her parents were paid for her services.

One house servant in Jos is not necessarily in itself an important status symbol, since many schoolchildren act in that capacity in return for room, board, and a small allowance. However, having five servants can raise one's prestige considerably, and this is probably the essential reason why Isaac retained more persons than he minimally needed. He had to have someone to guard his property and equipment, but it is probable that he held onto the Kanuri and Ankwe men as reminders of more prosperous times; their presence contributed at least a semblance of success to his business. For these two men there were also advantages to the arrangement since Isaac provided them with an assured source of income, if small, and a place to sleep. They did little actual work; the Ankwe man found occasional unskilled labor employment, while the Kanuri was beyond employable age.

At Umuahia, in the Eastern Region, Isaac owned a sixty-acre plantation of rubber, cocoa, and palm kernel trees, which he had acquired from his mother in 1942. He also had a stake in lineage property at Aba, the other partners being descendants of his paternal grandfather. Isaac's uncle supervised this lineage property, which was about one mile long and a quarter-mile wide, and grew oil palm trees. Isaac received a small share of the profits. Rest houses were maintained for lineage members at this plantation, as well as at his ancestral home in Opobo Town.

Soon after we met I asked Isaac to show me his photographs. His entire collection was wrapped in bundles of brown paper, for, he explained, his present meager accommodations were temporary and he did not plan to display his pictures until he was settled permanently. The pictures were largely of church meetings, tribal union send-off parties, and christenings. The very large number of pictures, and the fact that the persons shown in them were well-educated and many of them wealthy, indicated that Isaac had either achieved modern African elite status or would soon be included in that social category. Most of the people in these pictures were of his own tribe, but commonly included were people from Sierra

Leone and Ghana as well as Efik from Calabar and some Ibo. With the exception of the Ibo, these ethnic groups shared the advantage of an early contact with Europeans with a subsequent early introduction of Western education. Thus these persons are prominent among the modern African elite. The professions, occupations, or skills of the men shown included a postmaster, a chief clerk of the Jos Local Authority, a high-ranking politician, a wealthy African tin miner, a doctor of medicine, a university vice-chancellor, and other senior civil servants or business men. Most of the men wore formal Western dress. Sometimes Isaac volunteered the information that the husband of a woman in a picture was prominent socially or professionally. His emphasis on rank or accomplishment was a strong hint of his own orientation toward elite status. The pictures of Isaac's congregation at St. Luke's Anglican Church in Jos showed almost no Yoruba, except for the clerical officials, even though Yoruba usually account for more than half of the congregation. Actually, most of the Yoruba members form an informal but separate congregation with services conducted in Yoruba, thus their absence in Isaac's pictures.

Early in our acquaintance Isaac invited me to the Annual Harvest Bazaar given by his church. This gave him a dual opportunity to be seen with a European guest and to impress me with the prominent members of the church who were his friends and acquaintances. He explained that this year he was not to be the one to "open" the annual giving. Some years ago when he was chairman and "opened," he had donated forty guineas (about $120). It was a blow to Isaac's pride that this year he was able to give only a few guineas. Perhaps he wondered when he once again might be able to achieve comfortable financial circumstances so that, being recognized as an affluent member, he would be honored by his congregation with an invitation again to be the chairman of the Annual Harvest Bazaar.

Having prominence and prestige as a good Christian, an upright and an outstanding member of his congregation, as well as being a member of the modern African elite, were the personal satisfactions that Isaac sought, and he tried clinging to the gains he had made in these directions. He was no longer able to make the generous donations he had given in the past to his church, and he did not subscribe a tithe, which would have brought him honor, for doing so would reveal his income. Instead he gave his donations piecemeal for Sunday collections, on special occasions like Easter and Christmas, and sometimes as a personal thanks-offering. Since he was still a prominent member of the community and of his congregation, he was sometimes invited to attend services at St. Piran's, the Anglican church in Jos with a predominantly European congregation that held the distinction of once having Queen Elizabeth and Prince Philip attend its services.

As a member of St. Luke's Church Parochial Committee, Isaac was active in financial and non-ecclesiastical church matters. When the church outgrew its old quarters, Isaac was assigned to draw up plans for a new sanctuary. His suggested innovations in design and in use of materials and methods unusual in Nigeria, but common in Western countries, met with more conservative criticism than he had anticipated, but he hoped that the opinions of Europeans like myself would support him in his efforts to have his plans accepted.

Isaac's behavior followed the Christian ideal. He and his family attended church services whenever able, and they held their private services each morning. When a friend of his, a wealthy Efik man who was an electrical contractor, fell seriously ill, Isaac and he expressed the solidarity of their friendship and their mutual concern through a Christian religious idiom; together they prayed for God's blessings and gave thanks for His past goodness. Isaac described how he had once been at this man's home when an important contract came in the mail. The contractor, his wife, and Isaac all got down on their knees to thank God for His benevolence, and there were other occasions when these three knelt to thank God for the blessings they had received.

Isaac and his wife Cecilia had been married according to native tradition and custom, but in 1956, ten years after their arrival in Jos, they had their marriage blessed in church. Isaac said: "We both decided to have our marriage blessed in St. Luke's Church, although we place greatest importance on the [native] ceremony recognized by our people in our home town. Without doing it traditionally, all the issue would belong to the wife and not to the husband. We wanted the church blessing just to have religious recognition and to entitle us to all church benefits."

Isaac gave the impression of trying to plan his life as if he were blueprinting a building. He laid his long-range plans carefully, and his daily activities followed a strict routine. He rose customarily between 4:00 and 4:30 in the morning, washed, and then practiced breathing and meditation exercises as part of his spiritual regimen. By 5:00, the children were up and the family all said morning prayers. Isaac then bathed and assumed his business activities, interrupting these only for breakfast. He stopped for lunch around one or two o'clock. After lunch he napped for an hour, and on waking once again did breathing and meditation exercises. Then he either continued his work, visited friends, or attended a union or church meeting. He returned home before supper, bathed again, and in the evening after the children were asleep, visited a friend, or stayed at home reading engineering, inspirational, spiritual, and metaphysical books. He usually went to bed about ten or eleven o'clock, after a final meditation for the day. Isaac said he tried to keep a similar schedule when he was working in the bush.

In Jos, he and his family followed the same routine on weekends as during the week, except that they went to church after breakfast on Sunday, and after lunch the children returned to church for Sunday school while the parents attended a tribal union meeting if there was one. The union meetings lasted from two to five o'clock, after which the family prepared to attend evening church services.

In apparent contrast to his orthodox Christian behavior, Isaac called himself a clairvoyant, and frequently liked to discuss a subject he called "occult science," which he considered actual and effective. He had a library on the subject, with books from England, India, and the United States. As he explained to me several times, there are higher forces or "intelligences" which, in turn, are divided into lesser and greater forces. To exploit their power, one must first have a calling and then devote a life of study to it. One of his ambitions was to be able to control these powers. In confidence Isaac told me he had spent over two hundred pounds pursuing his studies of the supernatural. He had studied with native doctors of different tribes, but mainly with Calabar (Efik-Ibibio) men. He said he belonged to no secret societies but was a disciple of particular masters, and had been initiated into some of their secrets, which he was sworn not to reveal. The skills of these masters included the ability to live underwater and to communicate with underwater people, to travel anywhere in the world instantly by touching water, to destroy a man through his image, to be magically protected from bullets or swords, and to become invisible. Isaac claimed he could read a person's mind by looking into his eyes (a natural intuitive gift which he had developed through mystical training). He regarded Cabalism as the highest form of spiritualism and the Jews as the masters of this art, which accounted for the great scientific discoveries and other achievements among Jews. Because of their study of the Cabala and because of their sincerity and suffering, the Jews were singled out by the higher intelligences who imparted knowledge, insights, and great discoveries to them. For example, he believed that Einstein had been able to develop his theories through this supernatural communication; now that Einstein was dead he had become a higher intelligence and would single out another hard-working scientist and reveal to him new discoveries.

Isaac's mysticism was syncretistic, combining into a personal theology traditional and Christian religious beliefs, as well as those of other religious and mystical systems. He strongly believed in native juju, dreams, and astrology; by his bedside he kept a "dream book," in which he recorded all his dreams, believing them to be omens. We may wonder how Isaac came to hold these beliefs, especially since he had received considerable Western scientific and technological training. He had evidently always held a positive predisposition toward traditional religious beliefs, and some personal experiences apparently validated them for him. In fact, an experience that occurred when Isaac was about 12 years old made a deep impression on him and firmly rooted his inclination toward mysticism and spiritualism.

He had come upon an old and unknown Brazilian[2] woman drawing water from a pump, and he had offered to carry the water for her. The woman invited him into her house and asked him to write his name on a blackboard in chalk. She counted the number of letters, made some computations, and told him he was about to leave his present school for another, that his father was going to be swindled, and that Isaac would travel overseas before he died. She then told him to return with two plates and two knives, which he immediately obtained from his father. Over the plates the woman cast a spell to ensure that whenever and wherever he traveled, no harm could come to him. The knives were to be used by Isaac to gain foresight.

Isaac's father supported his son's interest in mysticism and allowed him to buy an astrology book, which Isaac carried to school. When the principal told Isaac to relinquish the book to him, he refused. His father backed him on his refusal, saying he would rather transfer his son to another school than have him denied access to his own books. All the parties were adamant, and so Isaac entered another school. Isaac pointed out that the first prediction had thus come true. Isaac also said that his father had indeed been "swindled," but since the swindle (his father's trouble with the United Africa Company that helped breed Isaac's Anglophobia) had occurred just two days prior to the woman's forewarning, it was therefore not entirely in the nature of a prediction, although she was unaware of the incident.

Isaac placed one of the knives under his pillow before school examinations, and he claimed he was thus able to know in advance what questions would be asked, and so achieve scholastic success. He said he would use the plate when the woman's prediction of

2. Brazilians are the freed slaves of African ancestry who returned from Brazil to the West African port cities of Accra and Lagos, during the nineteenth century, where they were valued as skilled craftsmen.

travel overseas materialized. He was certain his destination would be the United States, where, it will be remembered, he wanted to study modern American civil engineering methods.

The manner in which Isaac acquired his "ideal" wife and the means by which he assured the health and well-being of his children further illustrate his faith in and reliance on traditional supernatural beliefs and practices. When Isaac was still in his early twenties, his parents began prodding him to marry, although they had no particular girl in mind for him. He was then working as a civil engineer for the Public Works Department in Enugu, where he had a mistress. She had been divorced and had left her two children with her former husband. On hearing of this relationship Isaac's father insisted that it be terminated. He was against his son's living unmarried with a woman, feared trouble from her former husband, and he foresaw the possibility that Isaac would feel obliged to marry her if she bore him children. Acting quickly, his father recommended several girls, none of whom Isaac wanted. In July of 1943, when Isaac was 25, he went home on leave and visited several schools there, looking over the female students with the hope of finding a potential wife among them, but he met with no success. Several days after returning to Aba, he had a dream in which he saw people he had never met. From his son's description, Isaac's father recognized them as distant relatives, long dead, who had left a daughter whose whereabouts were unknown. There was another relative in the dream whom Isaac did recognize; this man surprised them with a visit the following morning. When they discussed this coincidence they concluded that the dream had been an omen. Isaac related: "The relative who visited us said that this daughter, who is now my wife, was living with her brother. He [the visitor] was a godson to the woman in the dream. The brother was at Opobo and so we went there. I narrated the dream to their family. Then they said that a lot of strange things had also been happening to them. I expressed the desire of following up the dream by proposing marriage."

Three of Isaac's children had died within twenty-four hours of birth. After the second death, Isaac and his wife went for examinations at a hospital in Ikot-Ekpene. The doctor found them both perfectly fit and saw no medical reason why they should not have healthy children. This set Isaac to wondering. Upon his return to Jos he went to a diviner who told him that the efforts of a spirit seeking reincarnation by entering the bodies of his children had killed them. The diviner predicted that Isaac and his wife would lose three children—this was inevitable—but the number to die beyond three could be controlled if the proper rituals were performed. The spirit would have to be led astray through deception; the diviner advised Isaac to disguise each of his children with a small scar on the cheeks and thus delude the spirit into looking elsewhere. The age of the children or the exact time when the scarring was to be done had to be forecast independently for each child. All of Isaac's children except the last two have been accordingly marked. The diviner also predicted that Isaac would rear eleven healthy children; this was as inevitable as the loss of the other three.

The diviner was a Fulani, whose method was to gaze into a bowl of water. Following this experience, Isaac went to Opobo and told his uncle what had happened; the uncle called an Ibibio diviner who, by gazing into a mirror, confirmed the Fulani diviner's statements. Then Isaac consulted two more diviners, an Ijaw and an Ibo, both of whom confirmed further what the others had said. Isaac followed their instructions, offered gin and cooked food sacrifices to the molesting spirit in the ocean near Opobo Town and at a crossroads in Jos, and spoke the proper ritual expressions.

Isaac's third child, his daughter Constance, lived. When his wife conceived for the fourth time, Constance became ill, ran a fever, and was "frightened by phantoms." Her fever continued after the fourth child was born and increased after the new baby died. When Constance was quite ill, Isaac called an Ibo diviner to the house, a man whom Constance had never seen. When she saw him, she ran away screaming and the diviner told Isaac he had the same old trouble. He prescribed a cross-roads sacrifice and gave Isaac a charm to place there. Isaac went to a cross-roads near the cemetery in Jos between midnight and one o'clock, did as the diviner told him, and sacrificed a white chicken. As soon as all this was done, Constance's fever subsided. She lost her nervousness and was well thereafter. None of Isaac's other children died.

After we had become better acquainted, Isaac spoke more freely of his political and religious views; in his mind, the two were connected. He became emotional during one informal conversation, expressing anger toward white missionaries, whom he described as "tools of the imperialists and colonialists. When the British couldn't penetrate and hold an area they sent in missionaries, who subverted the traditional religious, political, and moral orders." He went on to caricature missionaries who ignore the startling supernatural phenomena of traditional African juju. The exploits of native magicians, who make a sandbank appear out of the sea, cause thunder and lightning in a clear sky, or on a clear day create a fog and cause it to approach (but not cross) a line drawn on the ground, left the missionaries without explanation, and they therefore decried them as "heathenish and untrue," although some of their own white brothers practiced magic surreptitiously. (Isaac believed that the proper attitude was to recognize native jujus as intermediaries between man and the one God.) He concluded his argument against white missionaries by insisting that those of today are still servants and spies of foreign governments. Although they attempt to conceal their true activities, Africans now recognize them for what they have always been.

Isaac's deep commitment to spiritualism led me to believe that he held a theory of spiritual causation and, indeed, he did express such theories from time to time. However, it can only be conjectured whether Isaac placed greater faith in spiritual causes or in material-political explanations for the course of his personal fate. Many of my informants showed inconsistencies of this sort, and it is possible that contrary views are often held but expressed separately according to the context. Had Isaac's spiritual-material ambivalence been questioned, he probably would have solved the dilemma by suggesting the view that seemed most real to him at that time.

As an example, when I once suggested to him that a rival Ibo contractor tried using juju against him out of envy (as Isaac's personal friend had told me), he vehemently denied the possibility. He said people would be afraid to do so because they knew he could read their thoughts and could not face him if they contemplated such an action. Furthermore, he insisted, no evil juju could work against him because he led a clean life and he held no evil thoughts; any such attempt would therefore rebound to the detriment of the other party. Isaac pointed out that the business of his competitor was now also poor and concluded that all southern contractors were doing poorly because of the effects of the Northernization Policy.

At another time Isaac said he had not been hurt so much by Northernization as by his own neglect of his spirits. True, Northernization seemed the obvious cause of his past seven years of financial strain, but the true cause, he thought, was that during his prosperity he had neglected to thank his spiritual guides. Recent suffering had taught him not to neglect his spirits, and he thought he was now at the end of his bad luck. Soon he should expect to receive many contracts, but most likely in the Eastern Region.

Although oriented to becoming a member of the modern African elite, Isaac could hardly be considered detribalized. He had always intended to retire to his ancestral home in Opobo Town, and for as long as he had been in Jos he had visited Opobo at least once a year; he always tried to be there at Christmas to see all his relatives and old friends who also gathered for this annual reunion.[3] We had not been long acquainted before Isaac began to express pride in Opobo history and traditions, especially in the glorious period under King Ja Ja's leadership (1870–1887). He said that Opobo people, as well as being chauvinistic, had a strong sense of history and proudly preserved all sorts of records—particularly old family records. In view of his strong sense of family pride and ethnocentrism it is not surprising that Isaac insisted that his children marry only Opobo Ijaw. On the other hand, his particular concern

3. For a description of these homecomings, see Plotnicov (1964).

about his children's marriages may seem curious, considering that his own mother and his father's other wife were both Umuahi Ibo. But Isaac felt great pride in his birthright as an Ijaw, and he tried to instill this feeling in his children, encouraging them along these lines by instructing them in Opobo history and traditions. He showed another indication of his ethnic pride when he said that he and his wife had given their Ibo nursemaid an Ijaw name to make her feel one of the family. "In most cases such children [servant girls] retain their new name. They feel it is a privilege to have an Ijaw name, because our people are regarded as more civilized. Any [non-Ijaw] girl who has been trained by an Ijaw family readily finds a husband at home because she has acquired our way of living."

Isaac was alternately hostile to and imitative of Europeans. He partially reconciled this ambivalence by attributing the European qualities he disliked to the English and those he preferred to the Americans and Russians. He was often inconsistent. For example, he took pride in his knowledge of Latin, and quoted Latin phrases; but his Latin teacher, whom he greatly admired, was English. Similarly he expressed affection for one of his British administrators in the Public Works Department. Isaac told several anecdotes illustrating how this man had stimulated him with challenging engineering problems, taught him more than was required of a supervisor, and, recognizing Isaac's abilities, given him responsibilities normally reserved for foreign engineers. This was the same man who had sought to protect Isaac's career by having him transferred from the Eastern Region to Jos.

Isaac objected to the colonial policy (no longer prevalent at the time I was in Nigeria) of segregating European residences and discriminating against Africans in European clubs and hospitals. Here he was expressing his antagonism because he was ineligible to belong to the elite group of Europeans—a source of resentment common among the modern African elite.

Isaac took great pride in recalling that he was at one time wealthier than most of the Europeans he knew. In fact, he could even be boastful about his financial prestige, as when he related the circumstances surrounding the purchase of his DeSoto station wagon. He was walking through an automobile showroom on his way to buy parts for one of his trucks, dressed in greasy, dirty work-clothes and looking like any other Nigerian mechanic. In the showroom was an English Senior District Officer, who paid no attention to Isaac until he asked the price of the new American car on display. The Englishman looked at Isaac as if to say, "How could this crazy half-ape dream of owning such a car?" Isaac deliberately spoke loudly and asked for particulars about the car. The salesman, knowing Isaac, treated him seriously, while the S.D.O. stared in amazement. Isaac said that in the end it took some doing to acquire the car. He had difficulty in obtaining a special import license because the car was non-British, but after many months it was his. One of the first things he did when it arrived was to dress in his best European clothes and drive to the office where the S.D.O. worked. An American car in those days was unusual in Nigeria and invariably attracted a crowd. Isaac observed with pleasure how the S.D.O. peered out his window at the admiring crowd thronging about the car.

With much amusement Isaac also related how he would drive leisurely to Kingsway Department Store in the morning to watch the reactions of the European shoppers. Dressed in shorts (not in chauffeur's uniform), he would get out of the car, slam the door shut ceremoniously, and walk slowly into the store. There he would turn and watch as the English women asked each other who was the owner. When they discovered he was an African, they began examining the interior closely to see how dirty and ill-kept it was. To their surprise they found it immaculate. Then they would "chatter about the car to their husbands, who probably could hardly afford a bicycle had they remained in England, and the envious husbands would say they thought the car too large, or they didn't like the enormous fins in the back, and so on."

Isaac was also prejudiced against certain African ethnic groups (even though he included among his best friends representatives of these very groups). The group against which he expressed strongest hostility were the Hausa, who were politically dominant in the North and were the architects of the Northernization Policy, but he was also hostile toward Ibo, Yoruba, Efik, and people from Sierra Leone and Ghana, who are prominent among the modern African elite. His hostility toward them may reflect his envy and his inability to secure equal standing among them as a modern elite member. Those tribes for which he sometimes had a good word he credited with superior traditional magic abilities. For the most part, he thought southern tribesmen politically unscrupulous and central Nigerian tribesmen thieves and rogues.

Isaac's intense ethnocentrism was related to his hostility to European and African ethnic groups. His bitter experiences with European Negrophobes, and with the discrimination against him as a southerner by the Northernization Policy, impelled him to adopt a superficial parochial posture that prevented the expression of his deeper sentiments of ethnic integration, sentiments evident in his choice of personal friends.

Since ethnic groups in Nigeria are so closely associated with political parties, the sentiments Isaac felt for particular ethnic groups were, as we might expect, carried over to political parties with which they were identified; but, just as Isaac was inconsistent in so many other areas of his life, so too he was inconsistent in this one, and his political polemics abounded with contradictions. He was most consistent in his oft-expressed bitterness against the Northern Region government because of its Northernization Policy, but he could also say that southern Nigerians would find allies against the "feudal rule" of the North among those enlightened northerners who had received their education overseas. These persons, however, are precisely those who benefited most from the Northernization Policy. On one occasion, he had within fifteen minutes shifted from expressing the view that the political leader of the National Council of Nigerian Citizens, Azikiwe (Dr. Nnamdi Azikiwe, the first President of Nigeria), and his counterpart in the Action Group, Awolowo, had made a secret pact against their common enemy, the Northern People's Congress—although at the time the N.C.N.C.

and the N.P.C. held a political alliance—to declaring that the Action Group was employing bestial and Nazi tactics in the Western Region, where that party ruled. Similarly, although he often praised Azikiwe as a clever politician and diplomat without whom Nigerian independence could not have been achieved, he also accused him of hypocritical and deceitful behavior toward the Ijaw. While he loved to talk about politics, and was active in the political affairs of his home town, he protested his aversion to politics generally, because they involved one in half-truths and unethical behavior. He excused his N.C.N.C. membership and support as expedient or necessary for business reasons.

When we first discussed friendships and extra-kin social interaction, Isaac said: "I have difficulty making friends in a place like Jos. Back home in the East many people know me and I have many old schoolmates. They're used to me, and they know my ways. But here in Jos I'm always on tour so people who meet me and would like to befriend me don't get a chance to. They send me invitations to which I can't respond. They come over to my house only to learn I'm out of town. And I myself feel more comfortable with my own countrymen or those people I've known for a long time, who understand me and tolerate my idiosyncrasies."

Isaac had close friends in Jos, whom he had pointed out to me when we looked at his photograph collection. He listed in the following order, according to their degree of closeness: a Catholic Owerri Ibo, 32, a free-lance law clerk; a Methodist Calabar Efik, 60, electrical engineering contractor; a Muslim Okrika Ijaw, 38, pharmacist and owner of a chemist's shop; and a Yoruba Anglican cleric of St. Luke's Church, 32. When Isaac was in Jos, he might see his Ibo friend two or three times a day at either's house. Sometimes they stayed up together until midnight discussing topics such as politics or mysticism, on which they shared the same views. The man helped Isaac as a typist-clerk, and Isaac reciprocated by occasionally lending him money and giving him food. They frequently ate together at Isaac's home.

His Calabar Efik friend was among the foremost of the modern

African elite in Jos. He and Isaac became acquainted when Isaac worked for the P.W.D. in Jos; this man had appeared at Isaac's office one day and introduced himself as the close friend of a relative. He told how he had been ejected from Maiduguri for fighting with a European Negrophobe, and Isaac told him that he had recently been forced to leave the Eastern Region for similar reasons. When these two "ex-rascals," as Isaac put it, learned that they shared a pride in being African, and that they both had stood up to slanderous expatriates, a mutual affection immediately developed between them. The Efik man told Isaac that since retiring from government service he had been trying to establish himself as a civil and electrical engineering contractor. Isaac told me that he had introduced the man to his boss and had helped him get his first contract. Since his new friend was not trained in civil engineering, Isaac helped him with his contract estimates and in return was introduced to influential people. When the Northernization Policy seriously affected Isaac's business, the Efik's business flourished because most of his contracts were with the federal, rather than the northern government. Isaac said that the man had once invited him to join his business as a partner, but Isaac suggested postponing this step until his own business was established in the East. The Efik friend left Jos in 1962 for medical treatment in England, and Isaac was asked to run his business during this absence. Isaac did so for only a nominal remuneration.

The only Ijaw Isaac called his close friend—the wealthy pharmacist—was one of the very few non-Yoruba southern Nigerians who had been converted to Islam; he had even made the pilgrimage to Mecca. He and Isaac first met in 1952, when Isaac had gone to his shop to buy medicine. They learned that they were not only of the same tribe but were also alumni of the same grammar school. Later they often saw each other at Ijaw Tribal Union meetings, and a friendship developed. When someone in Isaac's family was not well, he sought advice from this friend who frequently gave him medicine without charge. Isaac reciprocated by bringing him rice or firewood, which he got cheaply in the hinterland. He also helped his Muslim friend settle his perpetual marital problems with his three Ijaw Christian wives. This man was a chronic alcoholic, and during his binges Isaac and his Ibo friend would remain with him constantly to prevent him from behaving violently, which in the past had involved him with the police. When he sobered, they tried being with him as much as they could, to give him moral support.

Isaac met the Yoruba curate in 1959, and was impressed with his consistently upright behavior and his tact in handling church members. When he discovered that they held similar intellectual-philosophical ideas, Isaac cultivated the curate's friendship and became his informal adviser in matters pertaining to members of the congregation. The curate sometimes took part in Isaac's family worship services, and offered prayers on behalf of the family in church.

It should be noted that Isaac's close friends were all southerners of various tribes. They shared with him the attributes of modern elite status in wealth, occupation, or degree of Western education, and tended to share ideologies important to Isaac—e.g., mysticism or anti-European attitudes. Only one was of the same tribe as Isaac, and a Muslim at that. His choice of friends transcended his tribal ethnocentrism; that side of his personality was expressed through more formally structured relationships, such as that with his tribal union.

Isaac was president of the Ijaw Tribal Union a number of times, and when he was not president he still remained a member of the Executive Committee. He had also been president of the Opobo Clan Union in Jos almost continuously since its beginning in 1946. Even during those rare intervals when he was not serving as its president, meetings of the group were held in his compound. This voluntary association (limited to Opobo Town natives) is particularly important to its members for settling marital quarrels and other disputes, and Isaac took pride in his part, as arbitrator or as a member of a small judiciary committee formed for special cases, in settling these disputes.

Isaac said he had often been invited to join modern African elite organizations, societies, and clubs in Jos. At first he told me that he had declined these invitations on the excuse that his business required him to be away from Jos too often. He then added that he would join such groups as soon as he could. Later, he told me the real reason for not joining these organizations was that at present he was carrying out a personal project of spiritual self-development which would take three years to complete. He anticipated other such projects and felt that by the time he was fifty he would have reached a state of personal perfection. Then he would be able to be of service to his people, to the community, and to the country, both politically and socially. For the present he had to avoid clubs, lodges, and so on, because he might be obliged to drink at times when certain of his regimens required abstinence, or he might attend a dance and unknowingly have contact with a menstruating woman. Also, at a social gathering he might meet people who could provoke him into losing his composure, thereby interfering with his training.

It was only shortly before I left Jos that Isaac confessed his genuine inability to join these modern African elite groups. In 1962 I was helping him write letters in anticipation of his longed-for trip to the United States to work for a construction firm (the venture did not materialize), and one evening at my place he drank a considerable amount of whiskey "to ease his cold." Perhaps the alcohol stimulated him to "confess" his real reason for not being able to be, as he put it, "a more prominent social person in Jos": he was ashamed to receive and entertain visitors in his spare living quarters. He said he had once wanted very much to join the Masons and the elite social clubs, but to do so now would place him in the awkward position of having to reciprocate invitations and visits, and he was ashamed to invite people to his unfinished house. He fell into a reverie of what might have been had ill luck not befallen him. His house would have been completed long ago and filled with modern furniture, modern interior decoration, and modern paintings. His house would have been so fine that he could have invited Zik (Azikiwe, who was then Governor General) to stay with him when he came through Jos, and Zik would have accepted. (Isaac overlooked the fact that there is a special Rest House in Jos for the Governor General or equally important official visitors.)

It was interesting to note that once he had confessed so much to me in regard to his true feelings and social-economic situation, Isaac apparently realized that it was useless to try to deceive me through empty pretenses; his personality in relation to me underwent a profound transformation. After the drinking episode at my home and for the rest of the time that I knew him in Jos, he no longer presented a front of affluence and modern elite status, and he admitted he was near bankruptcy. This lack of money was at the heart of what we might consider to be his major social problem. He wanted to be elite and had almost secured the economic means for this position when he suffered a series of misfortunes. In his attempts to extricate himself from his economic depression, and to halt his slide downward in his social placement, he continued to meet new obstacles at every turn, which served to make his tenuous hold on what he had already achieved all the more difficult. The remainder of our interviews were frequent occasions for Isaac to pour out his heart and to lament his afflictions.

Several weeks before I left Nigeria I saw yet another indication that Isaac was no longer so much concerned with trying to convince me that he was—as would befit one of his social pretensions—a decorous and forbearing man. Desperate for immediate funds with which he could begin relocating his business, Isaac was casting about for possible sources. Having already obtained an overdraft, he was ineligible for a bank loan, but he thought he could collect on outstanding debts owed to him. On work he had done for the Jos Recreation Club six years previously, there remained an unpaid balance of £70. The bill was originally being paid off piecemeal, but with the founding of the Plateau International Club and the subsequent loss to this new club of many prominent and wealthy members concurrent with a series of severe financial losses through mismanagement, the Jos Recreation Club submerged into serious debt and was

barely surviving. When Isaac had approached the club's officers—
who were personal acquaintances, fellow members of his church
congregation, and persons who had repeatedly invited him to join
the club—to ask them to settle the debt, he was politely told that
a settlement was presently impossible; the attitude was clearly com-
municated that should he press this matter further his previous good
relations with the club's members might be jeopardized. Isaac, however, thought he was as much entitled to be repaid as the club's
other creditors, if not more so, since he had done the club's work
at nominal cost and hitherto restrained himself from liquidating the
debt. So he said, but it is likely that he had written off this debt as
a loss back when his financial condition had been more secure. By
reopening the issue he knew he was now risking being regarded
niggardly or revealing his true financial condition. Nonetheless, he
decided to initiate a suit. Although he thought his legal action against
the Recreation Club was justifiable, Isaac was not happy about it.
He was aware that the club was in poor financial circumstances and
that, as a sympathetic person, he should withhold his suit. At the
same time, he hoped that others were unaware of his own distressing
financial position. He wanted a quick and favorable court decision
so that the matter might be forgotten quickly by his friends. A favorable court decision would also justify his behavior and allow him,
he thought, to join the club at some future date. To lose the case
or have it drag out might make him unpopular.

Having decided to sue the Recreation Club, Isaac also determined
to sue the Nigerian Railways Corporation for misusing and damag-
ing some construction equipment they had rented from him. The
suit had no really firm legal basis, but if it succeeded it would bring
Isaac far more money than he hoped to receive from the Recreation
Club. He thought it efficient to employ the same lawyer to bring
simultaneous suits, and he thought he knew precisely the right person for this undertaking, an Ijaw who had recently come to Jos
after studying law in England. This fellow tribesman had acquired
an English wife, and several months after he had settled in Jos he
told Isaac that he felt his fellow Ijaw were avoiding him because

of his mixed marriage. Isaac undertook a personal campaign to integrate the couple into the Jos Ijaw community, inviting them to tribal union meetings, arranging for informal gatherings, and asking his fellow tribesmen to take all their legal matters to the new Ijaw lawyer. Isaac apparently felt that the attorney, deeply obliged to him socially, would feel committed to prosecuting his suits with especial vigor.

For a brief time all of Isaac's plans seemed to be proceeding well, but to his dismay the lawyer fumbled the initial actions. Because of the attorney's careless inaccuracies in filing the complaint, the suit against the Recreation Club not only was thrown out of court, but Isaac had to pay two guineas court costs as penalty. The lawyer had also overlooked a technical point in filing the complaint against the Railways Corporation, and instead of winning several hundred pounds as he had imagined, Isaac had to withdraw his suit rather than be liable for court costs in losing this case as well (although eventually he successfully sued the company). At this juncture Isaac gave his legal business to an Efik lawyer, who happened to be a relative of his contractor friend.

Isaac thought that in all decency the Ijaw lawyer should have apologized for his blunders; instead he demanded £20 as his fee. Isaac paid the money in smiling silence, but his indignation was boundless. In conversation with me he threatened to advertise the lawyer's incompetence and greed, and said he would see to it that this man would never have another client in Jos. This heated outburst was directly at variance with Isaac's usual display of calm in adversity and tolerance of weakness in others. His usual optimism deserted him. He lost charity, forgiveness, and forbearance—the decorum befitting his role of community leader was absent. When his composure returned, he told me that he regretted having employed the Ijaw lawyer and instituting legal proceedings against his friends in the Recreation Club. As always, Isaac wanted to remain on good terms with as many people as possible, because, as he rationalized, when African men reached his status as a father of many children, they began thinking about their children's future. These children eventually travel and meet people who know their father. If the father has made enemies, his children will suffer; but if he has made friends, people will be kind to them.

What kind of man is Isaac? Is he a man who, caught in the sweep of Nigerian national politics, was forced inevitably to become one of its victims, to become crippled economically, and to view without recourse the disintegration of his dreams of ambition in career and community, or is he a man whose inconsistencies and self-deception have contributed to his economic and social decline? Is he a man of strong traditional supernatural beliefs contradicting his avowed Christian tenets, or is he a man who, despite his education in engineering and science, cannot accept fully the twentieth-century orientation into which he was cast, and so cloaks his yearning for an idealized and more romantic past with a deep respect for Ijaw tradition and universal mysticism? Perhaps he seeks retreat as well as social gratification, for he characterizes himself in this way: "I want to live for deep scientific knowledge of both the physical and spiritual worlds. I like research into the unknown. What the common man is not interested in is where I find my pleasure."

Chapter VI

GANDE IKOWE: TIV

G ANDE Ikowe, the oldest male Tiv in Jos, considered himself
a prominent leader in the local Tiv community. By traditional
criteria of prestige, essentially based on age, his social position
should have been distinguished and secure. But Gande found that
the tribal values he had known and on which he relied were no
longer accepted by younger men, and he was dismayed when his
fellow tribesmen in Jos did not accord him the respect he regarded
as his right. Therefore, he looked forward all the more eagerly to
returning to his home village, where he believed the old ways had
not changed. Unhappily, life was different there too, and when he
did return he found that his old world no longer existed. The tragedy
of Gande's old age was to recognize his actual social role in a
modern world—a role that left him with little importance and worth.

Almost all the interviews with Gande took place at his residence
and were conducted through an interpreter. Occasionally Gande
made social calls on me, and then we would carry on casual conversations in a mixture of pidgin English and Hausa. When we first
met, Gande was working as a night watchman for a Yoruba lawyer,
the legal representative for the Action Group political party (a party
associated with the Yoruba of the Western Region). Soon after,
Gande lost his job and was unemployed for almost a year. His

qualifications were of little use to him in finding work; although he read a little Tiv and had a speaking knowledge of Hausa, he had no training in modern crafts or skills.

His poverty was apparent in his sparsely-furnished house and in the shabby clothing he and the members of his family wore. Although Gande gave his age as about 55, he was probably slightly more than 60 for, as a boy, he had witnessed the arrival of the first Europeans in his native area. He was born and reared in Mbatiev, a hamlet near Gboko in a section of Tiv country called Jemgbar by the inhabitants. Farming at home must have been dull for a Tiv boy such as Gande—viewing the changes going on about him, seeing the Europeans come in to build, observing their strange ways, and hearing stories of relatives who had fought in the Cameroons during World War I. Tribal war, the traditional outlet for young adventurous spirits, was now blocked, and older men's tales of past battles only served to whet a boy's appetite for thrills and glory.

When Gande was about 20 years old, his father died. He was buried in his compound, signifying that he was a "big man." He had been a leader in local wars, and was a wealthy man with much land, twelve wives, and many children. Gande's mother was his first wife. While his father was alive Gande heeded the constant advice of his family to remain at home and farm, but after his father's death, he left farming to become a porter for the local District Officer.

I was still in Tiv Division all that time, so I was always near my home. I was a carrier for the District Officer, and I carried his loads all around Tiv Division. I enjoyed my time with the D.O., so I didn't want to stay at home. Later, my brother and I were both working on the railroad when we were called home because our mother took sick. She died two days after we arrived. After that I left home for good. My mother's death had such an effect on me that I couldn't remain at home.

Gande joined the army around 1932, after seeing Tiv boys in smart uniforms marching and beating drums: "I liked that and that was why I joined them." He served in the army for about a year and a half and was given a medical discharge for tuberculosis. He came home and was again urged by his relatives to remain on the farm. He did so until the outbreak of World War II, when he again joined the army. "My parents were dead then," he commented, "and I could do as I liked." He fought in Burma during the war, as did many Nigerian soldiers. With excitement and obvious delight he described fighting tactics, at one point seizing a knife to demonstrate how a bayonet should be wielded. "We liked fighting. We were not afraid. We were singing when we went to fight. From the start we sang. We were not worried about dying. I said to myself that, if God wills it, I shall live." Gande said that pagan soldiers carried native medicine for protection during the fighting, but that he, as a Christian, did not do so. In a later interview he admitted that he too had carried native medicine then, and still does.

Several years before the end of the war Gande developed eye trouble, was again medically discharged, and returned to Mbatiev, where he was welcomed by his kinsmen with a traditional feast. At the time of his return, he must have been one of the few Tiv men there who could speak Hausa well, having learned the language in the army. This skill, with his military experience, made him valuable to the District Officer. He was employed to recruit Tiv labor for the tin mines on the Jos Plateau. He apparently impressed the District Officer favorably; when recruiting ceased, the D.O. made him a headman in charge of road works near his home. Shortly before 1950 the District Officer was transferred to Plateau Province, and Gande went with him to become a sanitary laborer cleaning barracks at a mining camp near Kuru.

In 1951 Gande left the mining company to take a job as a laborer with the Nigerian Railways in Bukuru. He told me several times about his work with the Railways, frequently citing the reasons for his dismissal after three years. The first reason was one he had probably told all prospective employers. He said he was dismissed because he had failed to return from a leave in the required time, remaining at home for more than four months when he had been given only three weeks leave. He claimed he had been ill. His petitions for reinstatement finally succeeded, but then he refused the proffered reemployment: "If I had chosen to remain with the railway, it would be as a newcomer, and they would also put me in the *poto-poto* squad. This is a group which is on twenty-four-hour call to be sent anywhere there is trouble along the line—anywhere, any time, on immediate notice. I had a family, therefore I thought it inconvenient to be going from one place to another." At various later times Gande altered and amplified his story. He once told me one of his wives had run away from him and returned to her home in Tivland, and settling his dispute with her caused his delayed return to Bukuru. His wife returned with him but, because she was prone to adultery, Gande refused to accept work that would prevent him from keeping a close watch over her. He said that he had fought hard to win his reinstatement, and was even given three months' back pay; but he had antagonized his immediate supervisor in the process, and thereafter his work was made intolerable. "If you're under somebody and that man doesn't want you, what are you going to do? It can only cause trouble. I could have killed him in anger. That's why I left the work."

He then went to work as a night watchman for the Antiquities Department Museum in Jos, acquiring the job through a fellow Tiv, who had been in the employ of the Director for a long time. He soon left this job to go to work for various employers as a gardener and night watchman combined, but returned to the Museum in 1958. He was dismissed in 1960, because, he said, punching the time clocks on his nightly rounds confused him. Museum officials said that he was sleeping on the job.

Gande's job history illustrates his highly transient character. However, he did express some pride in his abilities as a night watchman: "I know my work. I don't sleep on the job. I know the time when thieves work. I have my arrows. Whoever comes, I question him. If he doesn't answer properly I'm ready to use my arrows." He considered the small salaries he had received in the past as a watchman (£5 a month) commensurate with the worth of his work—a modesty rarely found among more sophisticated African urbanites—but when he was looking for work he refused several jobs because the offered pay was so meager. In one case, he said, the former night watchman had been wounded by thieves, and he was angry that he should be expected to risk his life for a pittance.

Gande felt that his most recent employer, the Yoruba lawyer, had shown no appreciation of his integrity and ability (he had caught two thieves while on this job, both of whom were sentenced to two months in prison) and had in addition dealt unfairly with him. Instead of paying him punctually at the end of each month, his employer had delayed payment until the tenth or fifteenth of the following month. Gande said, "As I have a family, this inconvenienced me, and I told him so. This angered him." In addition to continuing to pay him belatedly, he cut his monthly salary from five to four pounds; Gande objected, and the lawyer told him to leave, saying that his dogs could look after his property. Gande said he left without further protest, but to protect himself he made the lawyer acknowledge that nothing was missing from his house.

(The manner in which Gande obtained this employment, and lost it, is incidentally illustrative of some of the features of Nigerian "tribalism" and tribally-based political parties. Just as the Yoruba were at this time associated with the Action Group party, the Tiv were associated with the United Middle Belt Congress. It was shortly after these two parties formed the UMBC/AG Alliance that Gande, through his personal connections with local Tiv politicians and members of the UMBC, was hired by the Yoruba lawyer. When this political alliance was seriously shaken, as a result of riots in Tivland just preceding the formal acquisition of Nigerian national independence, the lawyer turned on Gande and deliberately created the conditions that made it virtually impossible for Gande to continue working for him.)

After this job, Gande was unemployed for almost a year, although for a short time I paid him to collect Tiv specimens of traditional craft for a museum. At first he was optimistic about finding suitable employment; but as weeks and then months went by, and his repeated visits to the federal government's Labour Employment Exchange were fruitless, the common long-term unem-

ployment depression developed. During this time living with him
were a wife, her baby daughter, and his teen-aged daughter by another wife, and in order to support them he was largely depen-
dent on aid from relatives and fellow Tiv living in Jos. When his
Yoruba landlord evicted him for failing to pay several months'
rent (and, incidentally, not holding Gande to this debt), Gande
moved his family into quarters where his wife's brother lived.
His brother-in-law paid Gande's rent there, and he, together with
Gande's sister's son, and a few distant relatives, gave him money
for food. Several unrelated Tiv regularly gave him a few shillings,
in accordance with the custom of giving money to an old man,
and were also alert for possible job openings for him. After many
months of unrewarding job-seeking, Gande was desperate.

Now that I have no work I am suffering. Sometimes I dream about
money. I see plenty of money on the ground. I pick it up, and somebody
from behind grabs it and runs away, saying that the money is his. I was
thinking that I'll never get anything in this world for, whatever I get,
somebody else will take it away from me. When I got up from that
dream, I was so annoyed I didn't even wash that morning.

Food prices and the costs of other things is a problem. It is food that
prevents us from buying plenty of clothes. If you take ten shillings to
the market, you can buy a nice piece of cloth. But for ten shillings you
can also eat good food for several days. There are some days we may
not take anything in the morning, because things are so costly. If we
haven't eaten anything that morning, we may have *gari* [cassava flour]
around noon, and then we'll eat again in the evening.

The animal protein in Gande's family's diet came from dried
fish, cow or goat leg, breast or head of goat, and—another indi-
cator of poverty—cow intestines. "As adults we can eat anything,
but we will occasionally buy an egg for two pence for my baby
daughter so she can have some good nourishment in her."

It was not until he was in his fifties that Gande had to rent living quarters; accommodations for himself and his family had always been provided by employers. During the four years he lived
in Jos, Gande moved in and out of several different places for various reasons, and even after he had lived for several months in the

same compound as his brother-in-law he again moved to a place where he remained for as long as I was in Jos, having accepted an offer of a rent-free room in the compound of a fellow tribesman at the other end of Native Town. Wherever Gande acquired living quarters, the physical conditions always represented the poorest in Jos housing. If the particular building happened to be roofed with zinc instead of thatch, it was not much of an advantage; while either thatch or zinc could keep out the rain, neither could keep out the cold. If some places had electric wiring, it made no difference to Gande since to keep the rent low he would not use electricity. Each of his successive quarters were mud-walled, and he and his family would occupy only one room, which was divided by a curtain to separate sleeping from living areas. In his last rented residence, which was typical of all the others, the zinc sheets of the roof could be seen from inside, for there was no ceiling. There was no provision for heating, and Jos can sometimes be extremely cold. Rain (and light with it) was shut out by hinged wooden shutters outside the single window. Drinking water was drawn from a well in the yard which was unusable in the dry season. Since the compound had no latrine or bathroom, the landlord was willing to rent Gande this room for 10/6 a month on the condition that he care for the compound.

In the following account of Gande's marital history, the chronology presented ought not be viewed as absolutely accurate, although the proper sequence of events and the time spans between them are relatively sure. This qualification also applies to other aspects of Gande's life, such as the birthdates of his children, and his work, army, and travel experiences, for he not infrequently offered contradictory dates for past events. Since Gande had no official records of his marriages or the births of his children (even though he did possess dated testimonials from several employers), it was necessary to anchor these and other events in his life to events in Nigerian history, such as the first entry of Europeans into his home district, the construction of the bridge across the

Benue River at Makurdi, and the short period during which Tiv
men were conscripted for tin mining. Unlike the other informants,
Gande's chronological framework for his past was weak, and it
required patient labor on my part to ascertain the proper order
of his personal history so that the temporal relations met the re-
quirements of Gande's judgment as well as internal logic and con-
sistency.

He and his first wife were married from 1926 to her death in
the early forties. Two of her children reached adulthood: an unmarried son who lived at home and a married daughter living in
Lagos with her husband and three children. The son was born in
1935 and the daughter two years later.

Gande met his first wife when he was traveling in Tiv country, first noticing her in her father's compound where he was invited to sleep. In the succeeding days he observed her movements
and, when he had come to a favorable conclusion, he asked her
father for permission to marry. Gande's father was well-known to
this man, who agreed to discuss the matter further when the family representatives on both sides were gathered. The marriage was
conducted in complete accord with Tiv tradition, including the
transfer of bridewealth in the form of traditional Tiv currency
—brass rods. Gande assessed that their marriage had been highly
satisfactory.

She was a good wife. She obeyed me and she gave me every respect. If
I wasn't home and she quarrelled with other women, when I returned,
I would bawl her out and she would keep quiet. In our place there are
ways of testing wives. For example, if a woman is unable to weed her
garden, we know she is not a good wife. When I gave my wife a small
garden plot, she did very well with it. She liked to work, she wasn't
lazy. She did everything with vigor. If she wanted to go to the market,
she would ask my permission first. When strangers [visitors] came I
would tell her and within ten minutes she would make everything. For
these things I say she was all right. I myself used to brag to my mates
that I had a nice wife. She was a good woman.

This first wife was not well when Gande joined the army at
the start of World War II, and he received word that she had

turned seriously ill soon after he had begun training. Gande was given two weeks' leave to return home. He took his wife to the hospital but the European doctor said the illness was incurable, so Gande brought her to her father's home to see if she might respond to a native cure. Shortly after he returned to camp he received word that she died. Gande was not permitted another leave then, but when he next returned home he performed funeral services at her grave.

Gande met and married his second wife in 1928, during a visit to his married sister. Seeing a girl whom he instantly admired, he extended the days of his visit, became well acquainted with the girl, and then approached her father for his consent. The father, previously acquainted and favorably impressed with Gande's father, was agreeable, but only on condition that a woman from Gande's lineage be exchanged in marriage, in keeping with the preferred form of traditional Tiv marriage known as "sister exchange." He would not take money. Gande convinced the girl to "elope" with him, and they ran away to Gande's father's compound. As expected, the girl's father and his kinsmen were soon at Gande's father's home, demanding the girl's return. Gande's father assured his visitors that his lineage was unable to supply a wife in exchange, and begged that his son be forgiven for his thoughtless behavior and that they accept bridewealth. When Gande's father quickly produced brass rods, a cow, and smaller livestock, the girl's kinsmen assented. The visitors remained as guests to conclude the formal marriage celebrations, and relations have been good between them ever since.

When I finished all this, I knew I had completed everything. I thought to myself that I have spent a lot for this girl, and if she isn't good then my money is lost, but if she is a help to me, then it really wouldn't have cost me a penny. After some months I saw that she was very good because she obeyed me (and she did well all the other things a good wife is supposed to do).

But sometimes my two wives didn't get along. Whenever that happened I called them and told them they were both good women and shouldn't quarrel. They sat and listened to me. I told them to farm together. They should eat food together. They should clear brush together from each other's farms. They agreed. These are the reasons why I liked them. Apart from that I got many children from them. I was more than happy.

Except for a brief period, his second wife has always lived in Gande's compound in Tivland. Residing with her during the period of this research were her two sons and the son of the first wife, all of whom farmed for her. Two of her daughters were married and lived in Tivland, and the third daughter had lived with Gande in Jos until she was married in 1962. This wife sometimes sent some of her farm produce to Gande, if a neighbor or relative was going to Jos. In speaking about her, Gande expressed his traditional orientation:

> She now has white hairs like me. I don't want her to travel with me because she has so many children to look after. If I went home, it would be as before [with excellent relations] between us; I would live with her at home. She is farming and she will feed me [thus meeting traditional ideals]. Her sons are now old enough to build houses. If anything should happen to her [like illness, while Gande is away], my brothers [close kinsmen] would take care of her. My brother, senior next to me, would be responsible for the entire compound.

> She came to the Plateau with me, but she stayed for only three months. I told her to go back because conditions weren't good here. In Tivland you can have ten wives and no money, but you can still live well by farming. Here you would be suffering.

It was late in the course of our acquaintance that Gande happened to mention the third woman he had married in 1932; he spoke of her in connection with fertility rituals for barren women. When asked why he had not spoken of her months ago when he was giving information on his marriages, he said, "I never mentioned her to you because she died without having children; therefore she's not considered as a wife. The reason I mentioned the names of the others is because they left children for me."

Happiness with his third wife was intense but short-lived. Gande met her when he was working at Gboko, which was then being developed as an administrative center. I asked Gande why he had wanted a third wife when he then already had two. He answered:

She, my third wife, was very beautiful. When I saw her she took away my life. Our people are dancers. Once people were dancing near the market and I went to watch. There I saw her. When I saw how she danced I was very pleased to look at her. I wanted to marry her. I met her and asked her if she had a husband and she said she had none. I told her I wanted to marry her and she said she had nothing to say about that and directed me to go to her parents. Her father said he knew my parents and knew them to be nice people so he asked me to return with bridewealth. I went back home and told my senior brother, and we returned together with the money. We delivered the money. My father-in-law said he didn't need plenty of money for his daughter.

She was a good wife, but the marriage didn't last long. She got womb [became pregnant] and died. She got womb after six months. The baby died in the womb. She stayed with the womb about eight months and never complained of any illness. One day she told me she was suffering from a headache and later she said her stomach pained her, and she couldn't see well. She told me the world was spinning. I tried to cure her with native medicine. It didn't help so I took her to the hospital, but she died on the way. The doctor operated on her and brought out the child. He said not to blame myself because if I had brought her to the hospital sooner she still would have died. The doctor asked me whether I would bury her there or take her back home. I carried her back. I handed her to her parents and they buried her on their land. I continued to see her parents occasionally afterwards. If I go home now I must still try to visit them because I know they weren't the people who killed her. It was God. God can do away with somebody at any time.[1]

The death of a spouse, or a separation, Gande volunteered, does not end the relationship established with her family, provided that relations had been good previously. In the honorable Tiv tradi-

---

1. In his remarks on the responsibility for his wife's death, Gande is addressing himself in reference to Tiv beliefs regarding witchcraft. Traditional Tiv believe that a person can increase his own quantity of supernatural power, parasitically, by acquiring *tsav* (the power that is one's natural endowment) from a close relative. To lose one's *tsav* is to lose one's life, to gain another's *tsav* is to increase one's own power and to use this advantage to gain wealth, long life, or other things people desire. But it is selfish, it is witchcraft, it is homicide, and it carries the danger of prosecution as a witch.

tion, Gande maintained contact with the families of all his wives, and said he intended to see them whenever he returned home.

When listing his wives, in formal interviews devoted to that topic, Gande also failed to mention the errant wife, the one he had married in 1944, and who was allegedly involved with his dismissal from the Railways. When he did finally mention her, in connection with another topic, he said she had become a prostitute and was living in a mining camp on the Plateau. Perhaps he did not include her in the discussion of wives because she did not bear him children, or perhaps he wished to avoid talking about her because she caused him so much trouble, or possibly he was ashamed of having erred in marrying her in light of her subsequent adulterous behavior. It was during World War II, around 1943 or 1944, when Gande was helping in the conscription of Tiv labor for the Plateau tin mines, that he met the young girl (he estimates she was about 13) who was to become his fourth wife. Gande was then traveling between the Plateau and Gboko and it was in Gboko that he first saw her. She was accompanying her mother, who sold cooked food to the labor conscripts. When Gande decided the girl pleased him and he would like to marry her, he approached her mother but she rebuffed him.

"I asked her why. She said I was traveling with Hausas. If I wanted to marry I should remain settled and farm instead of traveling like Hausas. She wouldn't admit me into her compound, but I wasn't stopped. I went to her father and explained everything to him. He called my mother-in-law [-to-be] and explained to her that my working in Gboko didn't mean that I turned from Tiv to Hausa, but that I was here for the benefit of the Tiv people."

By that time the bridewealth was no longer paid in traditional Tiv currency, and Gande estimated that it cost at least £47 to conclude that marriage.

We were given blessings for our marriage and people prayed that we should live peacefully, but all their prayers didn't amount to anything. I didn't get any value from her.

At first she was all right, but at Bukuru she started annoying me. She was a good woman for the first four years she stayed with me, but after that she got disobedient. She didn't respect me and I changed my mind about her. Once she went home to visit her mother and didn't want to return to me. I sent someone to fetch her. When she returned she was disobedient. She was running around with other men, so I sent her home. I thought she would lose her badness in her father's compound. She stayed one year. Then her father sent for me. He and her mother wanted to know what was going on. I told them she wasn't wife only to me. She isn't satisfied with me so let her remain there. I wouldn't force her to stay with me. She looks for others. That's why I gave her a year's holiday. Let her satisfy her curiosity. I told my father-in-law that such women kill their husbands, because if you don't kill yourself they'll tell their lovers to do it for you.

They lectured her, and they begged me to take her back. After we returned to Bukuru she ran away; I didn't drive her [away]. While I was away at work, she got money from some man and ran away. When I returned from work she was gone. She packed away with some of my loads [belongings]. I looked for her and people told me she said I sent her to Kagoro. I returned home and sat down. I don't like her.

It was time for me to go on leave. I went home and found her. She had gone to live with another man. The only thing that bothered me was that her parents might think she was still with me and if something happened to her I would be in trouble. I asked her if she would come back to me, but she refused. I went to her brother and together we took her to her father. I told my father-in-law he should ask her why she ran away. She didn't know what to say. They asked her if she had gotten enough to eat. She said yes. They asked her if she had enough clothes. She said yes. She answered yes to all the things they asked. Then they asked her why she ran away. She didn't know what to say. Then her father told her to go back to me or return the money I paid for her. She said she had no money and she started to cry. By that time I was fed up with her. I told my father-in-law that I didn't want anything back, I didn't want his daughter, and that I would never ask for the money. My father-in-law was afraid that I would sue him for the money in court. I told him not to worry and that is how I finished with her. But whenever I go to Gboko I still go to their compound and visit them.

I don't know what caused all this. When I knew that she was unhappy because we were childless I told her it was all right for us to continue staying together. That she was barren was no fault of hers but God's will. But she didn't want to stay with me.

Now she's a prostitute in a small village near here. She doesn't want to come to Jos because I'm here. When my wife [presently living with me] got a child she wanted to come to the naming ceremony, but I don't want to see her.

It was while Gande was still living with his fourth wife in Bukuru that he resumed a friendship with a man he had known in Tiv country and who was to become his brother-in-law by his fifth marriage. Over several years their friendship strengthened and one day, after having lived without a wife for almost ten years, Gande told him that he wanted to marry again, but that he could not return to Tivland to seek a wife. Since his friend was about to depart for Tiv country on a short leave, Gande asked him to look around for a prospective bride. When the man returned to Jos he brought a woman for Gande with him. Gande said he never expected it would be the man's own sister. This woman, like all Gande's wives, had never been married before.

Gande named the first child by this fifth wife Bapum, which in Tiv means, "They are criticizing." He said he chose this name for his daughter because people had criticized his brother-in-law for offering his sister to a man too poor to pay bridewealth. Gande asked him not to heed this gossip and gave him a little money as a token of his intentions to pay a full bridewealth when he was able.

Up until that time Gande had been living in the same compound where his friend lived, but on the day the marriage formalities were completed Gande and his bride moved to other quarters. By not living with his wife's brother, Gande at least tried to live up to traditional Tiv standards: "According to us Tiv people it's not good to stay in the same place with your wife's relatives. I moved out because I didn't want my brother-in-law to know everything that was going on between my wife and myself. I considered it wiser to stay far away from him so that we might meet only occasionally." However, when Gande was out of work he had to accept his brother-in-law's invitation to return, remaining until he was given a rent-free invitation elsewhere.

Gande was grateful that his present wife was willing to marry a man as old as he and, above all, that she had presented him with a child. This woman, an unsophisticated peasant girl in her early twenties, had never been away from home before and spoke no English or Hausa. She was a thoroughly efficient housekeeper and seemed unaware of the vices associated with urban environments. She was like Gande in her complete acceptance of traditional Tiv values and culture, which was one of the things Gande most admired in her. His almost complete orientation to the past was expressed in his conception of women as inferior creatures, and he claimed that he would not hesitate to beat his wife if she disobeyed him. He said, "What I used to do as a young man I still do. When I marry a woman I give her some rules, and if she agrees with them she will be a good wife. If she doesn't, then I'll tell her to fear her brothers." Gande's rules for his wife included keeping quiet when he was talking, obedience, acknowledgement of his leadership in the household, honoring the memory of his parents, and, when at home, working satisfactorily on the farm.

His justification for his appraisal of women indicated the syncretistic or changing nature of the traditional past to which he was oriented: "When we grew up my father told us not to tell our wives our secrets. Besides, when the first Europeans came to our place and taught us how to adore God, we learned one verse from the Bible [which said that] Jesus was sorry for women. They would suffer in this world. As He saw that women were not trustworthy, they would have to suffer. So I continue with my father's advice and other people do the same."

In his behavior toward his children Gande also turned to the past. Only two of his children had gone to school and these for a short time only. Boys, he thought, should remain at home to farm. Girls, being weak, and likely to misbehave, should not be let out of a father's sight until they married, and so he kept his unmarried daughter with him wherever he resided. "If I left the girls with my wives at home they might not behave the way I would like. Before

I returned home some of them might become harlots. At home they would do as they pleased. With me they won't do anything wrong. That's why I don't let them out of my sight."

Gande's eldest son, who was then about 30 years of age, had left school after reaching Standard III, but he could now read simple passages in Tiv and compute basic arithmetic. Several years ago he had abducted a girl he was courting before the final marriage arrangements had been made, and Gande had had to leave Jos to come to his rescue. As the head of the family, Gande assumed full responsibility for his son's behavior. He paid the court fine of £5 and the bridewealth for the girl, who had since given his son a daughter. His second son, farming at home with his brother, now wished to have a wife also, and was waiting for his father to fulfill his parental obligation by arranging for a bride for him. A third son, about 17, lived with his brothers, but Gande said he was too young to consider marriage.

His eldest daughter, about 32, was married to a Tiv chief in their district who was said to have about ten other wives and many children. She had no children, and Gande expressed pity for her barrenness. Tiv custom calls for half the bridewealth to be paid at marriage and the rest to be forthcoming after children have been born, so Gande was ashamed to ask for the rest of this daughter's bridewealth since she had borne no children.

His next eldest daughter had gone to school but never beyond Standard I. She was with Gande in Bukuru when she married a Tiv who served a European as cook. When her husband's employer was transferred to Lagos, she and her husband went with him. She now had three children. When she married, Gande had refused to take any part of the bridewealth, saying that his son-in-law should pay after his daughter had provided children. Now he was trying to collect via mail, but his son-in-law kept putting him off. Gande sent him frequent messages that he expected to visit Lagos soon, thinking this might produce favorable results.

A younger daughter, who was about 25, had married a Tiv farmer near Makurdi, who had paid half of her bridewealth. This daughter had been "good," for she now had a boy of nine and a girl of seven, and so Gande wished to collect the rest of the bridewealth. Recent news was that this son-in-law had taken a second wife, and did not appear concerned about making good his debt to Gande.

A fourth daughter, about 15, had been living with Gande in Jos. He once expressed regret that he had not had the money to send her to school, an indication that his ideas about the value of formal Western education were changing.

Schooling is good because I see how people who have been to school are earning big money and they give their parents some of it. They are the people ruling Nigeria now. Our parents used to say that schooling was not good for Tivs; we should be farmers. Even now I still believe that farmers have more money than government workers, but when I started traveling in big towns, I saw that the people who are not educated today, the world doesn't need. All these big posts are not for us [farmers] but for small boys [socially insignificant people] who have education. I don't know book, but when I joined the army, I almost got to U.K. and to see how big people enjoy themselves. If you are a farmer, nobody will know you, but if you are educated, then you will have a big post like Zik or Sardauna.

The fifteen-year-old daughter, an attractive girl, was courted in Jos by several Tiv men, and Gande asked her to choose her future husband from among them. She chose a man who was a prison guard who already had a wife and four children. Gande studied the man's character and decided he was good, but he cautiously added that, when somebody wants something from you—especially if he wants your daughter—he will appear nice enough. Only time would tell whether the man and his daughter would remain happily married. "If I had given my daughter away in the olden days, I wouldn't have had to worry about her any more, but now I have to think that maybe her husband won't be a good man or maybe she'll run away. In former times I could be sure she would remain with him until God took her life. Now I can only pray that they should live happily together."

Gande's doubts were well-founded, since shortly before my departure this daughter ran away from her husband and her whereabouts were uncertain. Gande had already received half the bridewealth, which he would have to repay if she did not return to her husband. In connection with this money, and the bridewealth debts due him, Gande perceived that his prestige, in traditional evaluative terms, was indirectly involved. He had validated his position of prominence, he thought, by having many children, but to maintain this position he had also to provide wives for his sons, and for this reason he sought to collect the outstanding debts. Tiv traditional standards also required him to complete the payment for his latest wife.

When I asked Gande whether, after he had collected all the bridewealth debts due him and had settled his own debt for his most recent marriage, he would use the money that remained (assuming there was a surplus) to relieve his present poverty, he pointed out that money received as bridewealth was special money and could not be used for any purpose except acquiring a wife, either for himself or for a son or for a close male kinsman.

Besides his immediate family, Gande's only consanguinal relative in Jos was his sister's son. Gande described how he should feel and behave toward his nephew, expressing the ideal classical Tiv mode of the relationship between the mother's brother and sister's son. Because the boy's parents were dead, Gande assumed a position of parental surrogate toward him, considering it his traditional duty to do so. He said that he also felt a very real affection for the boy, and that he and his nephew had grown even closer in Jos than they would have at home. However, Gande felt uncomfortable that the concrete actions expressing this close and warm relationship could not take traditional forms under the urban and modern conditions of Jos, suggesting that the expressions of the relationship which could take place here, much as these were valued, somehow debased the relationship. "At home," Gande pointed out, "the most important thing with us is farming. If my sister's son wants to take things from me, as he has a right to do, he may also buy a goat and call people to farm for me." But the exchanges and reciprocities between them now lacked the pleasant emotional content associated with the more familiar traditional items. The nephew gave Gande from 10s. to £2 each month. Occasionally he also wrote letters for Gande and read to him those received. Speaking of his nephew and the duties now incumbent upon him since the death of the boy's parents, Gande went on to say, "These are the reasons that I've been telling you why I would like to go home now. I'm the senior man and it's not good that I stay away. I'm needed there to look after my family. Instead, I'm here looking for money, but I haven't got it."

Gande felt most gratified about the relationship that had developed between his brother-in-law and himself. This man had helped him for several years, and after Gande's marriage to his sister he continued to aid him, both as a friend and as a relative. Although this assistance must have been conditioned in no small measure by concern for the welfare of the man's sister and her child, Gande thought that his brother-in-law had exerted himself on his behalf far more than was necessary, and he looked forward to the time when he could express his appreciation by giving gifts to his brother-in-law and other members of his wife's family. For him to be able to reciprocate in this way would also bolster the self-respect so obviously weakened in his position of dependence. Gande was proud of his excellent relations with his brother-in-law, and said that nothing could spoil their friendship. Yet, there was a brief period when the relationship was on uncertain ground. This man tried to involve Gande in several schemes, clumsy at best, by which they would dupe me into giving them large sums of money. A strong traditionalist holds absolute loyalty to his relatives in situations where a choice must be made between kinsmen and non-kinsmen, but traditional as Gande's orientation was, he was not absolute and inflexible in this or in other matters. Caught in the dilemma of betraying his brother-in-law's schemes or defrauding me, he warned me. To keep his brother-in-law from learning that he was being betrayed necessitated collusion between Gande and me. I had to respond in ways that would not expose Gande's duplicity. Of course, my interpreter was privy to all this, and it became a source of amusement to the three of us to joke about the man's persistence, and to devise counter-moves.

In most respects Gande remained a firm traditionalist, and, as wisdom is associated with age, he considered it entirely proper that people should come to him for advice, especially in matters concerning Tiv custom. People often did so, but, Gande pointed out, they did not always take his advice, and this was too frequently true with younger people. A man of Gande's age was also expected to visit Tiv people to inquire after their health, and Gande did so. He made special calls on the sick—"This is what people do in Tivland"—and if someone complained of an ailment that Gande could cure, he would give native medicine.

Gande had received instruction in native magic and medicine from his father, and he claimed he could cure gonorrhea, headaches, stomach aches, and fevers. By this time such knowledge had become rare, and because his skill was valuable, he attracted people who wanted him to cure their various ailments. He carried on his native medical practices only occasionally and secretly, because he had no license. Although this skill gave Gande prestige in the Jos Tiv community, his feelings about his practice were ambivalent. He was seriously considering becoming a genuine Christian and he felt he could not, as he put it, "have two gods." Sometimes he said he would not follow the old ways again; sometimes he reversed his position, telling me that if he finally went to his homeland to stay he would succeed to his older brother's position as native doctor, and he would then pass on his knowledge to his sons so that it might be transmitted over the generations. Sometimes he said he had discarded all his charms; sometimes he said he retained only those which had protected him when he was a soldier or a night watchman.

Gande apparently considered his homeland as an entirely separate world from his present urban milieu. Christianity and Christian behavior seemed to him appropriate in Jos; but in the context of Tivland, "native medicine and native magic are just like gifts from God. Tiv cannot do without them because there may be some years when the crops may not be good. At such times the old men will gather together to pray and then every crop will be nice."

For as long as he had to remain living in Jos, Gande wistfully expressed the hope that all his immediate neighbors might be Tiv men; then, as he put it, he could be easily found by anyone looking for him. This parochial sentiment reflects Gande's constant facing homeward, for the only people seeking him who would not know where he lived in Jos would be visitors from Tivland. Of course, he was most comfortable when in the company of Tiv, but this ethnocentricity was also related to his wish to be surrounded by the people of his tribe for only through them could he hope to achieve what he considered the measure of prestige and respect due him. Time and again he expressed such sentiments, as when he spoke of his obligations to render hospitality to visitors from his home town or to a Tiv in Jos who paid a call: "Many people eat with me. . . . They come here not to eat but only to see whether I'm alive and well. If they want to leave, and my wife is in the kitchen cooking, I'll tell them to wait. If people enter and see me eating, I'll tell them to wash their hands and eat. If they don't want to eat, I'll quarrel with them because it's our custom that if you're invited to eat, no matter how full you are, you should take something, small as it is, and put it in your mouth. Then you can leave."

Gande took credit for founding the Jemgbar Aid Association, a tribal union limited to persons who came from the Jemgbar district in Tivland. He said that as the oldest person from Jemgbar in Jos, he had felt obliged to call all the natives of Jemgbar together and urge them to form a union. They had agreed and elected him president, thus strengthening his self-image as a community leader. The association was founded in 1959, but its functions seemed to be limited to expressive activities like send-off parties and naming ceremonies, probably because a more inclusive Tiv Tribal Union already existed and provided instrumental functions. Very likely, the limited scope in function of the Jemgbar Aid Association was also related to the fact that the Jemgbar population in Jos was highly transient. All the members were unskilled workers and many were migrant laborers or subject to frequent transfers. Gande proudly showed me a picture of this group taken in 1959, taken in his compound on the occasion of a member's send-off party, with himself in the center.[2]

Gande was also a member of the Executive Committee of the Jos Tiv Tribal Union, which closely resembled other tribal unions in organization and function. In addition, Gande was a member of the Tiv Tribal Union committee of prominent men which met to settle disputes, and this duty also nourished his concept of self-importance. Married couples and others brought their problems directly to Gande, but he said that more important matters, and problems involving persons not from Jemgbar, had to be taken to the elected leader (called Chief) of the Jos Tiv population.[3] This man was younger than Gande. Gande considered that he himself should have been chosen, since he was the oldest Tiv man in Jos and therefore the most senior socially; but he explained this "anomaly" by saying that the other man was better acquainted with Europeans and their ways. Gande pointed out, though, that when this man was away from Jos he was his substitute. This example is but one of many in which Gande consistently demonstrated his desire for prominence in the Tiv community. Very often, when mentioning another man, he would say, "I am senior to him in age, but he is senior to me in wealth [or office, or occupation]." The traditional Tiv correlation of seniority in age with seniority in social status no longer remained valid, and this state of affairs was a source of disorientation for Gande.

As he could not yet return to his natal home and to the anticipated blessings of familiarity and security, Gande had to adjust to the social conditions of Jos. Here, one could not entirely avoid interacting with nontribesmen. With non-Tiv Africans in Jos, Gande's

2. Gande possessed only two other photographs: one of his sister and his wife taken in Tivland, and another of his daughter in Lagos with one of her children.
3. This man was not the president of the Tiv Tribal Union. A dispute which developed between Gande and the President of the Union is described later in connection with the naming ceremony of his daughter.

informal social relations were polite, but reserved and infrequent. At his last residence, a friendly and jolly old Hausa woman who lived across the street visited his compound daily. She frequently timed her arrival with my visits and there developed between the three of us, in this context, a joking relationship based on sexual themes. Sometimes she brought me gifts, such as eggs, and Gande said she frequently gave similar gifts to his wife. He admitted that she was a good woman, albeit she perhaps talked too much, and she was neighborly with his wife. I could not be sure whether he was pleased with her visits to his wife (who by this time was picking up Hausa rapidly) or merely tolerated them, for he cautioned his wife to avoid returning visits. He explained that someone might accuse his wife of acting as a liaison between this woman and a lover, but he partially dismissed this fear with the observation that the woman had no husband here and she was indeed a bit old.

Sometimes Gande accompanied his wife and daughters to church, but whether or not he went along, he could expect a visit of some congregation members each Sunday afternoon. These people were from tribes local to Jos, Birom, Jarawa, and others, and these visits, politely tolerated, were a source of painful boredom to Gande. Christianity was not a medium of friendship or social bonds for him, and the visitors had nothing else to talk about. As far as I could determine, there was only one context in which he took the initiative in interacting informally with non-Tiv. Perhaps two or three times a week he went to a nearby house where he could be sure of finding old Yoruba men passing the time at playing games of African drafts. Gande played with them, and frequently they were joined by persons of other tribes, including Tiv. It was clear that Gande enjoyed this. "You forget about everything else. The time passes so quickly that, before you know it, many hours have passed."

More clearly than with any of the other informants, Gande's evaluations of other Nigerian tribes and their members were rooted in the Tiv's historical relations with them and in his version of the tribes' present-day political affiliations. If the political party associated with the tribe was allied with the political party of the Tiv, then they were "friends"; otherwise they were not. Thus he could say of the Yoruba that, in spite of their extreme tribalism and untrustworthiness, they and the Tiv were now friends because they were engaged in a common cause against the political party of the Hausa. Gande defined "Hausas" as persons who come from the far North and wear big gowns, and equated them with Islam. He said they abused non-Muslims (calling them *arne*, which means "infidel" or "pagan") and gave jobs only to Muslims. Furthermore, according to Gande, the Hausa government was exploiting the Tiv people and forcing the Tiv to seek an independent government for themselves. He said that when a Middle Belt State was achieved, the Tiv could be friendly with the Hausa because the latter were otherwise easy to get along with.

The Fulani and Tiv were traditional friends, and nothing could spoil that relationship. According to tradition, a gift, however small, must be given by a Fulani to a Tiv about the beginning of each February. Although Gande believed that one should usually be friendly with friends of friends, the Fulani's Hausa friends could not be Tiv friends because of present political differences. He spoke of all the tribes he knew, whose members he had met in Jos, in this idiom.

Gande's intercourse with Europeans was almost entirely limited to employer-employee relations. For him, Europeans were never models for emulation. His feelings about them were on the whole neutral, although he distinguished between particular individuals as kind or mean, good employers or bad employers, intelligent or stupid. In another connection, he told me how grateful for their kindness and care he was to two particular District Officers for whom he worked. They had gone to great trouble to aid him, once when he was seriously ill, and once when he was badly hurt. Occasionally he voiced some anti-European remarks that sounded almost word for word like the propaganda of the political party with which he was associated.

Gande was indifferent or hostile to many of the cultural changes he had witnessed, but he did express satisfaction with some of the things Europeans brought. He thought it was good that slavery and pre-colonial tribal fighting had been abolished, that reading and writing were taught to Africans, and he had a special satisfaction with the concept of time-keeping. He thought it was wonderful that days could be divided into regular intervals, that these intervals could be tracked with mechanical devices, and that people could coordinate their activities by orienting them to the clock. He also appreciated European material objects, most of which were out of his reach. "Even if I could get them, I wouldn't know how to use them. I have no money to buy such things as cars, but I would like to have beds and good furniture, and I would like to be able to buy clothes and shoes for my wives and daughters so that when they go down the street I can feel proud when people say, 'They are Gande's [women].' I should like to have European shoes for myself. I like a clock, so I tried to get a small one [pocket watch]. I like nice enamel pots and pans. We can't make these."

At first I had no reason to doubt that Gande would be able to live for some time with the image of himself as an elder statesman of the Tiv community, widely respected for his age and the wisdom associated with it, who would one day return in honor to the hamlet of his birth. But in the autumn of 1961 his self-image was unexpectedly shattered by the failure of the naming ceremony of his baby daughter.

The Tiv naming ceremony, like that of other Nigerian ethnic groups, honors the parents who bring a new member into the community. Formal invitations may be sent out (I received one from Gande in the form of a sheet mimeographed by a Tiv working for a government department), but the parents are also expected to entertain any person who wishes to attend, and the more prominent the parents, the greater the number of guests who can be expected. In return for the hospitality of the parents, and in their honor, the guests present gifts of money in the name of the new baby. Goats will be slaughtered, meat, rice, and other food will be prepared, and beverages will be acquired during the preceding day. For the ceremony itself four prominent men are designated first-, second-, third-, and fourth-chairman, and a fifth man is chosen—for his entertaining abilities—to be the official "announcer." The chairmen are expected to present gifts of the highest denominations, ranging upward in value from the fourth to the first, while the announcer maintains some order during the period of gift-giving by the guests. Semi-professional musicians, mainly drummers who accompany their drumming with songs, are hired for the occasion.

When the guests have arrived and everyone is seated—men and women at opposite sides, and the chairmen in their appropriate place—the first chairman steps to the center and makes a small speech explaining the reason for the gathering. Then, from a bottle of gin, he pours a few drops on the ground as libation. All present stand as the local community leader says a prayer for the general welfare of the community and asks for particular blessings on the family being honored. Then the parents bring the child to him and he holds it while the first chairman makes a short speech, during which he names the child. The first chairman then takes the baby, holds it high for all to see, and introduces it to the guests. When he has handed the child back to its mother the people at the center return to their seats, and the announcer comes forward. He receives the first money donation from the first chairman, announces the amount, and places it on a tray at the main table. He repeats this for each of the other chairmen and a few prominent people among the guests. This concludes the formal opening ceremonies. Thereafter, people eat, drink, and sometimes dance.

The announcer's special abilities lie in having a voice with stamina to last through the afternoon and into the evening, a voice strong enough to be heard above the drumming and singing and din of the crowd. In addition he plays the part of a jester, brushing, blowing, and "cleaning" paper money and throwing, catching, and juggling coins. The announcer's comic routine may include pretending that the currency handed him has been manufactured on the spot, handling the coins as if they were hot coals, and fanning the paper money to "dry" the ink. The announcer is also the medium of communication between persons addressing one another, often translating their remarks into quips and parries. A person must donate some money, however small the amount, to have the announcer speak for him, answer a jibe, ask a question, or make a request for him. A competition develops with quality of wit and quantity of money matched as weapons. A man may give a shilling to request that a certain woman dance, and she may donate six pence for the privilege of refusing. This banter continues until people are out of larger coins and are "talking" with pence. Thus, the amount of money received as gifts at a naming ceremony increases.

As an old and (so he believed) respected member of the Jos Tiv community, Gande expected to be especially honored. He had no doubt that everyone from Jemgbar would demonstrate their respect and fraternal feeling for him by attending the ceremony and donating money generously. He had started planning the ceremony in May 1961, but by mid-August he found that he could not himself raise money for the food and entertainment, and he began to wonder if he would be able to have it at all. His friends advised him to go ahead, even if he had nothing with which to feed the participants. Then he received some financial assistance from his brother-in-law, and his sister's son was able to buy several goats at bargain prices in a bush market. Gande decided to hold the ceremony on a Sunday in early September.

In the meantime, an incident occurred which was to affect the outcome of the ceremony. A young man came into Gande's compound and got into a fight with the wife of his brother-in-law. Gande intervened to stop the fight, but the matter was brought to the Police Charge Officer, and from there it went to the Alkali Court. Gande said he had tried his best to convince his brother-in-law to dismiss the court case, but his brother-in-law was insistent, and Gande was required to appear as a witness against the young man.

The youth had come looking for Gande's brother-in-law after he had heard that this man was trying to have an affair with his wife. The fight ensued when the woman called the man foolish for allowing himself to be deceived by baseless gossip. The uproar brought Gande to the scene, and he tried to convince the lad to leave the compound and to return, if he must, when the man he sought would be home. He lectured the young man about his conduct, and warned him of the public opinion that would rise against him if he beat women. Gande said he told him to leave the compound several times, and pointed to the white hairs of his beard as a mark that he, Gande, should be respected and heeded, but the boy said he was neither worried nor moved by Gande's words.

After the man left, Gande went to his father to ask him to deal with the offender, but the man said he would have nothing to do with the problem. Gande's brother-in-law then decided to take the matter to court. When it became clear that the lad would have to stand trial, his father approached Gande and asked him not to testify against his son. Gande's negative response to this request was couched in terms of abstract morality and justice, but essentially, he admitted, kinship loyalty required him to support his brother-in-law. The case was delayed several times and not settled finally until some time after the naming ceremony.

The day of the ceremony came. Gande expected his guests to begin arriving at one o'clock and hoped to start the ceremony at one-thirty or two. But by two o'clock so few people had arrived that the guests had begun whispered commenting among themselves. By two-thirty the drummers who had been hired for the occasion began playing to while away the time. Nervously wiping his hands on a handkerchief, Gande began a heated discussion about the reasons why certain prominent people had not yet arrived. A slight drizzle fell from time to time, but the overcast day was not enough to keep people away. At fifteen-minute intervals the drummers would start playing, apparently without spirit, and then shortly leave off. Gande borrowed a bicycle, left and returned in about twenty minutes. His agitation, apparent all along, had not diminished.

At three-thirty he ordered the ceremony to begin. The program got underway fitfully, initially appearing that it might cease altogether at any moment. If events could, they were conspiring to keep Gande from deriving any pleasure out of this day. The announcer called out the name of the first chairman, who rose and walked to his place at the main table. The announcer, from a previously prepared list, called the names of the second and third chairmen; they were not present. The fourth chairman, when called, took his place near the first chairman. Substitute chairmen were found for the vacant positions, but they had not come prepared for the honor, so they could give only a few shillings when the announcer approached them for money. Gande later told me that there were supposed to be four lady chairmen, but the first lady chairman had been sick and could not attend, and the second lady chairman (who was the mother of the young man involved in the fight) did not attend and kept the remaining lady chairmen away.

As the announcer walked among the crowd people gave him money, and he announced the amount and spoke for the donors. Some, when giving money, had the announcer state that it was to be used to buy the baby soap or other articles. Others attached humor to their donation, as when a donor called for the privilege of asking someone to show his face. When it was observed that the women were giving infrequently and very little, a man paid to ask the reason. A woman had to pay to answer that the women had not been informed of the naming ceremony. Another man said, again making a payment, that the first lady chairman had been informed in sufficient time, but that she must have failed to tell the others, for she was not present. (Not until later was it learned that this responsibility had been delegated to the mother of the youth in dispute with Gande's brother-in-law.) After a while, the remarks between the men and women turned to banter, and, when one woman said that the ladies present were insulted that they did not have their own table, a man paid to have a table brought to them, whereupon the women started giving money more whole-heartedly. The affair was in sharp contrast to the unqualified success Gande imagined it would be.

At our first interview after the ceremony, Gande anticipated questions about the poor attendance and the absence of the leading women. He tried to mimimize the situation by saying that no one was obliged to attend a naming ceremony—a contradiction of his earlier statements—and that, after all, the important functions of the ritual had been served—the girl had been named and the people had prayed for her welfare. He looked for whatever palliatives he could find, saying he had been honored by my presence, and, since I was to write a book, "now her name will go as far as England." But my interpreter, never expert in diplomatic skills, volunteered the opinion that the amount collected for the baby, £19 10s,[4] was an insult to Gande. Gande agreed. He said that people usually got from forty to sixty pounds at naming ceremonies, and some got as much as eighty. Even those who were unlucky got as much as thirty pounds. "In my case all but one of the biggest people didn't come. They always used to come before, but because they didn't come, we had to choose some nobodies [as chairmen]. These couldn't give as much as if the others had come." Then Gande showed his distress, and for a moment seemed to perceive that his image of himself was not shared by other Tiv. "Those who came didn't reach 5 per cent of the Tiv people in Jos. I'm afraid they may be angry with me. Since I'm here in Jos, I never abused any Tiv man. I am the senior Tiv man in age here, but in other things, such as jobs, others are senior to me. In Jos I don't

4. Seventeen pounds of this amount immediately went to Gande's brother-in-law as half of the bridewealth for his wife. Because his wife had produced a child, he felt obliged to pay the balance quickly, and this he hoped to pay with the first half of the £34 he expected as the bridewealth for his daughter who was to marry the prison guard.

follow them but lead them, and they don't do anything without me."
Finally, the implications of the dispute in his compound came into
focus.

That boy's mother was the second senior woman and his father was
the second chairman [of the naming ceremony]. They did all this! The
father told the other men not to come, and the woman told the other
women not to come because they say my wife's brother is taking court
action against their boy. When I talked with his father he answered
that it was none of his business, but he said this angrily at the time, and
I didn't realize what he meant to do.

The women who came were told about it by my wife, but those who
came weren't serious. If they gave little, it means they have done
nothing. The women get money through their husbands and, if the
husbands don't want to do anything, the women can't do anything either.

Disgusted at the poor turnout and lackluster gift-giving, and
angry at the blow to his pride, Gande planned to air the matter
at the next meeting of the Tiv Tribal Union, and threatened to boy-
cott further meetings if he did not receive satisfaction. The affair
never reached the Union's agenda. The leader of the Tiv community
and several other prominent Tiv men in Jos persuaded Gande to
make a reconciliation of friendship with the youth's parents. Gande
rationalized: "I thought about what they said and decided to let
it go because in a naming ceremony people aren't forced to come."
He continued: "The chief of Tiv in Jos went and talked with the
boy's father privately. He denied keeping the people from coming
to my daughter's naming ceremony. He said he couldn't attend because he had to send money to his father and he had no money with
which to come. I don't hold him any grudge, but I don't know
whether he deceived me when he said he doesn't hold any grudge
against me. I'm still sure that he and his wife kept people away because all the people from their area didn't come and they make up
most of the Tiv in Jos. They're from Jechira." The man with whom
he had quarreled was not only the leader of the Jechira section of
the Jos Tiv community, he was also president of the Jos Tiv Tribal
Union. He and Gande had formerly been good friends, and Gande
expressed the hope that they might continue to be.

In analyzing the significance of this episode, I would suggest that Gande was uncertain whether he had inadvertently become involved in a dispute with a man socially more powerful in Jos than himself, or whether the man's prominence was irrelevant, and the crux of the matter lay in the fact that Gande counted for little in the community. If the latter were true, then Gande would have to confront the unpleasant realization that he had been deceiving himself with regard to his social worth, and would be forced to locate his actual social position. To be, even temporarily, without anchor in the system of social ranking, or to find his true position was far inferior to what he had imagined it to be, was too threatening to his ego, and so Gande did not pursue that line of reasoning. Instead, he considered that the entire matter was nothing more than a kind of political clash between himself and the leader of the Jechira people. His following in Jos had been far outnumbered, so he had lost. He preferred to think that such a catastrophe could never have befallen him at Jemgbar. The personally most satisfying explanation was that he had indeed been viewing his self-importance realistically, that the traditional cognitive and evaluative perceptions that he held and by which he ordered his life were still operative and shared by others, and the proof of this could surely be demonstrated at his home in Tivland where his position of superiority was vacant and waiting for him. He needed merely to return to fill it. He thought that when he returned, he would find that the world had not turned on its head, and that the view he held of himself was in harmony with the way in which others regarded him. One of the consequences of the naming ceremony was that it had acted as a catalyst for his feelings about returning home, where his dignity could be restored. Therefore Gande looked forward all the more anxiously to the time when he might go home.

Shortly after these events Gande received a visitor from his home area. When I asked him about his connection with this man, Gande expressed his fervent wish to be back at home. He said,

This man is my friend who came to visit his sister. He's a farmer; he doesn't like to work for pay. Formerly he worked for the government, but when he saw there was no money in it he returned to farming. He enjoys farming best because farmers believe all government workers have nothing. If you go to their houses in the morning, you'll see them only drinking tea. If you go in the afternoon, you'll see the same, while the farmers are enjoying themselves.

You see this? [Gande held out a handful of bennisseed.] One bag of this is worth £4, and he has twenty such bags, and he also grows yams and other things. Sometimes a bag of bennisseed will sell for £5, and he has got about twenty bags. Just imagine, five times twenty while government workers will be eating *gari*. [He showed some dried beans.] This is also money. [Then he picked up a huge yam and two ears of maize.] We farm these a lot and get plenty to eat. All these things my "brother" here has brought from home to give me.

My aim in coming to Jos was not to stay. The D.O. brought me here to do some few months' work, but only God knows what He does. He held me here. Now I pray that He let me go, that He lead me home to meet my family again. Immediately I touch home, so many people will ask me why I stayed away so long.

People like myself wouldn't go anywhere until we did our farm work during the rainy season. As a young man I made sure never to go away during the rains. If I happened to be away, I would return to help my people farm. When I returned from the army, I didn't let my compound remain neglected. I repaired some houses and built others. I tried to keep the place up.

At home we have large meeting houses in the middle of the compound. If I were at home today, I would build a hut like that in my compound and have that house for guests, because we believe that it isn't proper to entertain a guest in any other kind of building. Oh my, that hut would be even bigger than any you've seen in Jos, because here everything is costly. At home we have all the building materials right at hand. Here in Jos, if you want land, you have to buy it, but at home we don't buy land. Land is for everybody.

When I go home my sons will try to do everything for me so that I won't have to do a thing for myself. Small boys can remain in towns, but someone of my age ought to be at home. I left my home a long time ago. I want to go home; I'm tired of being away. Now, here, I'm suffering. I told you that one day I will leave Jos to return home, to go and farm. I don't know what I'm doing here in Jos. I don't have any money; I'm not able to feed myself.

When asked why he did not return home at once, Gande answered: "I left my home to look for money, and I'm still looking for it. I haven't got money to return. I have children at home, so if I return empty-handed, it will be useless. If I had sufficient money to go home and start farming, I would do so at once. I have plenty of land at home, which was my father's land."

I also asked him why he didn't appeal to his relatives at home for money so that he could return, he said, "No, we don't do that. I would be degrading myself. Every one of them at home thinks I'm making money. They would look down on me. They would laugh at me." I then asked him, "How much would you need to return with dignity?" He thought that £40 was minimally necessary, and that he could save this amount if only he could get a job. (As the only jobs obtainable for him paid no more than £5 a month, it was virtually impossible for him to meet this goal.) Gande explained further that he would be ashamed to have to depend entirely on his sons to farm for him; he wanted to be in a financial position where he could hire farm labor if he wished, thus demonstrating that he was allowing his sons to farm for him and not begging them. In the same way, he did not want to have to depend on his wives' farming to support him. And, not least important, he would be ashamed if he could not properly entertain all the visitors who would come to greet and welcome him upon his return.

Toward the end of 1961 Gande enthusiastically accepted my offer of temporary employment, which would consist of his assembling a collection of traditional Tiv craft and art objects for a United States museum. We laid careful plans, listing the items that should or could be got. By post we placed orders with craftsmen to make the things that were not sold in the market, and Gande notified his family to expect his visit. His joyous anticipation turned to concern, however, when he considered that he had no money with which to buy requisite gifts for his wife and other kinsmen at home. He needed money for other necessities as well. Together we bought shoes, cloths, and other gifts to take with us, and I gave money to Gande for his various needs, including tiding over his wife in Jos until his return. He had not been home since his troubles with his fourth wife, and his expectations were high. At home he expected to find things in their proper place and perspective. Before we left Jos he told me that he imagined there would be a grand reception for him on his arrival.

I drove Gande to his home town in mid-December. Three-quarters of the way on the road from Makurdi to Gboko we left the main road and proceeded for several miles on a dirt track to a point where we had to leave the car and walk a trail for about half a mile until we arrived at his compound. There I witnessed a tearful re-union between Gande and his family. Gande's wife wept intermittently for a long time. After we had both rested, we went over for a last time what he was to do and how we would communicate. Then I resumed my journey to tour the Eastern Region.

Gande's instructions were to proceed with his purchases and to remain in close touch with the young man who had first introduced us in Jos, but who had resumed residence in Gboko. I would return to him about mid-January to transport him and the objects he acquired back to Jos. He was left with money to travel around Tiv country and make purchases.

When I returned to Tivland, Gande could not be located, and my efforts to find him were unsuccessful. I remained for several days in Gboko as the guest of the young man who was to have been our intermediary. He had lost contact with Gande, but from him I learned that Gande received far less respect during his visit home than he had expected. Gande had told him that he had been ill-treated by some relatives with whom he had stayed in Gboko. They fed him poorly, kept bothering him for money, and made him feel unwelcome. When our intermediary invited Gande to stay with him, telling him that he would be a most welcome guest and that his wife would feed him well, Gande accepted but he never appeared. The young man suggested that Gande might have been ashamed to stay with him, a non-kinsman and a young boy at that, when he had kinsmen in the town whose duty it was to host him. To have accepted the youth's invitation would have indicated that his own kinsmen had rejected him.

Gande had left few ethnographic articles with the young man, and said that he was having difficulty in acquiring some of the objects. Many of the items that had been ordered for manufacture were not completed, people would not sell him objects of ritual and magic that he thought he could get with little difficulty, and those who learned he was purchasing for a European raised their prices tenfold. He had told the boy he needed more money and asked him to advance him funds, but the latter was unable to do this.

I wondered how people could have learned that Gande was making purchases for me, and whether his complaint about the discovery was a ruse on his part intended to gain money from me. While not entirely dismissing this possibility, I thought it unlikely, basing my assumption on our good relations in the past and on Gande's previous honesty toward me. On the other hand, it was Gande himself who had initially pointed out to me the necessity of making these purchases clandestinely, for many people believed it was against the law to possess ritual objects, and that they would expose themselves to prosecution unless contacts were made through trusted persons familiar to them. Gande had also warned me that if people learned that a white man wanted these objects, prices would be inflated. Arrangements were therefore made to have our tracks carefully covered, so that only Gande and the young man were aware of what was taking place. I doubted that the young man was the source of the leak, but even if he was, it was difficult to see how the information could have spread from him to persons in various parts of Tivland. The most likely explanation was that Gande himself was responsible. Why, I wondered, had he done such a thing?

The only answer I can offer is a speculation, for I never questioned Gande about the incident. From all that I learned, it was clear that Gande received a cool reception from his countrymen at home. Perhaps he thought he could regain a measure of prestige, if not envy, if he indicated that he had an important relationship with me, and that I had entrusted him with this special "mission." Perhaps he hearkened back to the time during the labor conscription days when he had assisted the District Officers and was given special privileges and powers, and he tried to recapture the power and social significance he had experienced then. I may never learn for sure what Gande thought and did, but if he had indicated that he was working for me, the responses to this information must have been quite contrary to his expectations, for he failed to acquire most of the ritual objects we had planned to buy, and he had great difficulty in buying even commonplace items at their usual cost.

At the beginning of February, about two weeks after I had returned to Jos, Gande sent his son to Jos with a message to his brother-in-law, instructing the latter to see me so that I could send Gande £20. He did not say how this money would be used. From my earlier experiences with his brother-in-law I considered it necessary to refuse this request, and I sent instructions to Gande to return at once to Jos with whatever purchases he had made. Several days later, Gande's wife came to me to beg for some money so she could feed herself and her daughter. She was big with pregnancy, but otherwise looked thin. She explained that she had been ill, and I gave her money.

Gande finally returned to Jos in the beginning of March, bringing with him most of the non-ritual objects we had sought. He never mentioned any grand reception given for him at home to commemorate his visit, and I did not question him about it. We had concluded our formal interviews and thereafter saw each other only occasionally, and during these visits he never brought up the subject of his visit home.

Gande finally found employment as a day watchman with the Public Works Department, which paid him slightly less than £5 a month. Before my departure from Nigeria, he visited me and announced with joy that his wife had given birth to another daughter. I congratulated him; we made our farewells and wished each other the best. In parting he said: "Surely I'll have many more children if God keeps me alive. I'll get many if I go home. When you pray God to give you something, if He wishes He may give you half of what you ask for or He may give you nothing. I pray God I may go home. I won't stay in Jos to die. I must go home."

Chapter VII

PETER ADAM EKONG: EFIK

P ETER Ekong, a lonely and nervous man in his middle fifties, was the most unreliable of all my informants. He often answered my questions untruthfully, and his responses and comments contained many contradictions and discrepancies. Frequently he failed to keep interview appointments and during one period, he deliberately avoided me on one pretense or another for a time long enough to make me consider replacing him with another informant. But precisely because of these qualities, and others that served equally to contrast him with other informants and thus extend the range of my limited sample, I proceeded with the interviews. He expressed strong high status aspirations—his criteria for upward mobility being European—but his hopes of advancement were shaken by events that occurred during the period of the interviews. Modelling his behavior as best he could on the European, he wore only European clothing to signify the modern African elite status to which he pretended. Still, he proclaimed pride in his "pure Efik" heritage, and was insistent that the Efik not be confused with Ibibio, to which they are akin, the latter in his view being distinctly inferior.

Peter's dishonest responses, his contradictions and inconsistencies, his evasive and superficial remarks, can largely be understood as consequences of a discrepancy between us about the nature and purpose of our relationship. Initially, he believed that he was introduced to me because of his prominence and leadership among the Calabar people (mainly Efik and Ibibio) in Jos, and that the intent of my research would not include probing deeply into his private life. He wanted me to maintain this impression of him, and he thought that our contact would be brief (thus making it more certain that I would maintain a favorable view of him), pleasant (insofar as he would have the pleasure and prestige of being sought out and interacting on egalitarian terms with a distinguished white man—a researcher, a scholar, and a person associated with an American university), and superficial (in the sense that he would be required to speak only generally about his people and himself). Relating himself to me in these terms, he tried living up to a status of notability he had not actually achieved. Often he provided stock responses to queries about his values and ideals. For example, he expressed his intention of returning to his place of birth to live out the remainder of his life, and enumerated the idealized economic and social attributes of living in Calabar. Peter even praised the magic wonders of the Calabar juju practitioners in the kind of detail he thought was sure to please the romantic fancy of Europeans. Our interviews, in English, were at first seen by Peter as friendly and informal social get-togethers that necessitated full reciprocity, and so were held equally divided between our residences; but as the concomitants of the interviews—beer and cigarettes—devolved upon the host, it was not long before Peter felt the financial strain of providing adequate hospitality, and we met more often at my place.

When Peter's first definition of our relationship required adjustment—in his experience I was not behaving toward him and other Africans in the way Europeans had or should—he concurrently altered his statements about himself, living conditions and family relations in Calabar, and his evaluation of Efik traditional culture; i.e., his comments about returning home progressively changed to the point where he declared he would never go home, except perhaps for short visits, because he feared he would be killed there, and he called the Efik "uncivilized" people who performed barbaric acts.

Peter was a trained and highly skilled motor mechanic. At the time of our acquaintance, he had retired from employment with the United Africa Company in Jos, after working for the company about sixteen years, and was now free-lancing as a mechanic. He considered his occupational skills as somewhat higher than those of a skilled artisan, and in describing his work with the U.A.C. he portrayed himself as a mechanical engineer without a practicing license.

He had been trained as an apprentice mechanic with the Nigerian (now Port) Authority at Bonny and Lagos. Just previous to this apprenticeship he had served as a teacher for one year at a Catholic secondary school of Calabar that he had attended and where he had achieved Standard VI. In 1931, on completion of his six years training as a mechanic, he received a Certificate of Competency and a job with the Authority in Lagos at £72 a year. He was laid off in 1933 when the depression forced the Authority to retrench, but he quickly found employment with a cold storage company, at £20 a month, maintaining ice-making equipment. At first located in Port Harcourt, he was transferred to Jos in 1934. After a year's employment with this company in Jos he resigned for a job with a lead-mining company at an increase in salary to £7 a week. He held his job at the company's location in Ibi, near Makurdi. He returned to Jos in 1938, when the mining company went bankrupt as a result of the collapse in the price of lead ore, and it was then that he started working for the United Africa Company, from which he retired in 1954. His initial salary with the company was £30 a month, and this increased to £48 by the time he retired. Peter said he had received bonuses and various allowances from the U.A.C. that substantially increased his earnings. For several years thereafter he worked as a lorry mechanic in the repair yards of the Nigerian Railways Corporation in Zaria. While in Zaria in 1957, he met a Syrian he had known from his days of U.A.C. employment in Jos. This man had a relative in Kano who was a buyer of agricultural produce, particularly groundnuts, and who possessed a large fleet of lorries used to transport groundnuts bought in Chad, Niger, and northern Nigeria to Nigerian seaports. Peter accepted the Syrian's offer to be the groundnut buyer's chief mechanic because it would involve working only half the year—during the dry season from November to April when the groundnuts were shipped—and because he could earn almost as much money during that time as he had been making at U.A.C. and the Railways working a full year. During the rest of the year he could free-lance. Although his various positions did not bring him wealth, they were well-paying jobs by Nigerian standards, providing him with the economic means for some material display and a measure of prestige as a highly skilled laborer with considerable job responsibilities.

From the time he first came to Jos in 1934, Peter had rented living quarters for himself and his family, but in 1940 he bought a house plot in the Native Town for £50, and started building a one-story concrete house. At that time building materials and construction labor were scarce, and their costs were high. Corrugated galvanized iron roofing sheets could not be found and he had to substitute for them tin sheets from opened four-gallon gasoline cans. Many of these, though rusty, still show the Shell trade mark. Peter estimated the cost of construction to have been more than £600. The house was completed in late 1941, and early the next year he and his family moved in.

Electric wiring runs throughout the house, and piped water is tapped in the yard and kitchen. The rooms are modestly furnished with locally-manufactured furniture. The living room, with an entrance directly to the street, held cushioned chairs, a sofa, and small tables for holding drinks. Peter had several radios, only one of which was in working order. A refrigerator that had long ceased operating was used as a cupboard. In the yard, protected by a roof, was a wood-burning stove that saw little use, since the family cooking was done in the traditional manner of pot-on-stones suspended over a small wood fire. A former bedroom that faced the street was converted into a shop for the sale of canned food, bottled beverages (including beer), cigarettes, candy, soap, and sundry items of the sort women petty traders display on stands set up before the entrance to their compounds. To one side of the interior yard were two rooms (one containing a clay oven) used for commercial bread-baking. Neither of these enterprises, which were run by Peter's wife, enjoyed continuous success. Peter claimed that the necessity for his wife to travel to Kaduna to deal with her children's and grandchildren's frequent problems, and her poor health which, when she was not attending an outpatient clinic, often prevented her from working, were the reasons why her trading activities did not fare better. It later became clear he and his wife also lacked the capital to run these businesses.

Speaking of his seasonal employment in Kano, Peter was quick to point out that, for £100 a year, he rented a house in Kano in a section of the city where Europeans, Levantines, and wealthy Africans live. His emphasis on its location was part of his initial attempt to impress me. When it later became obvious his ailing wife would not be able to accompany him to his place of employment I asked Peter whether he intended to maintain his former living arrangements, and he answered that since he was going to be alone it was pointless for him to continue renting the prestigious but expensive residence. Instead, he intended to room with an Ibo man he befriended in Kano, who lived near him. Peter's Hausa houseboy was also a status symbol, but a minor one, since he lacked training and skills in his work and served mainly as a general factotum. In addition to his pay of £2 a month, he was provided with meals and a small room in the yard near the kitchen. A more conspicuous indication of social superiority was a European car Peter had received from his son in Kaduna. It was bought from an expatriate who left Nigeria, and Peter drove it back to Jos where he put it up on blocks in front of his house, saying it required minor repairs. But there it remained, immobilized, throughout my stay in Jos, while Peter kept saying that he was awaiting the arrival of certain parts he had ordered. That parts for this fairly popular automobile were not stocked in Jos, or could not be quickly received from an agency in a nearby city, was quite unusual, and I suspected that Peter was simply unable to afford the upkeep on his status symbol.

Peter's mother, the only child of a wealthy man, and one of the most junior of Peter's father's many wives, was still living in Calabar, where Peter was born and raised. She had apportioned much of the property inherited from her father among her children, and Peter's share was managed by one of his older brothers, all who lived in Calabar. Peter described his mother as a Catholic and an "important woman" who held several native titles. She was once a wealthy trader, Peter said, but now derived a modest income from land she had retained which produced palm kernels, kola nuts, and other forest products.

His father, who died the year Peter was born, was the grandson, in direct patriline, of King Eyamba, a ruler of Duketown, Calabar. Peter proudly proclaimed that his father had achieved the top ranks in the native Egbo secret society, that he was a Royal Freemason (as well as a baptized Catholic like his mother), and that he had been one of the richest men in Calabar. He had received some Western education, had been an agent for European commercial firms in Calabar, and was purported to have been instrumental in establishing Catholic missions in Calabar. Although an apparently devout Christian, Peter's father was a polygynist. Peter illustrated his father's gargantuan polygynous achievements with the comment "He had so many wives, I never know them all. When I grew up somebody always telling me 'This your father's wife'." Peter also claimed that he had over a hundred half brothers and sisters, not all of whom he knew personally. Peter claimed that the eldest son of the senior wife had dissipated all of his father's wealth. According to Peter, his father had made out a will dividing his estate among all his children and had left this will (unregistered) with a fellow Freemason who, when he was about to be transferred from Calabar to Sierra Leone, handed the will to the eldest son.

In telling me about this, Peter wanted to indicate that he had been unlawfully done out of his share of his father's estate, and to voice his strong disapproval of polygyny and its disruptive consequences. "Marrying too many wives," he pointed out, "means no sympathy between the children of different mothers. When the father dies there's no peace; a lot of poisoning; everybody is quarrelling over the father's properties. Other houses [lineages or large families] in Calabar had the same trouble. I observe how people are selfish, they don't want to do good for their country or their family. Such things should be abolished from Calabar fashion."

During formal interviews on the topic of his courtship and marriage, Peter wanted to give me the impression that his wife's background was an enviable one, though perhaps not equal to his own. Her mother was Calabar Efik and a distant relative of Peter's. Her father came from Ghana, and had allegedly received police training at Scotland Yard; he was, according to Peter, the senior African police officer for Calabar and the British-administered portion of Cameroon. He was also supposed to have been a high-ranking official of the Royal Freemasons. Peter related that his father-in-law died in 1922 of poisoning while drinking with a Yoruba man. The accused murderer swore his innocence on native juju and then went crazy. (Poisoning and developing madness were common elements in Peter's stories; he said his eldest brother had gone mad after the father's wealth had been entirely gone through, although he did not suggest that his brother might have been poisoned.)

It was always difficult to determine the accuracy of Peter's statements. At first he told me that he and his wife were married in 1934, but he had previously mentioned tthat his eldest child had been born in 1921. He also said that when he had first met his wife, around 1920, they were both attending the same school and had been schoolmates for several years, which would imply that his wife was at least literate. However, on his Certificate of Marriage, dated 1939, his wife's signature appears as an "X". Later he explained that he and his wife had been lovers in 1920, and she had borne a son while he was away for his apprentice training. At this time, she lived with his family, who arranged for traditional native ceremonies sometime between 1920 and 1930. At one time he said he knew nothing about the details of this marriage, since he was away, while at another time he said the standard bridewealth of £12 12s. 4-1/2d. had been paid. At still another time he gave a different figure for the standard bridewealth. Perhaps it was because his wife was now so corpulent that Peter felt obliged to point out that she had not gone into the traditional southeastern Nigerian fattening room upon marriage. Peter, as well as her Western-educated father, opposed this custom. His wife had got fatter, he explained, each time she had another child. She had eight in all, four of whom had died at birth or in early infancy.

Although Peter thought it was unwise for parents to choose careers for their children, he expressed for each of his children preferences which reflected his own modern elite aims: "If any of them chooses to be a mechanic [like myself] I would object to it because the market for mechanics isn't as good as it was in my days. You'll not progress. The highest post you can get is supervisor. You can't go overseas to qualify as an engineer." Not long after we first became acquainted Peter talked of his aspirations for his daughter and his two sons, who were then attending school. He skillfully avoided mentioning a third son, his first-born, and instead concentrated on his other children. This eldest son had shown little aptitude for scholarship at school, and Peter had apprenticed him under himself when he worked for the U.A.C. This son was now employed as a mechanic with the Public Works Department in Kaduna.

The next eldest son, Ulysses, born in 1945, was attending Lagos Government School, and Peter hoped he would become an administrator. "If he spends eight to ten years in the United Kingdom, then he can come back to a good post." Peter hoped that

Caesar, who was a year younger than Ulysses, might eventually become a lawyer, but at the end of 1961 this boy was expelled from his school in Kaduna because of truancy. After Caesar's return to Jos, Peter complained that the lad had caused him all sorts of trouble and grief. He said he had invested heavily in the boy's education, but now Caesar did not want to return to school and was unsure what career to choose. Apparently, Peter had forgotten his own advice—"Occupation is difficult to choose for children. They may not obey or if they do they may not have keen interest. You can't force children."—for he had been badgering his son to return to school and to think seriously about his future: "I told him to decide on one thing. I told him that without sound education he can get no good job. He made us pay school fees for nothing. He giving us a very good headache." Several months later Caesar and another boy called on me and, using the device of a not-very-convincing story, attempted to borrow one pound. I did not mention this incident to Peter, who needed no prodding to express his disappointment in his son. He deplored the fact that Caesar was running about with "Ibo ruffians" and even warned me not to let him come into my house for fear he might steal something.

When Peter spoke of his daughter Cecilia, who was born in 1940, or when he looked at the pictures of her, his love for her was obvious. He was very proud of her scholastic achievements although she too had disappointed him. In September 1961 she had applied for admission to an American college and was also trying for a Nigerian Government Scholarship. Whether or not she received a full or part scholarship, Peter was certain that she would receive a college education, for he claimed he had sufficient funds to pay for it. With the qualification that a choice of career must be her own, Peter thought she might become a secretary, bookkeeper, or nurse; but most of all he hoped she would become a midwife: "Her money would come back quicker than sitting in office for three years before promotion and waiting ten years to become senior service. Midwife could work for a big hospital or be engaged privately." By early 1962, however, she was back home with her

parents in Jos with her illegitimate new-born infant. Because Peter
was then avoiding me, it was not until several months later that
he told me what happened.

Oh, she disappointed me. She had finished Kakuri College in Kaduna
and obtained her Cambridge Certificate. Even the Principal made arrangements for her to continue school in America. While she was going
to school and living in Kaduna, many people wrote me proposals to
marry her, but I refused them all because the girl was going to America
for further training.

She likes to spend her holidays with her older brother [Samuel, the
eldest son] in Kaduna and that's where she met this Tiv boy. He's
single, a student, and he gave her the baby. How it happened I don't
know. I asked my son [by letter] and he said he doesn't know how it
happened. All of a sudden she writes my wife that she isn't well, and
the next thing she is back in Jos with a belly and the baby was born
about a month later.[1]

Peter detailed his plans to meet the baby's father and determine
for himself if the youth was fit to marry his daughter or if he should
be taken to court for "spoiling" her. The young man had written
Peter that he intended to marry the mother of his child, and that he
hoped to meet Peter and the rest of the family on his projected
visit to Jos during his next school holiday. On several occasions
Peter had expressed the modern African elite ideal that his children
might marry persons of any tribe, provided the pair had com-
patible personalities and loved each other; he would object to any
marriage only if the family of the other party was of ill repute.
There was little likelihood, however, that Peter would receive a trustworthy report (or any report for that matter) about this boy's
family in Tivland, but at least he could judge the boy's character
when they met. If Peter approved of him, permission for their marriage would then have to be obtained from his church, since the

1. At still another time, Peter gave me a different version for part of this
episode. In November 1961 he received a letter from Caesar's school about
the boy's truancy and his imminent expulsion. Peter's wife then went to
Kaduna to investigate the matter and thus discovered Cecilia's pregnancy.
She then returned to Jos with Caesar and Cecilia.

groom was not a Catholic. The lad failed to appear at the time of his promised visit, and Peter continued to report the delays which kept him from coming to Jos. I left Jos before being able to witness their meeting, but prior to my departure Peter once again began harboring hopes that his daughter might still be able to complete her higher education—if she did not marry.

Samuel, Peter's eldest son, had gone against his father's wishes by taking a second wife. Around 1954 Samuel had married his first wife, an Ekoi girl from Calabar who bore him two sons, one of whom died during the time of my association with Peter. About two years after his first marriage, Samuel married a Nupe girl from Bida, after paying £10 to her former husband to legalize their divorce, and she also had a son by him. At his father's insistence, Samuel released the Nupe wife. Peter said that he had "forced" his son to give up the Nupe girl because the church could have ex-communicated him for bigamy, apparently forgetting, when he said this, about his own father's marital prowess. He had written his son "strong" letters and finally had to go to Kaduna to make certain his command was obeyed. Peter suggested to me that unlike himself, his son lacked deep commitments to his Catholic faith.

Although Peter used the dictates of the Catholic Church as the reason for his deep concern about his eldest son's polygyny, I believe he had an additional, if not stronger, motive. He had always held great expectations of being accepted into the ranks of the modern African elite although, as will be shown subsequently, he had been given many indications that he did not and undoubtedly would not measure up to such high status. Still, he never relinquished hope, and tried to control the important factors that would decide his fate in this regard. His children were one such factor and their achievements and behavior was an important determinant. Peter thought that the success of his children would enhance his own candidacy and, in keeping pace with the progress of Nigerian society, they would have to achieve occupations and social positions of greater prestige than his own. Otherwise they could rightly be regarded as remaining stationary while many of their peers were leaving them behind in the pursuit of upper stratum positions; i.e., they would be downwardly mobile in relation to the position held by their father a generation ago. As Peter identified with modern African elite attitudes, and as he rightly regarded the actions of his children as reflecting on himself, it was to his disadvantage, since it discredited him, that his son should attempt polygyny. To Peter this was "uncivilized" as well as un-Christian behavior. For similar reasons, Peter regarded the shame of having a bastard grandchild as a threat to his actual and potential social standing. It was also largely for this reason that he was ashamed of Caesar's delinquency.

Samuel's devotion to his father's values may have been as shallow as his commitment to Christianity. While there are Calabar voluntary associations in Kaduna, Samuel chose instead to join the Ghana Union, thus stressing his affiliation with his maternal grandfather's national group rather than the ethnic group of his father, which was a repudiation of traditional Efik patriliny. There were numerous other indications that Samuel and his father did not have the same orientations and the same drive for success and high social rank.

Following the death of Samuel's one child, his two other sons, five and four years old, remained with Peter and his wife in Jos. According to Peter, the older child had been with them "since he was three months in the belly of his mother. He don't know the father. He take him for a stranger." However, the younger brother had made several long visits to Kaduna, visits that Samuel had urged, and knew his father quite well. Peter said he would be responsible for their upbringing because Samuel and his wife did not know how to raise children properly. He felt they lacked understanding, common sense, and a necessary motivation and devotion. "Young men today are not like yesterday. They like highlife; they like to go to club, to dance. My son doesn't know what is happening in his house. He has also to go on tour so he is away from his house. He has no sense yet to keep the children." Concerning Samuel's support of the children: "We feel we don't like to burden them. He doesn't send money for the children's food or clothing. We take care of all that. When the children will go to school, we will pay the fees. But any time he wants to give something I will take it."

Peter added that it was customary for Efik grandparents to raise their grandchildren, and that he would have been raised that way if his grandparents had been alive when he was a child.

From a survey of the photographs in Peter's possession, I discovered that his social life had been much richer in the past. When he brought out his pictures of friends, kinsmen, and fellow tribesmen, he said he once had many more than the fifty-odd photos laid before me, but his children liked to play with them and had destroyed many. I was shown his collection at the very beginning of our acquaintance, and the large number of pictures in itself suggested that Peter aspired to modern elite status. This impression was strengthened by the social affiliations these pictures represented, and by Peter's readiness to point out the social prominence of the persons shown.

Several large photographs, commemorating his daughter's communion in the Catholic Church, were group pictures of invited guests. Many of these were members of the modern African elite in Jos, many were not members of the Catholic Church, and with only a few did Peter claim a remote kinship relationship. The ethnic groups in these and his other pictures included many southern Nigerian tribes, but with a salient absence of Yoruba. There were many people from Ghana (then Gold Coast), with some of whom Peter claimed a remote affinal kinship, but there were few from Sierra Leone. Most of the persons were Efik and Ijaw, with the next largest representation being Ibo and Ibibio. In showing the pictures, Peter provided social identifications for each person. If he could not stress someone's elite occupation, he emphasized other attributes: "This is Madam Okwe John, one of the prominent women in this country [Jos]. She is the women's leader in the Catholic Church and the leader of the Ibo market women"; or "This is Bassey Umoh, the 'Chief' of the Ibibios in Plateau Province."

One group of pictures, of which Peter was extremely proud, showed Ibibio and Efik costumed players. He explained that in 1952 the Calabar people in Jos had pooled their talents and resources, investing hundreds of pounds to buy traditional costumes and masks.

To supplement their own numbers, they brought musicians and players to Jos from Calabar. The public performances of these traditional masquerade-plays had been so splendid that they were written up in newspapers and magazines, and, Peter added, the Europeans in Jos were so taken with the spectacle that the Resident requested repeat performances at the local cinema and on the museum grounds. This may well have been Peter's most glorious hour, for he was at that time president of the group that undertook the enormous task, and afterward the group was disbanded. (I later discovered that the play was a social failure for Peter, since it had bankrupted the Calabar organization.)

In showing me these pictures and in mentioning his former connections with ethnic and modern African elite voluntary associations, Peter could not avoid being confronted with the contrast between his former active social life and his present relative isolation. He had a variety of rationalizations for his having given up the clubs, and one of the most elaborate involved his domestic life.

I used to frequent clubs and to stay until midnight, and when I came home the trouble started [with my wife.] I used to drink too much. That's what used to bring palaver [quarrels] between us. She has a quick temper. If she hears anything about me, she starts accusing me before finding out what she heard is true. For instance, I might be working on a breakdown sometimes, and I work straight through the day and into the night late. She don't know where I am, and she asks somebody if he see me at the club, and he, without thinking, says I'm there. Then she accuse me of going to the club and not telling her where I am when I was all the time working.

Our wives are very jealous. Supposing I go to the club and dance with women, buying them beer, and chatting with them. That sort of thing bring palaver. The wife don't know if they my friends or concubines. But if she doesn't know about it, there is no palaver.

In the world there are a lot of hypocrites and gossipers who will come and tell my wife all about it. Being women have no second thought, this might cause trouble. A man must be very careful what to answer her when this happens so as not to cause palaver in the house.

Peter slyly, and with apparent delight, indicated that he was an astute diplomat when it came to producing alibis. However, he had learned from bitter experience that there always existed untrustworthy persons who would bear witness against him by telling tales to his wife, and who would publicize aspects of his private life that proved to be embarrassing. He thus came to distrust intimacy and former intimate friends, and explained that it was for these reasons that he withdrew from former close associations. He described how sorely disappointed he had been with one close friend who had "ruined" him: "In Jos we saw each other every day and night. We met at each other's house. We ate here and we ate at his place. We used to go to the club together, and we would be together until late each night. He never went to dance without me, and likewise myself. But when my wife and I had palaver he would be present, and he would broadcast this to others. When I learned this I began to withdraw myself little by little."

During the 1930's and 1940's Peter had participated actively in the Jos modern elite African social club, but he now considered that it had not been worth the investment of money and emotional commitment he had put into it. Perhaps he had concluded that his efforts to ingratiate himself with others who would accept him as a co-equal were simply beyond his financial ability. A hint of such a feeling appears in his complaint that other members lacked hospitable reciprocity:

It's been a long time, many years, since I used to go to the African Club. When I used to go to the club, I used to have to buy beer for the people. That's expensive. People may not like to buy beer for you, but want you to buy beer for them. I'm trying to keep away from extra expenses. When I had money, I used to go to the club in the afternoons just after quitting work. Then I would go home to chop [eat] and go back to the club in the evening to play tennis or billiards until late at night. But now, sometimes I read a book, or go to the barber shop, or just take a stroll, just for the pleasure of walking around the town.

All the time he had been striving for prestige, he had been dividing his energies between the African modern elite community in Jos and his own Calabar ethnic community. In the case of the former, the truth is that Peter could never completely measure up to membership standards. His wealth was hardly sufficient to make up for his lack of Western higher education. His English speech was better than pidgin English, but crude in comparison with that spoken by many Africans. He was still an artisan, not an engineer. Other Nigerians, with the same shortcomings as Peter, had been able to achieve modern elite status, but in each case they had saving graces that Peter lacked: athletic skills, top ethnic leadership, leadership in local or national politics, etc. Also, since he had allowed his membership in the African Club to lapse, it would have been unseemly for him to attempt to return to this form of social activity, even if he had had the financial means to do so and the members had been willing to re-accept him.

Since he was a direct patrilineal descendant of King Eyamba of Calabar his chances for success as a leader in Efik-speaking Calabar tribal unions were strong; and as a consequence of his unrewarding experiences among the modern elite he concentrated his efforts on his own ethnic community. Peter and his wife became presidents of the men's and women's wings of the Efik Tribal Union. He said it had been founded in Jos around 1933 (a date that appears to be a bit too early), and that it ceased functioning in 1954 as a result of Peter's removal to Zaria and his later taking work in Kano. Peter's wife, who was sometimes within earshot of our conversations, and who occasionally offered information or her opinion, also declared that the Union could not function without their leadership. The functions of the Union, as described by Peter, were typical of contemporary West African ethnic voluntary associations. Its aims were to foster peace, love, and unity among Efik immigrants in Jos. It assisted its members in times of trouble and illness, and helped them find jobs. The society also tried to settle disputes between spouses, between members, and between members and outsiders, and performed burial services for its dead. Peter indicated he had played an important part in maintaining group solidarity. "At the end of the month we sacrifice a few pounds from the treasury to buy drinks and slaughter some goats, just to maintain interest. Sometimes I would shoulder the financial burden of this myself because I wanted people to come to enjoy and to remain friendly."

Despite his leadership, the Efik Tribal Union failed, and perhaps because of the unfortunate circumstances of its dissolution (the native play), Peter made no effort to revive it, although he claimed otherwise. In any event, revival would have challenged his status as a leader. For the same reason, he was unwilling to exercise his eligibility to join any of the other Calabar unions active in Jos. Such membership would have afforded him the opportunity to revive old friendships or make new ones, but he might also have been demeaned by having to accept a subordinate position.

The elaborate play given in 1952 began as a means of strengthening the Efik Tribal Union but instead led to its downfall. The performance was actually sponsored and organized by the Calabar Native Players' Organization (formerly called the Calabar Friendly Society), an organization that included in addition to Efik, members of other ethnic groups local to Calabar. Peter said he and his wife were presidents of this group also, and that its membership greatly overlapped with that of the Efik Tribal Union.

We had special players [semi-professionals] come up to Jos from home. They know how to make proper juju. This is native science. [He described one of the magical feats: a huge cloth lying flat on the ground suddenly rising to a height of two stories without any apparent explanation.] We in Jos had to subscribe money. We had masks carved in Ikot Ekpene [an Ibibio area]. We had to buy cloth, pay for the strangers' transport to Jos, put them up, and feed them. I gave twenty guineas. Others gave as much as they could.

We thought we might make some money from the play, but we lost money. Europeans and Africans came to see it. They bought tickets and made donations to the players, but we couldn't cover expenses. Many people who donated money originally couldn't afford to do so, and we wanted to give them back as much as possible.

We held general meetings and went over the amount of money taken in, but the treasurer refused to give back the proceeds. He said he wanted to prepare another play. We took him to court, and Agbakoba [a notably successful Ibo barrister in Jos] was our lawyer. [In doing so the members had broken one of the cardinal rules of ethnic voluntary associations: never take a fellow tribesman, and particularly a fellow union member, to court!] We won the case and he gave back the money.

People who gave one pound got back ten to fifteen shillings. That's how we split. People lost interest in such things, and they also were afraid of losing money again.

It was unfortunate for Peter's ambitions that his leadership had come to be associated with these events. From Peter's point of view, the performances had been eminently successful, for they had brought him to the attention and praise of the Resident of Plateau Province and other highly regarded Europeans in Jos. But from the members' viewpoint it was a financial failure, particularly for people who could ill afford such luxuries, and, even worse, it carried the seeds of the eventual disruption of their union.

If, as a result of these circumstances, the members' appreciation of Peter soured, he, in turn, may well have strengthened his developing ambivalent attitudes toward his fellow Africans and native traditions. Sometimes he expressed intense aggression and hostility, balancing his deprecation of Africans by idolatry of Europeans.

The Europeans came out here with one mind—to take us out of darkness and make us civilized. Europeans are well-cultured, well-educated. A European takes everybody the way he takes himself. He has the fear of God in his mind. He civilized, we primitive people. He took us from darkness and put us to light. He teach us Christian way of life. He teach us to destroy our idols and our medicine. He makes us to stop human sacrifices when some big man dies. I think it's a very good thing that Europeans came among us. Some people say they do us no good, but they hotheads.

When the Europeans come and see all the bad things we did, he could have left us alone. He come 4,000 miles, and he say he don't care about us and go back home, leave us stay in our primitive way. But no, he was self-sacrificing. A European doesn't hold grudges. If he wants to teach you something, he teaches you right away.

When it was suggested that Europeans, being only human, might have some bad traits, Peter answered: "Maybe in their own country they show bad things, but all the Europeans I met since my childhood I never find one mistake in any European." Toward his fellow countrymen, however, he could be highly critical. When I asked him to give his impressions of the ethnic characteristics of African groups represented in Jos, he expressed the greatest antipathy to those that constitute the core of the Westernized elite—Ibo, Ibibio, Yoruba, Ghana, and Sierra Leone—and tolerance toward groups whose members are singularly absent in the modern African elite— Hausa, Tiv, and Plateau tribes—suggesting that his attitude toward the more Western-acculturated groups was based on his own lack of success in achieving modern elite status. But within his ambivalence, he still sought contact and associated with persons of the former category.

When, toward the end of our acquaintance, he admitted that his troubles were piling up, I asked if he had a friend he might seek out for advice. He gave the names of the most prominent persons among the modern African elite in Jos, and said he would take the same problems to each one, compare advice, make his own plan, and then return to each for reappraisal. These prominent members of the Jos community were not his close friends; at one point he said so himself. In soliciting their advice he was not enhancing his own prestige so much as he was validating their positions as leaders in the community, for it was their social obligation to be available to anyone who requested their advice. When he later asked me for a small loan, I asked him why he did not approach these same persons. Peter said he would never go to an African for a loan: "I try not to disclose my secrets outside. I don't like going for financial help. It's a disgraceful thing. I might go to somebody like you, as a European. I fit to [can] disclose all my secrets to you. We Africans are still Africans. When you borrow from an African, he'll tell others. For the sake of that I try not to borrow money, but I freely help people—Ibos, Calabars—but I don't tell their secrets."

If, by not disclosing another person's secrets, Peter was identifying with Europeans or merely being virtuous (or perhaps both), he certainly did identify with Europeans in other ways. Although he had little contact with Europeans, he enjoyed the prestige of his few encounters with them, and he relished the details of these meetings. "When I worked for U.A.C. I sometimes had European guests," he said. "All our engineers and branch managers paid us visits. For them we could prepare 'small chop' and drinks, whiskey and soda, and some beers, but no stout. The chop would be tomato, cheese and sardine sandwiches, with fried groundnuts on the side."

Consistent with his admiration of the European, imperfectly as he understood the model, he pictured himself as a good Catholic, for he attended services regularly, donated a shilling or two when the plate was passed round, and even considered that he and his wife could have absolute trust in one another because they went to confession: if either had sinned severely, the wrongdoing would have to be revealed at confession and the fact that a misdemeanor had occurred would become known to the other when sacraments were withheld. He had also told me, shortly after we first became acquainted, that he had pledged £100 toward a church building fund, but that the gesture was contingent upon his receiving money owed him by the Syrian in Kano for work he had done the previous year. He was accustomed, he said, to giving big donations during church fund drives.

Many times he declared his wish to become a member of the Royal Freemasons, despite his religious affiliations. His expressed hope that this might someday come true did not diminish even after I knew his financial situation. "In such a society everyone helping you—even Europeans help you. If I should be a Freemason, I wouldn't have all this trouble now. As my life now fluctuating, I can go to any European or African member for money advance [a loan] or job. I can get help, and it would make my life easy. [What's more] you associate with big people, Europeans and Africans. When I go home, I'll show them my father's membership certificate to see if they will allow me to join without having to pay any heavy amount." Whether Peter really saw Masonic membership as a panacea for his various troubles is uncertain; regardless, it was an unrealistic view that membership (if he ever could achieve it) would provide him with the economic benefits he imagined it could.

It was in the context of his avowed full commitment to Christianity that he deprecated his native traditions and customs, especially those involving human sacrifice, polygyny, and the intra-familial conflicts over inheritance that occurred in polygynous households. On the other hand, he retained a belief in the efficacy of native magic, referring to it as "African science" or "native science."

He spoke so lovingly of the magical wonders and the magnificent spectacles to be seen in the traditional "plays" given in his home town at the end of each year that I decided to include Calabar in a tour of the Eastern Region that I planned to make late in 1961. When I told him of my intention, Peter was so pleased that he invited me to be his guest at his family home in Calabar. He offered to be my guide, saying that we would go together about the town and even into the bush to see the best plays, take pictures, and record music. He was sure his relatives would be delighted to extend me hospitality. To bring home a European as his guest would have been quite prestigious for Peter, and his anticipation of this glory had led him to invite me without considering the consequences. He said he would write to his family to expect us. I recalled his employment obligations in Kano during the time of the projected trip, but he said he would have no trouble leaving his work for a week or two. At subsequent meetings we laid plans for going down to his home town together in my car.

During October, a little over a month after he had first extended the invitation, Peter became increasingly less available to me as an informant. When I tried calling on him he was invariably "out." When I did find him at home, he often tried excusing himself from talking to me because he was "ill" or "busy." Later he said that during part of this time he had been to Kano making arrangements to resume his work. At one point he said he was uncertain whether he could make the visit now because he had not been home since 1954[2] and, because of his seven-year absence, he would be expected to give money and presents to his relatives and friends, and

2. He made this trip when he was given three months' leave from the U.A.C. When he mentioned this, I did not point out to him that he had previously said he had retired from the U.A.C. in that year, and that it seemed unlikely he should be given a leave under such circumstances.

he was not sure he could afford this extra expense at the time. About a week before my departure for the Eastern Region, even when it was clear that he would no longer work for the Syrian, he admitted that he could not take me to his home and that he was not even sure of a welcome there for himself.

Early in our acquaintance Peter had presented an idyllic picture of life in Calabar: one paid no house rent; food was plentiful; the family helped with the upbringing of children and helped pay their school fees, and so on. When I asked him why, since he had retired from full employment, he remained away from this heaven-on-earth, he said that the house he was building at home was not completed, that he was not yet ready for total occupational retirement, that he still needed money to see his children through college, and that he generally was not yet ready to plan specifically about his retirement. But toward the end of our association he admitted the drawbacks of living at home. One of the unhappy features was living close to relatives, who periodically call on you for money for themselves, or for money and food to stage various family ceremonies. Friends and relatives ask for outright gifts or loans which amount to gifts: "If you don't give them, you have trouble and, if you give a loan, you never get it back. People at home are always writing me asking for money—twenty pounds, thirty pounds—and I send them one or two pounds to keep them quiet." In addition, Peter said that people at home would expect a returning immigrant to put up a very big house for himself and to have a small business: "It's a shameful thing to go home before the building is finished. They'll say 'What kind of man is he who lives in his father's house and hasn't built his own house?' This is a first-class abuse in our fashion." For all these reasons, he said, he would remain in Jos and try to earn enough money to return home in style.

When I returned from my tour I again met with Peter and told him I had enjoyed my visit to Calabar. I had not met any of his relatives. He once again began telling me of his financial difficulties, and I asked why he did not tap his bank reserve of profits derived from his share of the family plantation in Calabar. Why did he not write to the brother who was looking after his interests? He responded that a brother, even of the same mother, would cheat one, and explained that since 1957 his brother had not sent him a penny. He had written to him about the matter, and his brother had answered that because of trouble with the laborers, and poor growing seasons, no profits had been made. Peter did not believe this account but claimed he could not leave his work to investigate the situation personally. (Subsequent remarks indicated that he was afraid to do so.) When his wife went home on a visit she had confronted Peter's brother who told her the same story; but Peter felt that his wife did not get a straight answer, for the foreman told her things had been going well. Peter said that in the past the profits he had received went toward his children's education, and that this money—had he been able to lay hands on it—might have been used to send Cecelia to an American university.

I pressed Peter further on this question and suggested that surely his mother or his other brothers would see to it that he was not denied what was justly his. Peter's answer was evasive, and he indicated that he preferred not to discuss the matter: "My mother can't read, so it's no use writing to her. My other brothers must know about this, and if they haven't done something by now, I can't expect help from them. There is only one thing I can do, and that is to go home and see my brother. If he can't give me a proper account, then I call all the chiefs of the district and the elders of the family [lineage]. Then they decide what to do. I can't take my brother to court. That's forbidden, and our chiefs won't allow that."

Much of what Peter had said up to this point in the interviews seemed to indicate that his behavior was directed toward acceptance by his family in Calabar. His goals, as outlined previously, tended to be those of the modern African elite, which would lead eventually to his returning home to his natal town with enough money to retire with prestige. If I had arrived at this conclusion, however, I was forced to qualify it after Peter made an almost vehement attack on his home people and the sort of reception he could expect from them if he tried to return permanently. It was just before my departure from Nigeria that I reminded Peter that he had lived in Jos longer than he had lived in Calabar, and on this basis might consider Jos his home. He answered that Jos was not his home:

I stay here because I fear poison at home. I haven't sufficient money to satisfy the people if I went home now. If I go home the way I am now, they'll be expecting me to be rich and give them plenty. Some of them might have an evil mind if I don't give them enough. When they come to greet me and I don't satisfy them, they'll try by all means to take my life. That's the only reason I keep here so long. When I go home, these people will come around day after day, and for days I have to entertain them with plenty of drinks and food. They think that when somebody goes to bush—they call this place "bush"—he gets rich, so they want to eat [share in] bush money.[3]

In effect, Peter was saying that he was a man without a home. Wiping his brow, he went on to tell how his own sister had been poisoned after she had quarrelled with another woman in the market. Making no distinction between chemical and magical poisonings, he described what a person marked for poisoning must watch out for:

They could put something in your food or drink. They could put it in their hands when they going to shake hands with you. They could put it in a handkerchief, and when they pass you on the street they could make like they wipe their brow, but the medicine is in the handkerchief, and it has your name on it so it goes straight to you. They can watch you where you pass urine and then pick up your urine. They can bribe a service girl at a bar where they'll take you to drink. They wouldn't hesitate to give her fifty pounds to wipe the inside of your glass with leopard's whiskers. That's very poisonous.[4]

There was no question in my mind that Peter was quite frightened at the prospect of returning home, although I found it difficult to accept all his reasons for so fearing his relatives and home townsmen, particularly since I was aware of how fond he was of tales

3. A discussion of the implications of such family tensions on the development of Nigerian urban populations appears in Plotnicov (1965).
4. An interesting parallel from Stanleyville is provided by V. G. Pons (1956:669).

involving poisonings. Unfortunately no time remained for me to probe more deeply into his relations with his kinsmen at home, which, I am sure, would have provided a fuller explanation.

At one time or another Peter had pointed to almost every social relationship and declared it untrustworthy. As for relatives: brother could swindle brother while other kinsmen (e.g., other brothers and a mother) stood by impotent or in collusion; children could neither be trusted to raise their own children properly, nor depended on not to blemish the good reputation of their parents; a daughter's suitor hardly demonstrated reliability, and was not a person in whom one could place confidence; and even a wife, perhaps because of the inherent limitations of her sex, could not always be depended on to be understanding. And as for non-kinsmen: one's fellow tribesmen were uncertain supporters of their voluntary associations, and a tribal union officer might repudiate the mandate given him; one could not expect equal reciprocity at social clubs, which were supposed to be composed of peers; and for self-protection, a man could not place blind confidence in acquaintances or even close friends. In short, people were either deliberately and maliciously untrustworthy or, because of shortcomings within themselves, undependable. Who could be trusted? Apparently, and for the most part, only those with whom Peter had little acquaintance and of whom he had little intimate knowledge—e.g., Freemasons and Europeans. Peter explicitly stated this but, of course, he clearly did not trust me to the degree he claimed, and one is led to wonder whether he was aware that those he claimed could be trusted were the very persons with whom he could be least expected to interact.

I do not know whether Peter viewed Levantines as Europeans or as a category apart, but his relations with his Syrian employer also concluded on a note of enmity and distrust. As a result of this experience, he had to admit to me that, in contrast to his initial presentation of affluence, he was in poor financial circumstances. Peter's narrative of this episode is filled with discrepancies and is hardly believable in places, but it is here presented as he related it to me, and I can do no more than point out some areas of ambiguity and offer alternative explanations.

As will be remembered, for several years Peter had had a contract with a Syrian groundnut buyer, who lived in Kano, to maintain his fleet of more than twenty lorries. In loose partnership in the same business with this middleman were several of his relatives who had fewer trucks, but who all together shared common garage and maintenance facilities. A few of these vehicles were in use throughout the year, but most were employed only during the dry season and stored the rest of the time. It was Peter's responsibility to make roadworthy those trucks that had been in storage, repair and maintain all the vehicles that were in use during the major period of buying and transporting groundnuts, and return to storage at the end of this period all those that were not to be used again until the following year. Each year the conditions of employment, remuneration, and other arrangements were contracted afresh, under the supervision of Peter's and the Syrian's lawyers, but much of Peter's earnings were in the form of "dashes" [gratuities] and bonuses, and thus kept off the books. When Peter went to Kano to draw up a new contract before the beginning of the groundnut buying season of 1961–1962, the Syrian (according to Peter's account) was willing to continue the arrangement and promised to send £500, to be delivered to Peter personally by a Hausaman, so that he could stock repair parts in Jos and provide advances to the crew, which he was to recruit. (The details Peter provided of his contractual arrangements from year to year were so replete with discrepancies that I considered it of dubious value to record them here. I should point out, however, that prior to his departure for Kano to renew his contract, Peter told me that whereas he had accepted expense advances from his employer in past years, he would not do so this time because it meant spending the money too quickly and not knowing how much he had really made at the end of the season. Instead, he intended to cover these expenses with his own funds. He did not tell me why he reverted to the old arrangement—although I learned by then that he did not have the resources to cover his initial expenses—nor could he explain, when I asked him, why the advance of £500 should have been conveyed to him by an informal courier. The Syrian could have given Peter a check for this amount when they met in Kano, or he could have sent a check for this amount by registered mail, or he could have made special arrangements for a draft at one of the Jos banks. If Peter was telling me the truth, then it would appear that the Syrian no longer wanted Peter's services and had found a ruse with which to put him off.) The Hausa who was to deliver the money to Peter failed to do so, and when Peter learned that this man had been seen at several of the mining camps on the Plateau he tried tracing him down. During this time Peter made himself unavailable to me and when next I saw him he recounted how he had spent many days unsuccessfully pursuing his quarry. He now said that the amount sent was to be £250. As the season of work was rapidly approaching, Peter was under pressure to obtain some money to hire his crew, and so he wired the Syrian of what had transpired and asked for another advance. When several more days went by and no word came from Kano, Peter expressed his concern that on the one hand he might be accused of receiving the money and pretending otherwise, and on the other that time was rapidly slipping by and it might soon be too late to find employment with another groundnut buyer if he could not return to work for his former employer. He thought he could make last-minute arrangements with a wealthy Hausa middleman at Wase, who had seven lorries. (My fieldnotes record that at this time Peter appeared tired and had lost some weight.) Peter was finally able to corner and confront the Hausaman who, before Peter's "witnesses," claimed the Syrian had never given him the money. At first Peter thought the man had gambled away the money, but later considered that perhaps the Syrian had tricked him. He later said his lawyer had begun proceedings to sue the Syrian for breach of contract and the money owed him for previous work.

By early 1962 Peter had long given up hope of finding employment with a groundnut buyer—he had not been employed by the Hausa middleman at Wase—and he was now seeking any employment. At this time he sought me out to ask me for a loan of £5 so that he and his family might at least have something to eat. When Peter returned the £5 he had borrowed, he apologized for not seeing me during the long interval and explained that he had found a job with a recently-opened tin smelter near Jos. The hours were irregular and the work was fatiguing; he was so tired after each day's work that he slept most of the time. He said he had sought employment as a mechanic, but the only decently-paying position available was that of a tender at the furnace. He was learning the necessary skills and was approaching the end of his probationary period. Peter said he was becoming accustomed to the heat of the furnace and the strenuous physical work, which his economic conditions forced him to accept, and he hoped his employers would make his job permanent. He had lost still more weight and looked visibly older.

Peter relaxed at a later interview—something he rarely did—and permitted himself the luxury of expressing grief over his troubles: the difficulties of his present employment, the treachery of the Syrian, and his disappointment in his children. He pictured himself as analogous to the Biblical Job: God had tested them, and neither would fail in his faith. He ended his speech with repeated expressions of courage triumphing over despair: "Everything comes from God. If He chooses to try me in this way, then I'm satisfied. I'm a man who always gives thanks to God, and I thank God for what he had given me in this job. [He had recently been given a position as furnace foreman, with an annual salary of £450.] If somebody do better than me, I don't envy him. That's the way God tests us. If I'm walking down the street with somebody and somebody comes along and dash my friend £50 and don't give me a penny, then I say it's the work of God, and if God choose to give me something He will do it. I must be satisfied."

It was important for Peter to pretend, to himself as well as to others, that he intended to retire to his home town; it gave him a means of dissociating himself from urban life, with all its uncertainties and tensions, and from the unfulfilled glittering promises which urban living was said to hold. Thus he could sometimes idealize the life in his home town. If he could he wanted to return home and live out the remainder of his life there as an important man, but he was uncertain of his reception. In Jos, his façade of wealth and importance had cracked and crumbled; the local ethnic and modern social institutions that provide many immigrants with a sense of belonging and social security were lost to him, and his social network had shrunk to a point that dangerously approached a border of isolation. He was a lonely man.

Chapter VIII

FOUR ADDITIONAL PORTRAITS

THE present chapter consists of biographical sketches of four other informants. No attempt is made to analyze each of these cases in detail, since the previous four chapters and the chapter following this one give descriptions and analyses of Nigerians who have cast their lives in an urban area. This chapter seeks to impress the reader with two facets of Nigerian urbanization that, while already mentioned, need to be stressed for their importance. The first is the wide variety of cultural and social elements that constitute the heterogeneous modern urban scene. Secondly, for those readers who have some knowledge of African cultures and peoples, the sketches in this chapter caution against the tendency to simplify a complex situation through the attractiveness of embracing stereotypes—views of persons as being typical representatives of their ethnic group or class. For example, there is a tendency to think of all Ibo who have taken up residence in alien areas as educated, fairly well to do, and aggressive in personality. The Ibo informant, described here, belies this straitjacketed view. Deviations from their ethnic norm, in one dimension or another and to a greater or lesser extent, are also demonstrated by the other three informants. I can assure the reader that I did not deliberately seek out atypical examples; the examples provided in this study reflect the wide range of variation present in Jos.

Musa Ibrahim Dan Zaria: Hausa

Musa was my only informant clearly employed as such. At first he had assisted me in translating Hausa records, for which he was paid by the hour, but when I discovered that I would not be able to continue interviewing another man chosen as a Hausa informant, I invited Musa to take the man's place even as he continued to receive his translator's salary. The arrangement pleased him, since although he was far from impoverishment, he frequently protested a need for money, and eagerly sought opportunities to supplement the small pension he received as a retired civil servant.

Musa was a proud man. He was exceptional among his generation of northerners in having received considerable formal Western education, and he expected others to be aware of his gift and to respect him for it. He carried himself with an erect dignity, and although his dress and general appearance conformed with Hausa tradition, his flawless English indicated that he was a man with no ordinary tribal background. In addition to his perfect command of English and Hausa, Musa claimed to understand and speak a little Birom, Jarawa, Fulani, Yoruba, and Arabic.

If Musa's Western education made him an atypical Hausa man of his age, his religious background made him even less typical: although when I knew him he was a practicing Muslim, he had been converted to Christianity as a young man, and had been an active devotee of that religion for some years. The reasons for his conversion and reversion became clear to me as I learned the story of his life.

Musa was born around 1902 in the small village of Turawa, about twenty miles east of Zaria. Soon after his birth, his family moved to the village of Taka Lafiya, about ten miles southeast of Turawa, where Musa was raised according to traditional custom. Musa's parents were Muslims who made their living by farming, and Musa's early education consisted of his learning how to farm and how to read the Koran. When Musa was ten or eleven, the man who was eventually to become his father-in-law came to Taka Lafiya, where his mother lived. This man, one of the first to have

contact with European missionaries, urged the people of Taka Lafiya to set up a Christian community in the town of Gimi. Musa's
parents were among those who were converted to Christianity and
followed him.

The move to Gimi was hardly providential for Musa's family.
When Musa was about thirteen, his mother died; six months later
his father also died, to be followed in death within the year by his
second wife, another Christian convert. The epidemic—Gimi was
at that time heavily infested with tsetse flies, and Musa attributed
the deaths of his kinsmen to trypanosomiasis (sleeping sickness)—
also claimed two brothers and a sister of his own mother and his
half-brother, the son of his father's second wife. Of Musa's siblings
who survived to adulthood—a half-sister and three full brothers
—they were both Christian and Muslim, some having returned to
Islam from Christianity. Some had made mixed religious and/or
ethnic marriages, but since Musa had maintained almost no contact with them, he did not know how his nieces and nephews
had been raised. The children were scattered, living in various
parts of northern Nigeria.

At the time of his mother's death, Musa, whose interest in Christianity had been whetted somewhat by the assemblies called by
native evangelists in Gimi, became a student at St. Bartholomew's
School of the Zaria Hausa Christian Mission, the only Christian
mission then permitted to operate in the Muslim Hausa area (see
A. Kirk-Greene, 1962). He remained there from 1915 until about
1918 or 1919. When he had completed his course work, he was
asked to stay on as a teacher, which he did. The missionaries liked
him, and encouraged him to study on his own after he had completed class work. One man taught him some Greek, and one lady
in particular, Miss A. M. Locke, devoted much time in tutoring
him for overseas examinations. The mission even paid his way to
take these examinations in Lagos, which was the only place in Nigeria where they were then held.

From a senior teacher he rose in 1924 to the position of Headmaster of the school. But three years later he was asked to leave
to become a clerk under a Welshman who was with the British

Cotton Growers' Association at Dutsen Wai, a railway stop on the Bauchi Light Railway, about forty miles east of Zaria. Musa felt Miss Locke, in collusion with the other missionaries, forced him to leave his school and the teaching he had come to love.

When she came out she brought about eight missionaries and teachers, who styled themselves the "Cambridge Group." When she came she met me there as the Headmaster. They advised Dr. Miller, who was then Superintendent of the Hausa Mission, that the school should be run under Miss Locke, because she was a teacher trained in England. Dr. Miller agreed to the compromise that she and I should work hand-in-hand because, as he put it, she was qualified and experienced as far as England is concerned, but I, as an indigenous man, was qualified as one with insight into the people, and was known by both the parents and the children. Of course, the decision was not favorable to the Cambridge Group, but they had to abide by it. However, they started to try getting rid of me.

One day he was called before the entire group of missionaries. He said he did not know why, and was frightened when at first no one said anything. Then Dr. Miller asked the Reverend Guy Bullen to speak for the group, but this responsibility was passed back and forth several times until Dr. Miller said:

As you know, the government has prevented us from going out of Zaria to preach the Gospel, but as we can see God moves in mysterious ways. He is opening a way for us. [He then asked Musa to work for the Welshman, whose clerks were embezzling from him.] You should not think that we are sending you there as an evangelist, and to depend on the Mission for your subsistence. You would work for the B.C.G.A. and receive your salary from them. But we say, "Ask yourself whether you really want to go."

Musa took the new position, and was pleased with his new employer, whom he described as a kindly man, considerate of the needs and sentiments of others. Indeed, this compassion eventually resulted in the European's dismissal. According to Musa, he had tried to cover up for a northern Nigerian employee who was being cheated by a clerk from the Gold Coast. This same clerk informed on the Welshman's attempt to "rebalance" the books. These events occurred in mid-1928 after Musa had been with his employer for a year, during which time they had developed a close and completely honest relationship. Musa could have remained with the B.C.G.A., but his relations with those of his fellow employees who had been antagonistic toward the dismissed European became strained, and so he considered taking another post. By coincidence, he received at this time two good job offers from his former employers at the Zaria Mission. But he was most pleased when he received a third offer from his Welsh employer, who had found employment with the Amalgamated Tin Mines of Nigeria in Bukuru. By this time Musa had been married several years, and his wife and two eldest daughters accompanied him to Bukuru.

At his new job he was regarded as a bit of an oddity, for he looked and dressed as a Hausa man, and Hausa were at that time limited to unskilled work and usually spoke only Hausa. It frequently happened that a European visitor to Musa's office would address him in Hausa, only to be taken aback by his response in perfect English. Unhappily, Musa's superior was one of the first Europeans to be dismissed when the economic depression of 1929 reached the minesfield. Musa, however, stayed on with A.T.M.N. until 1931, since some of the mining company officers were pleased with the idea of having an educated Hausa assistant.

Around 1930 the Zaria Mission again offered Musa a position. He turned it down, but in 1931 he accepted an offer from Dr. Miller to join him at a new mission station in Kano, and to become Headmaster of the school there. Musa could have remained with A.T. M.N., but he disliked his last European supervisor and, I suspect, he retained strong affections for Dr. Miller, who had been at odds with the "Cambridge Group" in Zaria. According to Musa, he had been removed to Kano through their machinations. The return to teaching was a delightful anticipation for him; however, he was disappointed in his hopes by the tribal discrimination displayed by the Yoruba manager of the school, who constantly favored the Yoruba faculty over the other members. Late in 1931 Musa and the other northerners on the staff resigned.

He quickly acquired a clerical position with the United Africa Company, but he was not happy with the work, and by this time he was convinced of his true calling—pedagogy. He said he was grateful when, toward the middle of 1932, he was taken on as a teacher at Toro Teachers Training College, which is located midway between Jos and Bauchi. When he left Toro, at the end of 1946 to become Plateau Provincial Visiting Teacher, he had risen to the position of Headmaster of the College. He later looked back on this period of fourteen years as one of the most satisfying in his life.

In 1952 Musa was sent to England for a three-month course in local government. On his return to Jos, where he had made his residence after leaving Toro, he was promoted to Supervising Teacher. This position involved him in the same work he had been doing as Visiting Teacher—helping to improve the quality of teaching in the schools—but gave him added powers and responsibilities. The last position he held was that of Plateau Provincial Adult Education (or Enlightenment) officer. He received this position in 1954, and at the beginning of the following year he was on the Queen's List, having been awarded the Certificate of Member of the British Empire. He was retired in mid-1957 at the age of fifty-five. During all this time, and later, Musa took correspondence courses in various subjects for no other purpose than the broadening of his intellectual horizons. For example, when the University College at Ibadan developed its program of Extra Mural Studies in Jos, he took several courses in economics.

During his retirement, Musa has tried to supplement his modest pension by assuming various temporary positions. For the regional and federal elections he instructed the election officers in their duties. He privately tutored Europeans in Hausa, and also conducted government examinations in Hausa proficiency. When I knew him, Musa wanted to return to a fully active employment. He said he needed the money, but more than that, he was in excellent health, vigorous, and deplored the periods when he was idle. He looked forward to an appointment as Warden (equivalent to a Dean of Men) at the Bukuru Trade Centre, and, considering his past record, firmly believed he would get this position quickly. But the job did not come easily, and when I left Jos, Musa was still waiting for the confirmation. Reflecting on the surprising delay, Musa thought that perhaps his friend, the Northern Minister of Education, was irked with him because he had turned down his earlier offer to take the position of instructor at the Maiduguri Crafts School. Musa would not go to Maiduguri because "it is hot as an oven there." Later, Musa suggested that the Chairman of the Public Service Commission might be responsible for the delay. He was rumored to be corrupt, and Musa thought the man might be waiting for a bribe before confirming the appointment.

As has been mentioned before, it was exceptional for Musa, a Hausa, to have been at one time a Christian. We have seen that although he was raised in a community of Muslims and naturally fell into their religious pattern, he went with his converted parents to Gimi, where he was constantly exposed to Christian proselytizing, and received his education in a Christian mission school at Zaria. When he entered the mission school, he considered that he had no choice but to adopt Christianity, since he was forbidden to pray as a Muslim. The school required strict adherence to its codes, and the children also tried to gain the favor of their teachers by showing an interest in Christianity and by informing on one another's transgressions.

As I acquired more knowledge I showed signs that I favored Christianity over Islam, although I did not then know much about the Islamic religion. I tried to please my teachers, but I remember one day, when we went out on our usual Sunday going around, I bought a halfpenny worth of meat and ate it, not knowing that one boy, who was trying to gain favor from our teacher, Dr. Miller, went and reported me for buying meat on a Sunday. So I was given twenty-two strokes of the cane on my backside. I'll never forget that until I die.

Musa was baptized around this time and became one of the school's best pupils. He said the heads of the mission had tried to persuade him to become a minister, but his only ambition at that time was to be a school teacher with the mission.

I remained a so-called Christian until I left the mission. In fact, I went to Toro as a Christian and I remained so up until the death of my first wife [who was an ardent Christian] in 1950. I did not convert to

Islam until about four years ago [1957]. How it came about is a matter of a long time.

From the date I left Zaria in 1927 until I converted in 1957 I had been together with Muslims. I moved with them, ate with them, and I dressed like a Muslim [actually like a Hausa], so anybody I told I was a Christian used not to believe me.

From the time I came to Toro I did not attend church services, and I wasn't getting any more Christian teaching or help. I remember speaking one day with my brother-in-law, who was then a teacher at Toro and is now its Principal, and I asked him what was our religion. We discussed this and concluded that we were not living as Christians, and so we laughed about it. Later, when I was Visiting Teacher, I once toured Pankshin and there met the Headmaster of the Provincial Secondary School, who was also a Zaria alumnus, and we had the same discussion. Well, from that time I concluded that we were, rightly speaking, no longer Christians in practice, perhaps in name only. Having realized the position, I decided to become a Muslim. There was no particular influence by anyone; I just decided by myself that I should not remain without a religious anchor. I don't condemn Christianity—not at all—but it is good only for those who practice it to their satisfaction. I, for one, can't practice it. Those who practice it with sincerity will undoubtedly find salvation through it, but the way I was living I could not practice it to my satisfaction.

I had been handicapped when I lived in Bukuru because there was no church to attend. It was the same at Toro. When I lived in Jos I didn't attend a single church service, although there was ample opportunity to, because almost all of my friends were Muslim. My brother-in-law at Toro and the Headmaster of the Pankshin school were in similar positions, and now they too are Muslims.

In Jos I have a good friend, Alhaji Arabi [one of the most prominent local Koranic scholars and Manager of Islamiya School], who once worked under me as Arabic and Religious Instructor in the N.A. School. With him and with another close friend, Mallam Abubakar Sokoto, and others like them, I often argued about religion. At some point I finally decided I should return to Islam. It was to Abubakar that I made the declaration of faith. To learn more quickly I bought a book that re-taught me how to make ablutions and prayers, when and how. The prayers are in Arabic but written in Roman characters.

Musa said he tried to pray the required five times a day, but when he worked he rearranged his praying times or said together at one time prayers ordinarily said at different times. This pattern reflected his avowed "moderate and reasonable" attitude toward religious dogma. He no longer ate pork (although he did not prefer it even when he was a Christian), but he thought he might take an alcoholic drink on those rare occasions when a toast was appropriate. He observed the Rhamadan fast and hoped he might someday make the pilgrimage to Mecca, but, in keeping with his religious moderation and his frugality, he said, "I won't do as some, selling my property in order to go. Going to Mecca is the last prescription, and for those who can afford it." Musa said that he had early developed an attitude of following the spirit rather than the letter of religious law, when he had fervently prayed for his brother's recovery from trypanosomiasis and had been disillusioned. Since his brother's death, Musa claimed he never called on any group, Christian or Muslim, to intervene with God or to ask for aid or comfort on his behalf.

Musa's "tolerant and reasonable" attitude toward things supernatural extended to cover areas of traditional native beliefs, such as using charms and talismans, practices condemned by both Islam and Christianity. He claimed that after he returned to Islam he had not acquired any charms, although he had occasionally done so when he was Christian; then he would purchase these from Koranic scholars, who made and sold them surreptitiously. He thought that they actually were worthless, but nonetheless they provided him with a measure of insurance. Thus, when one of his sons went to a school in a snake-infested area, Musa provided him with a bit of anti-snake rope (rope magically treated) sewn into a little leather container to preserve it. Another time, when Musa lived in Toro, his first wife became fatally ill, and treatment at the Jos General Hospital proved ineffective, Musa followed someone's suggestion that he consult the local pagan native doctors. He too was of no help, and Musa said he was skeptical throughout the entire procedure. Minor illnesses or injuries to anyone in his household have since been treated by Musa or one of his educated daughters with modern medications or first-aid procedures.

Musa himself would not implore God's aid to relieve illness in himself or any of his family, although he did not object to his children doing so.

All of Musa's children, with the exception of his youngest son, were born of his first wife, and of these children from his first marriage, three daughters and two sons, all but one son have remained Christian. Musa's first wife had been raised in the Gimi community of Christian Hausa, and they had known one another since childhood. Her parents were Christian converts and her father, it will be remembered, was instrumental in converting Musa's own parents. Musa developed an interest in her as a prospective wife when he was seventeen and a pupil teacher in Zaria, and she was one of his students. Her parents were then no longer living, and the marriage process and ceremony were entirely Christian. She had received enough education to qualify her as a teacher, but her only occupation during her married life was to do some petty trading, although she did tutor her two sons before they entered school, and Musa claimed this advanced them several years when they eventually enrolled. Musa was proud of her and remembered her as a good wife and admirable person. He said there had never been any misunderstandings between them. He told me, parenthetically, how much he appreciated the aid and comfort of his friend, the Chief of Jos, generously given at the time of her death in 1950.

Musa's second wife was in several respects quite different from his first. She was not Hausa but Ankwai, one of the many central Nigerian or Plateau peoples. She had no formal education other than the little reading in Hausa and English that Musa taught her, and, unlike his first wife, she had been married previously, although without issue. Formerly she had been a nominal Roman Catholic, but Musa claimed he made her convert to Islam prior to their marriage in 1951. Since Musa himself did not convert until 1957, a year before their divorce, it is instructive to explore the circumstances surrounding this marriage, for it points to some of the pressures leading to Musa's own conversion and to the potential difficulties in a situation in which members of the same family hold conflicting religious allegiances.

Not long after the death of his first wife, Musa went on an official tour of one of the Divisions of Plateau Province. There one of his colleagues and friends introduced him to a woman, and later explained that this woman was his ward and that the introduction was intended to relieve his widowhood, if both parties were amenable. Her guardian was a local tribesman who had converted to Islam and, from the circumstantial information Musa provided about him, it is reasonable to conclude that he would not see this woman married by a Christian, tribal, or civil ceremony. The ceremony was Muslim, and took place at the home of the guardian; Musa was not present. When this woman arrived at his home in Jos she was Musa's fully legal wife in accordance with Koranic law. In 1953 they had their only child, a son.

Musa conceded that this woman tried to be a good wife, but her step-children despised her, called her a pagan, and treated her with disdain. After several years she could no longer tolerate this treatment, and became bent on getting a divorce. Her behavior changed. She became disobedient, carried her petty trading outside the compound, and remained out late at night. She would leave the compound without Musa's permission, and would not come to him when he called her. Finally Musa asked her what she wanted; she told him, and he granted her a divorce. She returned home, but has not remarried, and now Musa wants her to return to him. He believes she will do so, since only one of her step-children still lives with Musa, and he himself has promised to guarantee his children's good behavior. He started to write to her about reuniting in 1960, two years after their divorce, and at the time I knew him he was sending their child on visits to his mother in an attempt to use him as a medium of reconciliation.

Musa's third wife, born in 1933, was younger than all but two of his children and was sixteen when she married him. She is Hausa, Muslim from birth, and was married once before, but had never had children. As with his second wife, he met his third through a friend, and married her in absentia. It was a little over a year after his second wife had left him that Musa jokingly suggested to a friend that he should do something to relieve his lonely existence. Arrangements were made for Musa to meet a girl who had recently been divorced. He was pleased with her appearance and agreed to marry her. His first marriage had cost him nothing and the expenses for his second came to about ten pounds; but for his third he paid out over thirty-five pounds for gifts, clothes, and other incidentals. It was ironic that Musa's monetary investments in this area were in inverse proportion to the amount of satisfaction he received. Unlike his other wives, she was not thrifty and did not trade. She was ignorant and illiterate, lazy and untidy. She could not, or would not cook, and was stubborn and undisciplined. While she was not especially quarrelsome, she was prone to sulk at the slightest offense, and was always complaining of illness and always wanting to return home on lengthy visits. Musa soon came to the conclusion that he wanted to be rid of her, but her father would always beg him to overlook her childish behavior and to be patient with her; she would eventually come to her senses. Musa is not a man of infinite patience and the two have been separated for longer than they have been together. He intends to divorce her.

Since he was not certain of a reunion with his second wife, Musa was seeking a wife during the time of our acquaintance, and indeed married one of two prospects available to him. Both were Muslim, had no formal Western education, and both were recently divorced. One was part Fulani, part Hausa, and had spent much of her time in Jos. She was about twenty years old, and had divorced her husband because of continuous conflicts with his senior wife. This woman's only child, a son who was just being weaned, was to remain with the father. The other potential wife was a woman in her late twenties, part Fulani and part Kanuri. Musa believed that her divorce could be attributed to her former husband's foolish behavior. She had no children, and Musa was not sure whether she may not have been married once before to yet another husband. Musa met her through a friend, with whom she was staying.

Musa was prepared to marry both of them, and to remarry his second wife as well, had his financial circumstances allowed it; but until he was assured of full-time employment he could marry only one. Otherwise he would have had to eject one or more paying or non-paying tenants from his compound, and he was reluctant to take such an action. He chose to marry the older woman, but he let the younger one know that if in the near future he could afford to marry her, and if she were still willing, he would like to do so.

It did not matter to Musa whether his wife was educated or not; nor did her ethnic origin concern him. He merely preferred that she be a Muslim, since he was anxious to avoid conflicts over religious differences. His own considerable education and intimate acquaintance with European customs did not move him to adopt European patterns of conjugal relations. He did not believe in sharing activities with his wives and considered that for himself to do housework would be demeaning. Neither did he wish to carry on the strictly traditional Hausa Muslim pattern of keeping his wives in purdah. Thrift, in his wives and himself, seemed to concern him more than other things.

Musa's three eldest children were married, but they were having assorted problems with their spouses. His eldest daughter was separated from her husband, a mining engineer, and would not consent to his request for a divorce. With her two children she held quarters in Musa's compound. She was employed as a nurse's aide. Her younger sister had married a Katab man who had been imprisoned twice for administering injections illegally. Since his last release he could not hold a steady job. They also had two children. This daughter had been dull at school, and Musa never held high hopes for her. The next youngest child, a son, had converted to Islam and taken a second wife when his first remained barren. The first resented sharing her husband with a co-wife, and it was not certain whether she would remain with her husband.

Musa considered a wife's ability to live satisfactorily with co-wives the acid test of marriage and advised his son to let his first wife go if she proved inadequate in this respect. Musa's youngest son of his first wife was engaged to be married to a Christian Hausa girl who was completing her secondary education. This son's academic career had been completely charted by his father, and he now held a comfortable clerical job with a department of the northern government. Musa's youngest daughter was studying pharmacy in Zaria, and had an excellent scholastic record. She was engaged to a young man studying at an English university, and since he was Muslim, Musa hoped that their marriage might result in a conversion of his daughter to Islam. His youngest son, born of his second wife, was too young to be thinking of marriage. He was doing well at school, and Musa was encouraging him to study medicine.

Musa's house was situated on a main thoroughfare in the Native Town. On one side of it was a house owned by an Ibo and occupied by Ibo tenants. On the other side was a house owned by a Yoruba widow. All of the tenants had been recently evicted because they were months behind in their rent, and because they were known criminals. Musa said he would prefer to have Muslims and northerners, particularly Hausa, as neighbors, except the "snobbish Sokoto Fulani." Musa's house was constructed of mud brick, and had a galvanized iron roof. It was relatively large, and held several tenants, all Muslim northerners, in addition to members of his family. When Musa retired from his post as Adult Education Officer he sold his car and converted his garage into modest living quarters. This room was now used as living quarters by transient northerners, single men who paid no rent to Musa but did errands and chores for him. Living elsewhere in the compound was a young Babur boy who acted as a servant for Musa, earning little more than his keep, since his only duties were to keep the compound clean and shop occasionally. Musa's brother, his daughter, and her children paid no rent for their quarters; they received their food free from Musa as well. Musa was trying to acquire a building plot upon which to build a house to be used solely by tenants. He was assured by his friend, the Chief of Jos, that he would be granted a plot soon.

His friendship with the Chief of Jos, a Christian Birom, dates back to his days at Toro, when he was the man's teacher. The Chief's residence is about a three-minute walk from Musa's house. Musa visits him irregularly and enjoys the occasions when they leisurely discuss politics and current news. Musa's other close friends in Jos are almost entirely Muslim northerners (of whom several are Sokoto Fulani, but apparently not snobs). Most of these men are learned in the Koran, and some have had a modest amount of Western education. They are almost all prominent locally, and one is a successful local politician. In his own life, Musa has relied more on such friendships than on kinship relations. It was through friends that he met most of his wives, and it is to them that he was grateful for many important services. Indeed, even though Musa had many blood relations, his effective kinship network was exceedingly narrow. He knew that his father had two siblings, but he knew the name of only one, and nothing more of his father's family. He remarked that "the only relatives I have that are alive are my brother, who lives with me, and my half sister who lives in Zaria." Except for his brother, he had not seen any of his consanguinal kinsmen for over ten years, and when he had had closer contact with them it was with a pattern of decreasing frequency. On the occasions when he had visited relatives he said he had always been careful to set aside a fixed sum of money to be spent on gifts. He was thrifty in all things, including his exchanges with kinsmen. He told me, "I seldom give more than a pound to the same person for fear that I may run short."

Musa was never interested in voluntary associations. When he was employed he did become a member of the Northern Teachers' Association, but he always declined invitations to assume office. As a civil servant he could not join a political party, but his sympathies lay with the Northern Peoples Congress, and for many years he occasionally attended their political meetings and rallies.

In 1959 he became a member of the party. It is illegal to wear political party badges or symbols, but Musa once showed me the N.P.C. party symbols stamped on the inner lining of his cap. Musa thought it was a splendid joke to keep this little secret "under his cap."

Musa no longer enjoyed studying and reading as much as he had in the past, and he spent less time at it. Still, he kept abreast of local, national, and international developments, and could speak knowledgeably about African national politics, the American Negro, and other current affairs, as well as such things that might be categorized as humanities.

Unlike most of my informants, Musa expressed his intention to live out his life in Jos, and he held no allegiance or emotional commitment to any other place. What held him to Jos were his friends, the position he held in the local community, and the comfort of the climate. When I asked him how he would like to see his future develop, he said he would like to win several thousand pounds in the football pool, build several houses for tenants, make the pilgrimage to Mecca, and be comforted in the thought that he had provided adequately for his children. But even with so much wealth he would still want most to return to his beloved teaching.

David Aba Kagoro: Kagoro

"How can anyone not love David?", his neighbor, who was my assistant, said to me at a time when he might easily have been exasperated with David's annoying habits. David frequently played his radio too loud and too late into the night, despite repeated requests for some neighborly consideration. Sometimes David fell asleep with the radio blaring, and my assistant's thumping on the walls, or banging on the door, could not be heard by him above the din. It seemed to his neighbors that David was always being visited by his friends—fellow tribesmen of his own age—who enjoyed as much as he talking excitedly, singing, joking, and laughing long into the quiet hours of the night. There were other disconcerting acts that brought against David and his friends such epithets as "bush people," "ignorant peasants," and "uncivilized." As much as he would complain to me, however, my assistant always pointed out that it was impossible to remain angry with David for long. David was full of youthful exuberance, happiness, and unadulterated innocence. His face normally carried a smile so genuinely sincere that it was contagious. But when someone would suggest to him that his irresponsible or inconsiderate behavior resulted in discomfort or inconvenience, as when I sometimes complained about his frequent failures to keep our interview appointments, his expression altered to one of contrition so profound that his confronter would himself experience a sense of guilt for having smothered this blithe spirit. David affected many people in this way.

He had many friends, and because of them I had to discontinue holding interviews at his quarters, since they were forever present and active as uninvited participants. Up to a point I could tolerate their attempts to answer the questions I put to David, or to "improve" his answers, but when they began translating my questions about David's conjugal relations and extramarital affairs to his wife (who spoke no English), I changed the location of most of the subsequent interviews to my place. Still, David's friends would often come with him to my quarters or would call for him in the middle of an interview. Since I could not change their gregarious habits, I eventually resigned myself to coping with them as best I could. Sometimes David and his friends appeared at my place with their native musical instruments, whether or not an appointment had been scheduled for that time, and proceeded to sing, play, and make merry, presumably on the assumption that I, like them, was always ready for a party.

David was acknowledged by his friends as an outstanding player of the dzundzum, a zither-like instrument made of reeds. He was indeed quite talented musically. I once found him practicing on a concertina he had just acquired. He said he had bought it from a fellow worker and was learning to play it because "he had interest." No one was teaching him, but he said he remembered how, as a boy, a lady missionary had played an accordion. In several weeks he had mastered the concertina, but his proficiency had stimulated his friends to try their hand at it, and thereafter it remained circulating among them. David could not bring himself to ask for its return.

Next to Kagoro, David spoke Hausa best; his English was about as good as the Efik informant's. Having lived in Port Harcourt and Lagos, he understood a good deal of Ibo and Yoruba, and could respond sufficiently to be understood in these languages. His little son, about four years old, spoke Ibo quite well, having picked it up from David's compound neighbors in Jos. David's wife could speak only Kagoro and a little Hausa.

David was born in 1938 in Kafanchan, Kagoro country, and raised there. He is the second oldest of six children who survived an infant mortality that denied maturity to four of his siblings. David's older sister lives with her husband and two children in Kaduna. All his other siblings and his parents live in or near Kafanchan. A younger brother and sister are married and have no children, and two younger brothers still attend school at Kafanchan. Both his parents are Kagoro and received a primary education, in Hausa, from the Sudan Interior Mission. His father is a Baptist pastor. David has three children, the eldest having been born when David was about sixteen.

His early schooling was at Kafanchan. After completing senior primary school in 1954 he attended the Bukuru Trade Centre and left the school in 1957 as a qualified electrician. Once during his time at the Trade Centre he wanted to quit. He had received a bad shock while repairing a power line, because someone had forgotten to remove the fuse. A classmate had died in a similar accident. "I thought the thing would kill me if I remained, but I thought of my future and decided to stay. Soon after that there was another boy who was very badly shocked. He was fainted for a long time. Then many of us wanted to run away, but the instructor made us stay with sweet words."

From 1957 to 1958 David worked for the Public Works Department in Jos, and during that time was a minor official in the P.W.D. labor union. His work entailed wiring houses and maintaining electric motors. In 1959 he joined Gottschalk's, a subsidiary firm of the United Africa Company, because he was offered the opportunity of further training. He was first sent by the firm to attend their school in Port Harcourt, where he was trained to service electric typewriters. After spending a year there, he was sent to Lagos to learn how to service electric business machines and duplicating machines such as the Thermofax. His course in Lagos ended in March 1961, when his company returned him to Jos. He said he was posted here because he is a northerner, and the company wanted to show that they were complying with the Northernization Policy. (His classmates at Port Harcourt and Lagos were all southern Nigerians, with the exception of one other northerner beside himself.) During the time I knew him, David was earning £141 a year, but his employers intended to send him to Lagos for another course of several months duration, after which he would return to Jos with his salary increased to £206. He was also repairing and cleaning typewriters in his spare time, which brought him several pounds a year.

When he was stationed at Port Harcourt, David was a member of the local branch of the Northern Peoples Congress. None of the members of this branch were Muslim northerners; all were from the Middle Belt area, most of them being Birom. According to David, by being N.P.C. members they were able to screen their true political beliefs, which lay elsewhere, and thereby protected themselves for job opportunities and advancements when they returned to live in the North. Membership in this branch also gave these men, who lived in an alien area quite distant from their home, a sense of cameraderie and a place for social gathering. David also told me that his tribesmen at home were basically not sympathetic with the N.P.C., but supported that party because otherwise they would get no government aid and amenities.

When speaking about his marriage, which took place early in 1953, David claimed his father forced him to marry his present wife:

My father was looking for a wife for me but I refuse ten girls before I marry this one, because I thought I was too young. Then he said if

I don't marry this one now he'll think bad of me. He told his brothers to find me a sensible girl, one who would know how to live with his son. I was at school then.

After they had made the arrangements I was informed to come and see her. I still didn't want to come. I was insulted by my friends to go and see her, and I went together with my friends. When we saw her my friends talked with her. I myself didn't say anything. My friends asked me if I liked her. My father asked me in their presence, and I said I was not up to age to marry. Then my father said if I didn't take this one he wouldn't agree with me. Then my friends told me to obey my father, so I agreed and my father had to pay my dowry. It was £12.

Then I went back to school and she stayed with my parents. Not long after, I was informed to come and marry her. Then everything was done and we were carried to church. All my sisters, who had married, were there. My friends had to come and advise me to go because I was ashamed. When we reach home, we find everything was done; people dancing. I was very ashamed. I didn't enjoy the wedding, but my friends enjoyed it. After three days I returned to school, and my wife remained at home with my parents. I didn't see her again until the following weekend, and every weekend after that I returned home to my wife.

Anyone seeing David's wife might think her a typical "bush pagan," although she is a Christian. She is about twenty-one, but uncertain of her precise age. Her face is decorated with elaborate cosmetic tribal scars. She has had little schooling, and in various ways expresses discomfort with living in a city. Her parents are both Kagoro; her father is a nominal Christian who has been married and divorced at least five times. He is a farmer, and his present wife is not David's wife's real mother; the latter had divorced the girl's father and remarried.

David has had little contact with his wife's parents. When he was in Port Harcourt he once sent his mother-in-law a pound note, and when he came to Jos from Lagos in 1961, he stopped off to see his father-in-law and his present wife. He gave the man a blanket and the woman a native cloth.

On the whole, David and his wife got along well. They sometimes helped one another: he with her housework and caring for the children, and she with his typewriter repairs. He liked his wife, particularly because she was thrifty, took good care of the children, obeyed him, offered him good advice, and helped keep him in line with good moral behavior. But there was one thing about his wife that frequently annoyed him: she continually clamored to return home to see her parents and siblings. While living with David's parents, she had often run away to her natal home.

David once came to an appointment looking downcast. It was quite unusual for him to appear so, and when I inquired if anything was troubling him, he told me it was his wife.

Last night she was crying. I asked her why, but she wouldn't answer. I asked her if something was wrong at home, but she didn't answer me. She said her heart was troubling her, but she didn't know why. [His wife was at this time in the early months of pregnancy.]

The other day she asked me permission to go home, and I said no. That may be the reason for her crying. She also said she wanted to see to her crops; yams and other things which she planted before coming here. During the time I was in Lagos she asked me for some money for farming. I sent her £3 which she paid some people to farm for her.

I won't let her go home, because then I won't have anybody to care for me. Sometimes I come home late from work, and there will be no one to help me. I could eat with my brother-in-law, but if I come home late he may have taken his chop by then. It would be hard for me to cook for myself.

My junior brother came here from home [on a visit], and maybe he is the one who told her about home. I told my brother to tell my parents to harvest her crops. He went home and they will do that.

David's wife wanted to bring the harvest to Jos for their larder and for sale in the market. Now David's parents would take the bulk of the crop and send a portion of it to him. She continued pressing him to allow her to visit her father, and David considered that since he was to leave soon for a study course in Lagos, she might then return home and remain until some time after she delivered her baby. He thought that if he had to return to Jos and wait for a period before his wife rejoined him, that he might get a young female relative to stay with him to do his cooking and his household chores.

David already had three children, and he wanted no more than four. His wife wanted many children, and refused his repeated suggestion that she take a native medicine to prevent conception. His wife, like other Kagoro women, was conversant with such things but would have none of it, and David did not know how to acquire it. He confessed that this area of difference between them sometimes drove him to consider extreme means, such as tricking her into drinking such medicine without her knowledge. He told me that he did not want more children because a large family would hamper his chances of improving his material standard of living; I would speculate, however, that his wish to marry a second wife, a childhood sweetheart, entered into his calculations.

David once told me that he had grown up with a Kafanchan girl who agreed, when they were both still children and playmates, to marry him. Time only strengthened their conviction that they should eventually be man and wife. David's father had been aware of David's attachment to the girl, but he objected to the marriage then because, he said, all of his own brothers had married Kafanchan women and he wanted his eldest son to marry a Kagoro. Thus he had insisted on David's marrying his present wife, and we may presume the reason David tried to avoid that marriage was the hope he could hold out until he could marry the girl of his choice. David's father was still against the union with the Kafanchan girl because it would be bigamous and therefore un-Christian, but David said his father would now go along with it since he had fulfilled his command to take a Kagoro bride. His childhood sweetheart was studying nursing in Kano, and within a year she would graduate. She then might be posted anywhere in the Northern Region. David had no idea when they might marry, but he was preparing the way by exchanging gifts with the girl and by pressing gifts and money on her parents. He said his wife favored having a co-wife to help her around the house, but obviously she did not understand what David's marriage with a nurse would entail. An educated woman with a professional career would not demean herself with housework.

David's eldest daughter was born at the end of 1953, while her father was still completing his primary school education. During the time I was interviewing David, she was living about thirty miles south of Jos with a tribesman who was the Headmaster of the school she was attending. David sent the man money, clothing, and other things, which more than covered her full support. This arrangement was made to keep the girl in a Baptist school after the deadline for registration at the Baptist school in Jos had passed. (David's father insisted that his son's children attend only Baptist schools.) David hoped that the girl might eventually become a nurse. His son was born in Jos, early in 1957 when David was employed with the Public Works Department. He was four years old when I knew him, and David was proud that he was learning the alphabet from his mother. He could recite up to the letter "H." David hoped that he might one day be a scholar at a university overseas. His youngest child, a girl, was born in mid-1959 in Kafanchan, when David was still at Port Harcourt. (His wife was then staying with his parents.) Perhaps she too would become a nurse. Even though he was anxious that all his children pursue Westernized careers, David was at the same time concerned lest they forget their tribal heritage. "I'd like them to know our people's history. I'd like them to know how we were before. I'd like them to speak and to know my dialect well. I'd like them to know all my relatives, all my friends, and all my townspeople too. I can tell them our stories. I'd like them to know some medicine so they can protect themselves, but not wicked medicine."

Living with David at the time I knew him was a girl of about twelve. He called her his sister, but she was actually a cousin, the daughter of his father's brother of the same mother. She was attending the Native Authority School; her father could not afford to send anything for her support, because he was a low-salaried school teacher with many children. He lived in a small hamlet south of Jos and sent his daughter to David in order that she might take advantage of the educational facilities in Jos. She would visit her family on holidays, and when living with David she helped him and his wife around the house, washing clothes, ironing, marketing, cooking, cleaning, and taking care of the children.

David's brother-in-law, a young man, lived near David, but was practically a fixture in his house. He frequently ate there and, somewhat less frequently, asked David for a shilling or two. When he came to Jos, David found him work as an apprentice shop-boy with a large European firm. A fellow tribesman, an old friend of David's, had a room to himself in the same compound. Although he remained friendly with David, he spent little time with him. Between the two, they frequently harbored fellow tribesmen and townsmen who visited Jos looking for work. Together they also helped find these men jobs. Sometimes David borrowed money from me to help such men—money that was always returned. Such visitors, or guests, always ate with David. Occasionally he found them a nuisance, as when one borrowed his clothing without permission and left it full of lice. But David said nothing, and the man continued to wear his clothes.

Sometimes visitors from home are an asset. When relatives come they often bring yams, beans, and groundnuts. When his mother came she brought with her these items, as well as rice, maize, a fowl, and additional ingredients for cooking. David always reciprocated such gifts whenever he visited home. In addition, he sometimes sent his parents money, either as a gift or for some specific purpose such as hiring men to help with the farming that his father did in addition to his church work. The gifts of food from home were always welcome, because David rarely had enough money to buy good food. Since coming to Jos his wife had only once bought a fowl or eggs. Usually their animal protein consisted of cow intestines and meat bones, which David admitted were the cheapest kinds of meat.

As a skilled worker, David earned comparatively high wages, yet neither his normal diet nor his house furnishings and other material possessions reflected his income. For his entire household he had but one rented room, which was meagerly furnished. He and his wife slept on a narrow iron bed, separated from the rest of the room by a curtain, and his children slept on mats on the floor. The concrete floor lacked a linoleum rug. David's two most costly possessions were his radio and his bicycle. On his income, David could well afford to feed his family better, rent more ample living quarters, and furnish these quarters more substantially. Why then did he not do so? The answer is simple: the money that could have brought David's household better food and furnishings went as outright support or aid to kinsmen, tribesmen, and friends, or was used to maintain these relationships at a high level of solidarity.

David's sessions of conviviality with his friends, all of whom were from his own or a neighboring tribe, provide an interesting example. David had about six very close friends and perhaps another six to ten whom he saw frequently but did not designate as his very best friends. These men often ate at one another's homes —if they happened to drop by during a meal—but more often drank together. They met almost every night either at their own homes or at one of the palm wine bars in the Native Town. Each, in turn, acted as host or co-host for a particular evening, not in a rigid system of rotation, but in one determined by the exigencies of who had money that night. If it had been their custom for each man to pay for his own drinks, the total amount they spent for palm wine would have been considerably reduced. As it was, each man was constrained toward generosity and reciprocity.[1]

At such gatherings he and his friends would talk about their personal careers and those of their acquaintances. They would pool their information to help a friend find employment, or they might plan to pool their money for some investment, although the latter was always planned on a minor scale. They would talk about old times, gossip, and talk about women and current exploits, but rarely would they talk about politics, and then only if those present shared the same political affiliations or ideologies. Sometimes

1. I do not believe that a concept such as that of rational economic behavior is applicable to this situation. David was not in a position to choose between various economic ends—such as between improving the living standard of his household and hosting his friends with palm wine—and limited means. No choice was involved. As long as he accepted his social position, and the culture of the sub-society of which he was a member, it would never occur to him to behave otherwise than he did.

they dreamed that they might all invest in real estate so that they might all live in the same compound. During such get togethers, friends might raise personal problems, usually involving their kinsmen, and the group would try to work out a solution.

Many of these problems were frequently the topic of discussion when these men met with others of their area at their tribal union gatherings. Meetings of this association were held on a Sunday afternoon of each month, and men and women met separately. David actually belonged to two tribal unions: a Kagoro union called Zdoryang ("stand up"), and a union composed of several culturally and geographically related tribes called the Menzit (or Nanzit) Union. *Menzit* is a Kagoro term meaning "our people," and the union consists of the non-Muslim peoples of southern Zaria Province, including the Kagoro, Kafanchan, Manchok, Marwa, Katab, Kaje, Kwoi, Kadoko, Ninzam, and others. David said that "every man from southern Zaria is a member, nobody is outside," but the statement cannot be taken literally. It is intended to mean that membership is not compulsory, but that every tribesman should feel himself a member whether or not he pays dues and attends meetings, and that he should support the union in spirit and with money. Similarly, any tribesman is eligible for union aid, because he holds his membership by virtue of ethnic origin and not through formal induction. The union performs the functions normally associated with such groups, although in a weakened form. David's Kagoro union met the same afternoon as the Menzit meeting, for after the formal meeting of the whole group the individual ethnic units met separately.

As an employee of one of the United Africa Company firms, David was also eligible for membership in the U.A.C. Club—a social and recreation club—but he provided the excuses that he was not yet in a financial position to do so, and that he would not want to have such membership until he was firmly settled in Jos. The latter excuse was also given for his not joining, and infrequently attending, the Youths of Christ, a social and educational missionary organization. Still, David feels he is a firm Baptist, and much of his energy goes into religious activity.

When he first came to Jos, David began attending the Baptist Church that held a predominantly Yoruba congregation (mainly from Ogbomosho), but since he did not understand Yoruba sufficiently, he went thereafter to the Sudan Interior Mission services, which were in Hausa. David said they were still preaching the same word of God, and that he did not alter his denominational affiliation by changing churches in this way.

With the exception of his tribal union meetings, David's Sundays are devoted to Christianity. After arising in the morning, he listens to the religious broadcasts on the radio. Later he meets with kinsmen and friends and together they attend services. His wife and children attend the same services, but go there and return separately. After lunch, David and three or four companions —close kinsmen and friends—go about the Native Town preaching the gospel to Muslims and pagans. They have had little success.

When we talk to them they answer us with bad manners, but we give them kind words so they will know our religion is true. We take Bible and hymn book, but nothing else [such as the literature of the Jehovah's Witnesses] to present to them. We ask them to come and confess in Church, and then to baptize, and then to turn to good way.

One Hausa man said that Jesus Christ was a false prophet; the True One is in heaven, while Isa [Jesus] is the false bush god. He said the one we follow is the one of Roman people. They were serving idols. We said it is not so. We would keep on arguing. If we can't get their heart, we would pray for them, and we would come again next Sunday. Some please us to stay and listen, while some do not. I used to do this since school days.

Sometimes we meet the Watchtower people [Jehovah's Witnesses], and they argue with us. They tell us that our way is not the right way. We tell them, why should we Christians fight each other while Hausa people see us and say our way is not truthful? We tell them there is only one Christian God. I not deep in Bible, so I can't argue with them. They can quote verses, and I'm not good at that.

David was aware that his behavior was not consistently Christian. "Religion forbids to drink, but as we are away from home we do drink." This moral inconsistency did not trouble David, nor did his occasional adultery. I could observe no consistent pattern in the contradictions between David's Christianity and his traditional beliefs. He claimed that traditionally he could have slept with the woman he intended to marry before they were married, but as a Christian he would never do so. Yet he was planning to enter into polygyny, rationalizing that since his father had consented to this marriage if he first married his present wife, doing so could not be completely morally wrong. David was also firmly convinced of the efficacy of traditional magic. He himself had used love potions when he was a youngster, and had also made medicine to protect himself against poisoning. If his wife or children were seriously ill, he would send them to the most reputable native doctors of his natal area. "My father doesn't like me to go to them, but my mother do see them," he told me. On the other hand, he would not trust a native doctor in Jos. "I always go to the hospital if I'm sick. I also pray to God. I only go home if the hospital fails to cure the sickness." David mentioned that a relative had once given him medicine to wear which would protect him against magic needles projected at him. "But I don't want to wear it because our religion forbid it. We never carry medicine in pocket like Muslim. I don't want to annoy him, so I tell him I wear it."

Almost without exception, David was pleased with the civilizing (as he put it) changes in Nigeria brought about by missionaries and Europeans. The exceptions were exemplified by individuals who would probably have fallen short morally under any conditions. "Some people, the more they educated, the less respect they give to their parents. It is wrong. Some men don't feed their family, but go drink somewhere while their families are dying from hunger. They don't clothe their families." David, of course, considered himself free of such abuses.

David held clear ideas of what he wanted from the future. He wanted to invest some money in real estate—perhaps with his father in Kafanchan, perhaps by himself or with friends in Jos—so that he could be financially comfortable from the derived rents.

And, he thought, someday he would like to learn how to drive and to own a car, "so I can cool my body from walking all about."

David Njoku: Ibo

David Njoku, unlike most Ibo in Jos, was in a poor financial position when I first began the interviews. Like other Ibo, he tried to be a thrifty person. His bank passbook showed that by November 1956 he had been able to save £168, but since that time of relative prosperity he suffered a series of personal misfortunes and had been reduced to impoverishment. When I met him, David was about fifty (he did not know whether he was born in 1910 or 1912). His facial scars indicated that he was a western Ibo; he was, in fact, from Issele Uku, on the western side of the Niger River. At the time we were introduced, one of his wives had just died in childbirth, and he had been out of work for some time. It is likely that David's many difficulties prompted one of his compound neighbors to introduce us; he probably thought that I could help David financially. Because David had no formal education, and could not speak English, this neighbor wanted to serve as interpreter, but I found that David and I could communicate adequately in pidgin English. David, of course, spoke Ibo best, but he spoke Hausa almost as well. He also understood Yoruba and Edo, and knew a great many greetings and useful phrases in many northern Nigerian languages, since he had travelled extensively in the North and had been in and around Jos since 1926, or for more than half his life.

David's father, a farmer, died before he could remember him, and David was raised by his father's brother. This uncle was of a different mother, and mistreated David, giving him an exceptionally heavy burden of farm chores. Therefore, when he was about ten or twelve, David ran away from home. He walked to Warri, a distance of about one hundred miles, where he knew he had relatives. He found one he had known at home and stayed with him. This man found him an apprenticeship with a carpenter. He remained with the carpenter only about half a year—the man was kind to him, but his wife was stingy with food. He decided to go to Lagos, because many people were going there for employment; still he had to remain in Warri for several months in order to save enough money for passage on a boat. At Lagos he sought out another relative and stayed with him until he found employment with a European as a houseboy. He stayed in this position for about a year, but during that time he kept hearing that Jos, in the North, was the land of golden opportunity, and when another of his father's brothers wrote to him from Jos, inviting him there, he decided to go.

He arrived in Jos in 1926 and stayed with this relative. The man bought and sold lorries, and also had a small fleet that he used for transportation. David was apprenticed as a driver and motor mechanic under him for one year. He received no pay, but was given instruction, food, and a place to sleep. In 1928 he received his driver's license and went to work for a European firm that supplied coal to mining companies. (At that time the heavy mining machinery was run by coal.) During the 1930's he held a succession of jobs with African transporters—Hausa, Yoruba, and Ibo—and one with a European gold mining company at Minna. From 1939 to about 1945 he drove for the A.T.M.N., and then, for about five years, he worked for a small private European mining outfit that went bankrupt in 1959 and was bought by an African. One of the European owners of that company taught David how to open and maintain a savings account, and it was during this period that David started developing a sizable bank account. Unfortunately for David, the new African employer sought to reduce wages by firing and hiring rapidly, by getting rid of men with seniority and high salaries and hiring new men at starting wages. David regretted being forced to leave his position. He had not only been earning good wages; he and his family had lived in rent-free quarters at the company labor camp, where his wives were able to earn some money trading, and where David earned some additional money by growing Irish potatoes and maize and raising a few cows, goats, sheep, and fowl. After being dismissed, he left his family at the labor camp to seek work in Jos. From that time until about late 1960, he could find only temporary employment as a chauffeur or lorry driver with Hausa or Ibo employers, and during this time he had been forced to move his family to Jos.

His testimonials, from European miners and mining companies, all stated that he had held onto his job for two or more years, that he was a careful driver, honest, and of good character, and that he had been discharged through a general retrenchment. Like most informants, David took pride in his occupational skills. In telling me the names and tonnage of the lorries he had driven since receiving his license, he must have hoped that I would be instrumental in finding him new employment; nonetheless, he clearly felt pride in his superior abilities as a driver and mechanic.

Since moving his family to Jos in 1960, David has lived in three different places, all of comparable quality. He left the first place because the landlord raised the rent, and left the second because the landlord refused to repair a leaky roof. His present quarters were on a main thoroughfare in the Native Town. David rented two adjoining rooms, each identically 12 x 12 feet in a two-story house of concrete block with a zinc roof.

Both rooms were used for sleeping, but the "back" room also served as a storage area, while the "front" room doubled as a reception room. It was here that most of our interviews took place. This room held three cushioned chairs of local manufacture, one of which, slightly longer than the others, served as an extra bed for overnight guests. Next to one wall was a narrow iron bed. On another wall was a pendulum clock (an item almost every town dweller tries to acquire), and an alarm clock stood on a shelf. Some simple stools and small wooden tables for beverages stood about the room. On the floor was an old and spot-stained rug. A radio in one corner failed to work for lack of batteries. David also owned two hurricane lamps, and an old spring-wound gramaphone. In this room slept David's sister, visiting from Enugu, and his new-born son who had lost his mother. The second room was cluttered. It held two wide iron beds, a kitchen table loaded with cooking utensils, and, piled on top of one another, trunks, suitcases, and boxes containing all of the family's movable property. Although there was hardly room to move about, the rooms were kept clean. The compound yard, where all the tenants cooked and washed, was clean and uncluttered. David shared the house with Ibo, Yoruba, and Efik tenants, all of whom appeared to be getting along well with one another.

I met David during a period of mourning, which was why the several pictures he owned were hanging facing the wall. These pictures were mainly of himself and his wives, or himself with his European employers and fellow workers, but one was of the Chief of Issele Uku, whom David called his senior brother, but to whom he traced only a remote relationship.

David is indeed a direct patrilineal grandson of a former Chief of Issele Uku, but his grandfather had an extraordinarily large number of wives, and his father was the child of one of the most junior. His father was so lacking in royal prerogatives that, to David's knowledge, he belonged to no societies and carried no titles, but he had married many wives, many of whom he also divorced. David did not know how many wives his father had had, nor who all of his co-siblings were. His father had received no formal education, and was not a Christian. When he died, he was given a traditional burial beneath his house.

David took some pride in the fact that his mother had been her husband's senior wife. She was buried alongside him when she died sometime during World War II. Like her husband, she came from Issele Uku, held no titles, belonged to no societies, had received no formal education, and was not a Christian. She traded in the market. Of her many children, only four survived to adulthood: two daughters older than David, and a younger son. All had married and had children, but only the youngest remained at Issele Uku.

In 1936, when David was about twenty-five, he wrote home to

his sister to ask her to arrange acquiring a wife for him. A girl was chosen, and when David went home to meet her, he was pleased. He paid her bridewealth, and undertook the financial burdens of the traditional marriage ceremonies. Like his subsequent wives, she had never been to school, and like them did some petty trading. The one drawback to their otherwise good marriage was that she was barren, which caused her humiliation and grief. After almost twenty years of marriage she persisted in asking David's permission to return home to Issele Uku because she had no children, and David allowed her to go. She died there quite suddenly at about the age of forty, just a few months after I met David. Just before she died, David had complained that her kinsmen were forever getting money from him. He always sent them money as gifts, but they would then ask for additional money to send children to school, to bury a relative, or for other needs. David called this drain on his money a waste; the burden of demanding affinals was ill-suited to modern urban living. But David's first wife had also been of some financial help to him. When she was with him her trading contributed to the family budget, and when she went home she assumed responsibility for the construction of David's retirement house. While she was home, and during the time David was unemployed, she would occasionally send him one or two pounds from her trading. She had been living in David's lineage compound, and she was buried there.

David's second wife died in Jos in April 1961. She died giving birth to a boy, who lived. (Ironically, she and David's third wife conceived at about the same time. The third wife went home during the pregnancy and delivered a stillborn girl.) This second wife was still in her twenties when she died. David was uncertain whether he had been married to her for eleven or thirteen years. He considered her his favorite wife; she was a very beautiful woman, "slender and fine." She came from a village near Issele Uku. David had gone home for a visit, also thinking that he might find a second wife who might bear children. He said that the very first time he saw the girl who was to become his second wife, he fell in love with her beauty. David assumed the full cost of the marriage payments and ceremonies, nearly fifty pounds in all. She lived with David in near-perfect harmony, and when he was out of work she helped support the household with her trading. David, however, also found her relatives a difficult burden to bear. For example, he told me that when her younger brother had come to live with him, he had apprenticed the boy to a tailor, supported him, and paid for his materials and tools. When the boy completed his apprenticeship, he stole his sister's gold locket, worth £8, and fled back to his own home. When David reported the theft to the boy's family, they did nothing more than to ask him to forgive the boy.

When David's second wife seemed to have turned out as barren as the first, he decided to marry once again. Again he wrote to his sister, who picked a wife for him. David went home to make the final arrangements. By this time the bridewealth had risen closer to sixty pounds. David assumed this cost as well as those for the various ceremonies. This marriage took place in 1955. Within three years she gave birth to a son. The delivery was difficult, and required a caesarean operation after two days of labor. The child was healthy, but when David's wife became pregnant again, her family ordered her home lest she have another difficult delivery. At home she received native treatment. After she gave birth to the stillborn girl, she remained at home until David sent her money to come to Jos to care for her co-wife's baby. At the time I knew her, this woman was in her mid-twenties. She too had helped David by doing a little trading, and she was helping in this way now. An Edo woman from Benin (who lived in the compound and was married to an Ibo man from Awka) helped David's wife in various ways. Sometimes she gave her a bundle of firewood; at other times she would send food for the children. On Sundays she lent David's wife some decent clothing, and frequently she allowed the woman to tend to her trading stall in return for a little cash. David said that his wife formerly had many cloths, but that when she went home she gave them away, piece by piece, to her relatives and friends.

He did not expect much from a wife in the way of companion-ship: "So long she know how to cook and keep house clean is enough." But they did go to church together, they visited towns-men and relatives together, and, occasionally, they played at African drafts together. He thought all his wives had been good women and that he had got along well with them. "Other wives see women for street wearing new clothes or gold and made palaver for their husband, but my wives never do that. I never quarrel with them, I never flog no one." Several times during our discussions about his marriages, David could not keep from weeping. The association of their deaths with his own plight in lacking employment was bitter. "These two wives I lose now, that paining me too much," he said. "You see me for tears come for my eyes. When I think of them it hurt me too much. If I get money, I never live for this Hausa country again." Of course, David occasionally did have disagreements with his wives—perhaps because his food or his bath water were not ready for him when he returned from work, or because the house was not cleaned to his satisfaction—but they were low-keyed and short-lived, his wives usually offering an acceptable reason for this error.

When David's second wife died in Jos, neighbors and relatives in Jos and from elsewhere came to console him, and to aid him in whatever way they could. During the first few weeks of mourning, townsmen and relatives, individually or in small groups, came, stayed awhile, and left. There was forever a coming and going, with from six to ten people present at any one time. Many of the men who visited were employed, and so appeared after five or six in the evening. Some would give David a few shillings or more. While David was awaiting the arrival of his third wife and her two-year-old boy, a neighbor woman from his natal area took care of his deceased wife's two children, and she or other women of his compound would also cook for him. The Jos hospital fees for the baby's delivery came to £2 12s. A young Efik man, another neighbor, gave David two pounds, and the townswoman who cared for his children gave him twelve shillings, enabling David to discharge this debt. David considered this money a loan, for he expressed his intention of repaying these people after he became employed. The Issele Uku Patriotic Union paid the burial expenses and provided the refreshments after the funeral. His tribal union allowed David to continue his membership without paying dues during his period of unemployment.

A week after David's wife died, his brother, who lived in Issele Uku, arrived to stay with him, and about a week after that, his sisters—one from Enugu and one from Lagos—came also. Shortly after his sisters arrived, the brother returned home, and the sisters, after remaining with David for about two weeks, began to indicate their wish to return to their families. They wanted to wait until David's third wife arrived, but she was late in coming and did not appear until after the sister from Lagos had departed. David considered himself alone responsible for financing his sister's return to Enugu. He also wished to send his son of his former wife with her for an indefinite period. David spent several days going about the town trying to get together enough money for train fare and food for the journey, and by borrowing, begging, and selling small items of his personal property he somehow managed to send them off. When I asked David why the child could not remain with him, he said that his wife, who had just arrived from home, found that the child's presence made her too sad. She could not bear to look at him without crying for his dead mother.

Over the following weeks, the number of David's visitors, and the financial support he had been receiving from them, took a sharp drop. There were few men at his home, although women and girls frequently attended the baby. David felt that he needed the company of men and their help as much as he had before, for he had still found no work and was behind in his rent. One of his relatives, a patrilateral cousin who was an Inspector of the Nigerian Police in Jos, had stopped coming. He used to leave a pound or more after visiting David. Another relative, who held a well-paying position at the Labour Exchange, had also made himself scarce at David's quarters.

I knew that these people, as well as other relatives and friends, had been helping David in various ways, giving him solace, money, and seeking employment for him. David, however, was unable to find work and after I had known him for several weeks, I asked him about the help he was still receiving. His support had been drying up rapidly and his response to my inquiry about it was one of disgust:

I no friends. I no fit people should tell lie about me or know my secrets. [By this David meant that he was ashamed of his poverty and misfortune. He regarded these as his "secrets," and thought that others would derive satisfaction from his plight.] So far I have no money I don't want friends. For my compound I never show myself. All the people for my compound know me for gentleman because they no see me at all. I no let show them my secret. That's why I go hide myself. I a poor man, and it a shame for me to go to a friend because he have to give me chop money [with which to buy food]. Now I just home and chop for myself [eat alone]. I no like for go and publish myself all the time for outside. When people see you fall down, they laugh. Sometimes I see some of them [those who had given him aid] pass when I for outside. They see me and for shame they must come inside my house, but they sit small [briefly] and then go leave. Some ask me to come for their home, but I no fit. I be ashamed.

David went on to tell me that when he had had money, he had given generously and continuously to those who needed his help, doing so without being asked, but now he thought there was no justice in kindness. He felt the consideration he had demonstrated in the past was not being reciprocated.

The time I have money I train many people [sent many youngsters through school], but now they grow up and not one help me. Some of them come for Jos, but they no fit to come to me. I hear someone see them drinking for bar. People come to me and say, "Na look! Your brother [kinsman or townsman] come for Jos, na he be for bar. He no fit dash you?" [The implication here is that a person who could afford to lavish his money on frivolities should give priority to a kinsman in need.] When I hear that I fit to cry. When I think how I waste money for so many people I get mad.

Even at the time we first met, David expressed disappointment in his relatives. Early in our acquaintance he gave me an account of how a younger relative had caused him considerable financial loss. During World War II, and for about a decade thereafter, David earned good wages, had steady work, and was able to deposit a good sum of money in a bank account. Except for the fact that he still had no children from his wives, this was for him a time of prosperity, security, and great expectations. Around 1956, a younger relative from Issele Uku came to Jos looking for work and stayed with David. David paid an Ibo acquaintance £6 to take on the young man as an apprentice driver. The apprenticeship lasted two years, during which time David housed and fed his kinsman. David paid for the boy's driver's license and got him a job with his own company, but when the firm started retrenching workers the young man was among the first to be dismissed. For a while he was able to find employment with other companies, but he could not hold onto a job. Then the lad started applying pressure to David to buy a lorry for him. He pointed out that many Ibo who sought to improve their income and help their relatives were buying lorries and employing their relatives to drive them. If David did likewise, he would make much money and become an important man. David's wives agreed with the young man. "But he not make me big," David said, "he make me down. I lose all my money."

In 1958 David bought an old Austin lorry from a European firm which, he claimed, first asked £150 for it, but later raised the price to £200, stating that another buyer had offered that much. David borrowed £50 from a townsman (who has since been repaid) and bought the lorry. He put a new roof on the truck, painted it, and rehabilitated it as best he could to make it roadworthy. These repairs, as well as its license and insurance, came to an additional £200, and David said he paid the expenses entirely from his own resources. When David gave the lorry to his kinsman he was still living in a labor camp away from Jos, while the young man was living and operating out of Jos. The lad made trips throughout the Northern Region, but David was in a poor position to supervise his relative's activities, and he claimed that the young man duped him:

He run my lorry for half a year. All this time he tell me motor need fix. He say this to me, but I not for Jos to know what is true, what is lie. He cheat me proper. He come tell me this break, that break, motor spoil. It cost me so much to fix. That why he can't give me more than £2 for his last trip. This happen all the time. He make £150, he bring me £30. Maybe he cheat me, and maybe he really break lorry.

David compared his own driving habits with those of the relative he employed:

I drive easy. For Wilson [one of his former employers] I drive same Thames lorry for nine years, and even then it look like new. I know everything about motor, but he not a mechanic. He not worry about greasing, that why motor go bad. He didn't know how to drive proper. When he drive he break springs. He not hear bad noises. He not fit to look inside when he hear something is loose. He break motor, he suffer car. He cheat me proper. Because he can't drive, he can't keep job. He always sacked for new company after two months. He always bending mudguard. He drive too fast on bad road with heavy load. He not consider these things. He never check nuts after he come back from trip. If nuts not tight, you lose 'em. People tell me he run too fast.

When the lorry appeared beyond hope of repair, David's young kinsman brought it to a junk dealer in Jos, and left it there. David came to Jos to see what might be salvaged. After inspecting the lorry he hoped to realize some money from the sale of parts. The lorry was pushed to one corner of the yard. David's hopes for even the slightest compensation were not realized. "Tief people take many things inside: kicker-starter, generator, switch. Maybe mechanic take these parts, sell 'em, say tief people take 'em. I no see it. I leave it for God. I haven't any profit at all from it. The boy [his kinsman] still here for Jos, still come to see me. He come the other day, but when I see him my heart not fit."

When the lorry stopped running, and David was out of work, his family was still staying at his former employer's labor camp while he sought work in Jos. He would find temporary employment and then return to check on his family. As long as his wives were permitted to remain there he could manage economically, for he paid no rent and his wives did a little trading to help him financially. The new African owner eventually chased David and his family from the camp, and he had to settle then in Jos. Because he would not be allowed to retain his livestock in the city, he sold some animals and slaughtered others, deriving a little money from the sale of the meat. Both of his wives had conceived at this time, and since it was cheaper for him to live with only one, David allowed the other to return home to deliver.

Three weeks after his second wife died in childbirth, David shaved his beard and announced to me that the first phase of his mourning period was ended, and that he could now leave his house to seek work. He had previously found temporary work with a wealthy Hausa, Alhaji Salami, and he first sought reemployment with him. The Alhaji owed him some money, and David thought that even if he did not get work or some of the debt owed him, the Alhaji might still give him a few shillings as dash. Alhaji Salami told David his car was still being repaired, and that he was not yet in a position to clear his debt. He did not know when the car would be running, and when David asked for a little money for food, he said he could not afford to give him anything at that moment. David's repeated visits to the Alhaji brought the same response.

He thought that his best chance of finding work was to have his friends and relatives seek employment for him. They would spread the news of his availability and bring news of vacancies to him. He said he intended walking about the town in his black shirt; when friends saw him, if they did not already know of his misfortune, he would tell them, and he thought they would pity him and therefore be eager to help him find a job. He said he put his hopes in friends, in God, and in me to find him any kind of work; he hoped most of all that he would be hired by a European, because an African employer would not treat him as well.

It was at this time that he received word of the death of his first wife at home. When I saw him he appeared almost in a state of shock at the unforeseen turn. "Now my first wife died. What I going to do? I can't hang myself. I surprised. This year, it too much for me. That baby for Enugu [his two-year-old son] still worrying me. Money, money, money, no work. So what am I going to do?" David began seeking employment on his own, but it seemed to him that wherever he went he was bedeviled by the Northernization Policy. He finally found work with a European small mining operator, but he deplored the conditions of the job. He started working at seven-thirty in the morning and did not return home until seven or eight at night. He worked a full day on Saturday, and was liable to be called for work on Sunday, receiving no pay for overtime. He complained that an experienced and good driver like himself should be getting twelve to thirteen pounds a month—and with overtime, about seventeen pounds a month—instead of the eight pounds he was receiving. This job lasted about four months.

David had told his employer that the steering mechanism of the Land Rover he drove was defective and must be repaired. His employer was willing to make the necessary repairs, but a new African manager who wanted to ingratiate himself told him that he could get a driver who could handle the vehicle without its requiring repairs. David protested to his boss: "It not fit to take car to bush with bad steering. Should be bad road and then car turn over, then who fit to blame? Me? I never catch accident for thirty-two years since I'm driving." Nonetheless, another driver replaced David—and the car did turn over when the new man took it into the bush.

When David was again unemployed, and could not find work with government departments or commercial firms because he was a southerner, I asked him if he would consider seeking employment in the Eastern Region, or in the Ibo ethnic area of what was then the Western Region. He said that he did not have the money with which to return to the South, and that he felt morally bound to remain in Jos until all his debts had been paid. After several more weeks of unsuccessful seeking he turned to me in desperation. He wanted me to relieve his misery and accept his proposition to get him a small lorry or kit car (a pickup truck). It would have to be bought from a European. "If you buy from African, no can last," he insisted. With his lorry he could freelance for small mining operators and recoup his losses within six months. He assured me that I too would profit from the venture. He claimed he knew the minesfield well, and many operators knew and trusted him. He could carry tin ore, provisions, and laborers for them. David believed my explanation that, even were I in a financial position to help him, my legal status in Nigeria prevented me from undertaking any commercial activity. David continued seeking work and, before I left Jos, had been able to find part-time and temporary jobs as a driver.

I learned that David had got his job with the European mining operator through a Hausa, a man he called his friend and with whom he was a fellow worker several years ago. It turned out, on further inquiry, that almost all of the jobs he had got came through such acquaintances, and not through fellow tribesmen or kinsmen. During his years on the minesfield David had made many non-Ibo friends, and they had often helped one another in finding jobs or staying with one another when looking for work. Here was a comradeship that crossed tribal lines. However, his friendly relations with non-Ibo did not detract from David's strong traditional orientation nor his ethnic loyalties.

For example, David took pride in the fact that at his family compound at home nine generations of people were buried. He wanted to be buried there, and he thought it was proper that his wives should be laid to rest there also. His first wife was, but the one who had died in Jos he could not afford to ship home for burial. The Jos cemetery in which she lay was not a "real cemetery," like the one at his lineage land, nor were the funeral ceremonies held for her in Jos "proper," as were those which took place at home. Nor was the wake held in Jos the real thing. At home people would cut banana fronds to dance with. In Jos there are no banana trees, and even if there were, it is illegal to cut trees. At home guns and small mortars would be fired, but this too was not allowed in Jos. At home a big drum would be sounded and people would march through the market to signify that an adult had died. Many cowry shells would be thrown to the attending crowd, and a goat, a fowl, and other offerings would be sacrificed at the shrines of the ancestors. Similar sacrifices would be made at the place where the wife used to bathe; but the titled men and priests to perform these rites, and the places where they must offer their prayers, were at home, not in Jos.

David said he was bound to perform the proper burial ceremonies for his departed wives. These funeral services, called second burials, can only be done at his natal home, and he estimated they would cost him about sixty-five pounds, an amount he thought he could save if he worked steadily for a year. He said these ceremonies must be performed to avoid misfortunes which the displeased ghosts could bring; but no one would lend him so large an amount for such a purpose. David was in a desperate situation, for if he failed his dead, he would begin having nightmares, his skin would itch and trouble him, he or members of his family would fall ill, and his remaining property could be damaged, stolen, or lost. He would know, of course, what the cause was, but he felt he would still go to a native diviner for confirmation.

However, he had faith only in the native doctors at home—those in Jos were frauds—and it was for that reason that he would never seek service from a native doctor away from home. If David or anyone in his family was ill, he would always go to a clinic or hospital, unless he was at home or he suspected that there was a supernatural cause for the illness and that it could be cured only by practitioners at home. Maintaining this blend of traditional orientation and empirical objectivity, he once told me he would like his children to grow up to be professionals—perhaps doctors or engineers—but he also wanted them to know traditional lore.

When the pickin [children] begin grow small bit, then time for hear teaching. For evening time I put 'em down for hear story. I tell 'em for family fashion, tell 'em how family begin, tell 'em wonderful stories of things what happen for our people and for our town. Sometime, evening time, we wait for quiet time, teach 'em how world be, teach 'em how to pick proper wife, look round before put hand [court or claim a wife]. I tell 'em they shouldn't play with so-ŝo-girl because her family branch our brother [kinsmen]. All that we talk 'em.

When I first started interviewing David he reported himself an unbaptized Roman Catholic. In Jos he attended Sunday services at the Catholic church occasionally, but out in the bush he could attend only the available mission services, which were invariably Protestant. David was not deeply committed to Catholicism and his second wife, a baptized Catholic, had not been buried by a priest. He himself once told me that when he finally retired to Issele Uku, he would not attend any church, because he believed in the efficacy and validity of his ancestors' religion.

However, during the year in which I knew him, David underwent a radical conversion. He developed a pattern of attending church regularly—no longer the Catholic church, but the Cherubim and Seraphim (a syncretic church). Furthermore, in contrast to the general pattern of a wife bringing her husband to a church or separatist church she had already joined, it was David who brought his wife to the Cherubim and Seraphim. He told me how he came to join this group during an extremely trying period of his life. His explanation of his conversion emphasized the expressive activities of solidarity and support that were provided in this congregation.[1]

Some of my townsmen to go that church, and when this thing happen to me they come here to pray for me. From there I start to join them. I go there [to church] everyday. My wife and I go every morning from nine to ten-thirty. In evening time we go five-thirty, close by seven. Saturday we go ten at night and come home two in the morning. Sunday morning nine we must go again. If I got job and go for bush, I can't go, but other times I always go. When I go for bush, I tell them [the members], then they pray for me to go and come back well.

Over there we just kneel and pray. You can go there to pray for job, money, health, family should be well and not hungry. [I suggested this could be done in any church.] No, you can't! You can't go to

1. See the discussion on the social and psychological functions of religious groups in Chapter III.

Roman Catholic church and lie down and everybody come round you and pray for you. Roman Catholic Church no fit to do that.

Everyday some people pray for me and I pray for some people. People also pray for my wife. My wife take the pickin and people pray for them. Anything worrying you, then you talk to the people. Then everybody stand up and pray for you. Some of our people [from Issele Uku] there, and then more different, different, different [tribes]. Plenty Yoruba, Calabar, Ibo, Shosho [peoples of central Northern Nigeria]. We call each other "brother." If I get money then I sew my own white robe [the uniform of the church].

In contrast to his earlier statement about returning to traditional supernatural beliefs and practices when he finally retired home, David now held that he would rejoin this group in Issele Uku, where a branch had been established.

He had no idea when he might return home. He wanted to erase the debts he had incurred in Jos, and he was ashamed to return home with nothing to give his relatives and others who would expect him to throw a lavish "big chop" in celebration of his homecoming. He insisted on returning and retiring properly, and had laid the way for his return home during his more affluent days, when he had begun building his retirement house on his lineage land. He had invested about five hundred pounds in its construction, and it would be complete when the ceilings and walls were plastered and the windows installed. The work was done in stages —whenever David had saved some money for this purpose—supervised at first by his relatives and later, by his first wife. David would know that he had overcome all his difficulties when he could return to this completed building "in proper fashion."

Pam Choji Kwol: Birom

I have been focusing these personal histories on some central concern, or major problem area, of each informant. Pam Choji was most concerned with maintaining his important administrative post, and the material security it provided, which he believed was threatened by persons who held enmity toward him within the local government administration. He also thought that political factions within his own tribe were a source of danger to him in his job. His office permitted him a measure of wealth and respect not only far superior to that common for his own Birom tribe and rural background, but quite superior to that of most residents in Jos of any ethnic background. Pam claimed he was not so much ambitious to advance his position as he was to maintain the gains he had made, for he had risen rapidly in his career. Such immediate political success is not uncommon in Nigeria, especially in the Northern Region, where qualified young men are few. Pam told me of his ascent:

I came to Jos early in 1958 to take over as ————. Prior to that I was District Head of Kwol. When I was *Da Gwom* [Birom for "Chief of"] Kwol, I was found to be an exemplary District Head. My district was the only one in the whole Plateau Province that ran smoothly and accomplished things. On the strength of Resident Weatherhead's recommendation, I was appointed ————, when the previous one was dismissed for stealing Jos Native Authority property.

The man Pam replaced was the son of one of the most powerful Birom political leaders, a man whose own position had once been threatened by a group of young men from several Plateau tribes. Pam Choji had been among those who had unsuccessfully tried to oust him.

I became the District Head of Kwol in 1953 because I was the obvious choice after the previous District Head had been dismissed for fraud. He was convicted for receiving land compensation for a farm he claimed was his and which belonged to someone else. He is my lineage brother, and I was the only one in the family who had sufficient education for the job. [Pam was only nineteen at the time and many considered him too young for such a responsible position.] I was the only well-educated person in my family, and I had the necessary traditional knowledge because my family was a traditional one. The people felt that with my Western education, I could better cope with modern trends.

The District Council I headed was so outstanding that the Resident sent out a circular letter to all the N.A.'s throughout the Province, stating that if they wanted to modernize their councils they should send observers to the Kwol District Council.

Pam does give the appearance of a modern-oriented young African, and for a long time I was in doubt about the extent to which traditional beliefs influenced him. His assertions that he never went to native doctors or used native medicines inclined me to believe that he was unique among Africans in rejecting supernatural beliefs. Then one day he told me he had heard about a strange creature seen at the Jos airport: a two-mouthed, four-legged man who was being kept hidden. He ordinarily lived in a cave and shunned people, yet now some people were taking him on a tour of the country. He was capable of telling anything at all about a person, and he could cure the lame and blind. Pam believed that the prodigious creature truly existed.

But if Pam is to be designated a traditionalist or a modernist, it is necessary to indicate precisely in which ways he is oriented in either direction. He is actually bipolar (as this account will show), but in dress, the first indication of a person's self-image, he is almost absolutely a traditionalist. Pam does not wear or own any Western clothing other than undergarments, socks, and shoes. Most of his suits were tailored in what might be called a modern mixed Yoruba-Fulani style. Meticulous about what he wears, Pam always selects expensive imported materials, some sent by friends from England, which he has tailored according to his own designs. He prefers caftans, and his taste is conservative—he prefers subtle color combinations and a harmony between the texture and weave of the material and the pattern of hand-embroidered designs.

I had known Pam Choji socially before requesting his assistance as an informant, and my initial estimation that he was widely known and well liked did not change. His friends call him *Sarki* [Hausa for "Chief"] or *Da Gwom,* and they express in the name feelings more of endearment than respect. A consensus of opinion ranks him as one of the most friendly and generous persons among the young modern elite in Jos. He is not one to put on airs, and I have witnessed him be polite to a boorish young man whom he later, when we were alone, characterized appropriately. Pam is a gentleman.

Pam was uncertain of the year in which he was born, but he thought he was twenty-seven years old at the time of interviews. Assuming this estimate to be correct, he was born in 1934 in Kwol, a Birom village which is in Jos Division of Plateau Province. He was one of his parents' five children (three daughters and two sons) who survived to adulthood. Like himself, Pam's brother and sisters were married and had children. The eldest sister, who had three children, died in 1956. Pam's parents both died in 1948, his father of leprosy. His father was about fifty and his mother was about forty-five. They had been simple farmers, had received no formal education whatsoever, and were traditionalists in their religious beliefs. His father must have been comparatively wealthy (for a Birom), since a horse was killed when he died, and its skin placed in his grave. He came from a Birom priestly lineage, but had himself never held sacred or secular office.

For a Birom of his time, Pam Choji had received considerable formal education. After seven years of attending school, which did not include university or college experience, he became District Head of Kwol. After a year as District Head, he took a leave of several months to attend a course in local government at the Zaria Institute of Administration, and two years after he had settled in Jos he took a course in administration at the British Council Summer School in Kano. Pam had fluent command of Birom, Hausa, and English, although he was self-conscious about his stammering in all of them. He said he stuttered worst in Birom, so badly that he was sometimes unintelligible. His brothers and father had the same difficulty.

Just before I left Nigeria, Pam came to tell me that the Jos Native Authority Council had recommended him as a candidate for a course in local government given at a university in England. Pam was quite excited about this, and it seemed that it was merely a matter of time and formalities before he would be studying in the United Kingdom, but it was not long before he encountered considerable difficulty. On the basis of his past record, the Resident had highly recommended him, but Pam's enemies in the N.A. tried various means to block his departure. They tried to recommend someone else in his place, and they tried to deny him a leave of absence from his post. Pam was also required to take a Nigeria-wide competitive examination, and in this he did not do very well. He was therefore placed on a list of alternates, and was not among the first Nigerians to participate in the program. (He later wrote to me that in early 1963 he was finally able to go to England to take the university course.)

When Pam and I first became acquainted he tended to deny that he held strong ambitions of rising further in public office, but as our interviews proceeded this modesty dimmed. There were several goals which he hoped to achieve—considering his abilities, neither the goals nor his hopes were unrealistic—and many, if not all of his life decisions were calculated to enhance his ambitions. Becoming Chief of Jos held high priority among them. To make his ambitions more possible, Pam had to be careful of committing errors of commission or omission. He had to avoid affiliating with certain political parties, avoid accepting administrative positions that might block further advancement, and avoid cutting ties with persons who might aid him in the future, and he had to cultivate friendships and contacts that would serve as supports, and even make the right choices with regard to marriage. In his own estimation, he had thus far made few mistakes in his behavior, choices, and actions.

Pam had once been invited to train for the position of an Assistant District Officer, but he turned this offer down because he would be "under the thumb of an Emir or Chief, and if you tried to bring in some reforms you would be discouraged. If you persisted and wouldn't take his hints, you'd be gone forever. Then your career is ruined, unless you tried going into politics, and then you couldn't be with the leading party." (The Emirs and Chiefs in the Northern Region were associated with the ruling Northern Peoples Congress, whose ideologies Pam did not uphold. If he were to run for political office, Pam's chances of success lay with the N.P.C., but his sympathies lay with, and his friends were members of, the opposition parties.)

Within the administrative structure of Jos Division, Pam had risen as far as any appointed official could go. He held the topmost grade and had reached the maximum annual salary of £564. While holding this office, he was also petitioning for a change of grade in which his salary would begin at £590 and extend to over one thousand, and his chances of getting this grade change would be considerably enhanced if he went to the United Kingdom for the course in local government.

Pam felt that if he lost his job while he was still a young man he would go into politics, but that he would have to enter them at the federal level in order to lessen the difficulties he perceived in Northern Region political involvements. On the other hand, he thought that if he remained with his present post and eventually retired from it, he would return to his natal area to live out the remainder of his life free of political and administrative activity, spending his time instead in looking after his property and investments at home.

It would be a betrayal to my people and a degradation to my prestige if I, who was once a District Head and who comes from a chiefly family, were to remain in Jos after my service with the N.A. is completed. After serving successfully in all my capacities, it would be a source of pride to me to live in my own District. I would be highly regarded, it would be considered dignified.

Pam not only desired to become Chief of Jos, he thought he had a good chance of getting the position. He once said, "That position isn't hereditary, and some people are saying that I'm the best qualified candidate." This chieftaincy is associated with Jos Division, rather than with the city of Jos, and because of the large predominance of Birom in the Division, a Birom has always held the chieftaincy. However, when the present Chief of Jos tried to make the position hereditary, the other tribes of the Division, and many Birom, protested so vehemently that the Ministry for Local Government, in Kaduna, declared that the position would be open to any qualified candidate who was from a tribe native to Jos Division. Pam Choji had played one of the more important parts in the demand for a non-hereditary chieftaincy. Unless the present Chief is removed from office for malfeasance, he will remain Chief until he retires voluntarily or dies in office, but since he has had several serious illnesses in the past few years, many considered that the position would soon be open. However, at the time of the writing of this chapter, the old Chief of Jos was still in power, and I am told that his health is apparently improving with age.

Pam had married twice; he took his first wife in 1953, and his second in 1955. Both his wives are Birom women, both live with Pam in Jos, and the three live together harmoniously. Pam's first wife comes from Kwol, and is about two years younger than he. They first met in 1947, in primary school, and became childhood sweethearts. Their courtship and marriage followed traditional Birom lines. However, necessity and, to some extent, Pam's ambitions forced certain modifications in the traditional marriage customs. For example, Pam's father was seriously handicapped with leprosy at the beginning of the marriage negotiations, and so the responsibilities of the marriage devolved upon Pam's older brother. Again, Pam should have worked on his father-in-law's farm, but he did not do so, initially because he was attending school and subsequently because he had become a District Head, for whom farm work would have been unbecoming. His older brother and other kinsmen substituted for him in this obligation. Further, Pam's wife did not come to live with him until a month after he took office as *Da Gwom* [District Head of] Kwol. This also involved a breach of custom. "Traditionally a *Da Gwom* candidate needs a wife, for the installation ceremony requires his wife to take part. My wife wasn't part of the swearing-in ceremony, and in this respect I broke with tradition. I was also by that time a Christian."

Pam's first wife had gone no further than her elementary schooling, which had given her some instruction in Hausa, and she spoke no English. Other than housework, she does no work, and no longer trades. Pam said she had once undertaken petty trading, selling milk, tea, soap, and sundries, but people bought things on credit and failed to pay their bills. Later, Pam supported her sewing lessons, but they were abandoned when the seamstress tutor left Jos. Pam regards his first wife as admirable in almost all respects. Only one trait of hers annoys him; she constantly wants to visit home.

It's very expensive for me to let her go all the time. She can't visit her parents with empty hands. At the same time she wants to take my son. I don't like the idea of taking him because they have no idea of hygiene. Neither the house [a mud hut] nor the food is hygienic. It's not good for a child.

His first wife's first child was still-born, but her second was, during the time of this research, a healthy six-year-old boy. Since having her second child, she became pregnant again, but her complaints of illness led to an abortion at the Catholic Maternity Hospital. Subsequent examinations have concluded that she should be able to continue having children. Pam said he rarely saw his first wife's parents, but he occasionally sent them a little cloth and a few shillings, especially during the farming season, so that they might hire some additional labor.

Pam's second wife was about a year younger than he, and had been married and divorced twice. Before marrying Pam she had had three children, all of whom died. Since her marriage to Pam she had had a girl, in 1957, followed by a boy in 1960. She did not come from Kwol, but from a village nearby, and the manner in which Pam arranged this marriage reflects his concern with matters that may in any way affect his career.

I met her when I was District Head and President of the Kwol District Court. She came there to divorce her first husband. When I saw her in court I became interested in her, and I decided to marry her because I felt that she was a well-mannered woman. [In court she told how badly her husband treated her.]

From her comportment in court I was convinced that she would be a good wife and housekeeper, but for me to start courting her directly, as President of the Court and the person who decided the case, was indelicate. I had to maintain the dignity of the Court. I couldn't marry her directly so I arranged with her to marry someone else. Her second husband didn't know he was being used this way. She walked into the man's compound one day and two months later she walked out and I married her right after that.

Of course she didn't come directly to my house. When she left her second husband she went to her parents and complained that she didn't want the man. Her parents said that since he hadn't paid for her they would look for another husband. I sent my senior brother to arrange the dowry bridewealth with them. By then she was having a child by her first husband, so I paid £11 instead of £16. If I had paid sixteen, I would have been the father of the child, but in this way the child was to have gone to the first husband, if it had lived. The dowry was paid to the first husband.

My junior wife possesses the same good qualities as my senior wife, but she's more sympathetic. What I mean is, well, for example, my co-tenant is an Ibo man, and when his wives went home she took it upon herself to make hot water for him in the morning or to make tea for him or to wash his dishes.

In lauding his wife for such acts of consideration, Pam also expresses his own attitudes of neighborliness and inter-tribal good will.

His second wife had never gone to school (she spoke no English), but his first wife taught her how to read and write in Hausa. This is indicative of how well the wives get on together. Together they attend Sunday services at an almost exclusively Birom congregation. Whenever they visit other Birom women in Jos they go together. (There is a concentration of Birom in Pam's neighborhood.) Pam says they are friendly and try to do things together in part because they want each other's company, and in part because it signifies their solidarity. Pam is deeply concerned about his wives' congeniality, which would explain why he once became upset when this symbolic solidarity was threatened.

The previous Christmas he quarreled with his first wife over a holiday dress. He gave his wives money to buy new cloths for Christmas, and was under the impression that they would have identical costumes, but his first wife bought a different kind of cloth. Pam wanted the identical dresses to serve as symbols of his wives' equality and solidarity. He interpreted his first wife's behavior as a gesture that she might want to appear superior to her co-wife. But such incidents in Pam's household are uncommon. More typical are the indications of cooperation. For example, Pam and his wives were planning together the basic architectural design of the house Pam intended to build in Jos. All three, together, had decided that they wanted to set aside a little area that would serve as a shop where both wives could sew and carry on petty trading. Pam promised to buy them sewing machines as soon as the house was completed.

Even though Pam was happy to include his wives in some of his planning, he kept some areas of conjugal relationship closed to them. Pam's wives did not know how much he earned, and the manner in which he gave them money for household and personal expenses was strictly within a traditional Birom pattern. It was he who bought such major food items as grains and yams, and he gave each a fixed monthly allowance for other food needs. If they ran short, he would give them a little more. And when the wives requested money to buy clothing for the children or to obtain some other household, family, or personal need, Pam remained the comptroller. Pam also had a personal social life which he did not share with his wives.

My wives do get annoyed with me sometimes, generally because I come home late from drinking, and sometimes very drunk, and then I disturb them. From there they may suspect that I'm chasing some woman—which is true. They usually tell me that as a responsible person I ought not to be coming in late or to be spending money lavishly, and that I ought to be putting something away for the security of the children. If they really knew I was chasing [women], they wouldn't like it. One day they accused me of having a girl friend, but the girl they accused wasn't my [girl] friend. She was my friend's girl, but they never believed me that she was his girl friend.

Pam had no wish to marry a third time, but said that if he ever did, he would probably marry a Birom girl, and one that was raised in the traditional manner to be industrious and courteous. Not an insignificant consideration was the fact that a Birom girl would require a small bridewealth. "I would prefer a fairly educated girl because she would understand me better and respect me in a modern way of life. She could be easily taught to welcome V.I.P.'s into my home, and if I'm convinced that she could cope with the situation, I would take her to parties and dinners." When I told Pam that he would have better luck finding an educated girl from another tribe, he answered, "She must be a Birom girl! I would better understand a Birom girl than a girl from another tribe. If I married someone else, I would not be respected by my family. It could also be used as propaganda against me if I were a candidate for the position of Chief of Jos. Other Birom would think I don't respect Birom tradition. But if I were a politician that might strengthen my position. But the girl would have to be from a Plateau tribe."

Pam's children, in accordance with Birom tradition, had his first name as their last name, just as Pam's last name was his father's first name. His eldest son, Gyang Pam, had begun attending St. Luke's Junior Primary School, rather than the N.A. School (where Pam could have easily enrolled him), so that he might, in accordance with his father's wishes, receive some religious instruction. "Secondly," he said, "at the N.A. School there are mostly Hausa and Hausa is mostly spoken. I want him to learn to speak English well." Pam would like to see Gyang marry a Birom girl, but he would not object if he did not, as long as the match was suitable. "Nor would I object if he wanted to become a Muslim. I wouldn't object at all. I'm not that keen a Christian. I'm tolerant." Like all informants, Pam wanted his children to receive a university education, provided he were able to finance it if scholarships could not be obtained. He thought his son should choose to study the subject of his own interest, but Pam said he would be pleased if the boy were to study law, since that was his own favorite profession.

He also wanted his four-year-old daughter, Gatok Pam, to attend St. Luke's School, and he wanted her to attend a university, preferably one overseas. "I want my children to have an opportunity of mingling with different peoples and learning more about different ways of life. I'd like my daughter to study medicine because, as a female, she has courtesy and kindness. If she were intelligent, I think she would be a good doctor." He would prefer seeing his baby son, Taki Pam, go into teaching because he thought that siblings should take to different professions.

In addition to his wives and children, two unrelated Birom boys live with Pam. These are children of friends, and they were ten and twelve years old when I knew Pam. Their fathers are farmers in Kwol. They had lived with Pam a little more than a year, in order to be able to attend the N.A. Senior Primary School. This arrangement will continue until they leave school. Pam feeds them and sometimes gives them clothing, but their parents are primarily responsible for clothing them, buying their school uniforms, and paying their school fees. However, Pam said that he had been paying their school fees, and he does not consider that his friends will be indebted to him with money for this favor. Sometimes these friends express their appreciation by sending Pam some of their farm produce for his family. The boys also help out around the house by cleaning, washing, and heating Pam's bath water.

Within his means, which is considerable by local standards, Pam liked to live well. He owned a slightly-used car that he had bought for £470, and his living quarters were pleasantly and adequately furnished with linoleum carpets, locally-manufactured cushioned furniture, small tables, book cabinets, a radio-phonograph, and other items which taken all together indicated a standard of comfort far above the average in Jos.

When Pam first came to Jos, in 1958, he was forced temporarily to take inadequate accommodations. A second place, in which he lived for ten months, had more space for his family, but still was cramped. Pam's current living quarters were rented initially from a Birom politician of one of the opposition parties, who had previously lived in it with his family. The politician sold the house to two Ibo who did not live there but rented its rooms to five families. In addition to Pam's family, these included another Birom family, two Ibo, and one family that came from a Plateau tribe near Pankshin. The house is substantially built of concrete block and has an iron roof. Pam rented four rooms: a bedroom for each wife and their children (Pam slept alternately in each bedroom), a parlor, and a guest room. The last was used by the two Birom school boys and for storage.

Mentioned earlier was Pam's considerable investment in personal attire. His other investments include real estate and productive property. He was building a new house for himself in Jos which would cost over seven hundred pounds. In addition to property at home, which he owns jointly with other members of his lineage, he owns a completed house in a town near Kwol that he built in 1957 specifically for renting. It holds three Ibo families, a Yoruba family, and the local office of one of the opposition parties, all of which brings in a rent income of about ten pounds a month. He has also bought about twenty acres of barren land on which he has planted a crop of trees. When these mature in a few years, they can be cut down and used as poles to carry electric wires for mining companies, and the branches can be used for firewood, which brings a good price in Jos. Finally, he has invested in a small herd of cattle and smaller livestock, which is cared for at home by his older brother. A substantial portion of Pam's income, however, goes for conviviality with friends over beer and extra-marital sexual relations.

People seeking Pam after office hours generally find him drinking beer with male friends in a pub; invariably, several girls are also with him. Women are his weakness, and he appears to be their weakness as well. Pam's reputation as a womanizer is well earned. People who knew Pam would sometimes express amazement that a man so lacking in physical beauty could possess such a wealth of charm.

According to his own account, he developed his interest in women after leaving school, for during his school days he was brought up in a missionary way of life to believe that sexual relations were immoral. Since leaving school he has behaved as if he were over-compensating for the enforced continence of his youth. He has had girl friends for as long as he has been married. At the time of our interviews he sought out a new bedmate once or twice a week, but initially his relationships could extend for several months or longer. He mentioned that when he lived in Kwol he was with a particular

Yoruba girl long enough for her to be regarded as his mistress. She wanted to marry him, but he refused. "For a whole year she tried persuading me to marry her, but as District Head, and being a Birom, it was impossible for me to marry her, a non-Birom. Otherwise I would have married her." In these affairs Pam was always courting some danger. Pam related one incident that was costly, and could have been even more disastrous. "I had another girl friend who was Hausa. She also came to my court to get a divorce from her husband. After I gave her a divorce I asked a friend to see her for me. He did and she agreed to being my friend. I had to contact her through a friend, because a District Head can't go around chasing girls on the street." This affair cost Pam £50, and nearly cost him his job. The girl's former husband learned what was going on and claimed the exorbitant amount of £50 as his bridewealth. If Pam did not pay this amount, the husband threatened to take the matter to the Alkali Court and claim that Pam engineered his divorce. It was clearly blackmail, but Pam paid and the matter was kept private.

In addition to not wanting to have mistresses now because he preferred variety, Pam pointed out that the responsibilities of his present job and the expenses of his family were too great for such sport. In Kwol he had lived in his family house, which cost him no rent, and he had farms of his own so that food cost him little. In Jos living was too expensive.

Although aware of the financial and social inconveniences that could result from his adulterous behavior, Pam seemed unwilling to abandon it. When I once asked him why he continued his extramarital affairs with other women, his answer was bluntly simple:

Just to have sexual intercourse with them, that's all. Sometimes you meet somebody in the pub, and from there you start arranging. Generally these are waitresses. Sometimes you may hear from a friend that there's a beautiful girl at such and such a place, and you send him to call her for you. If you see a girl who appeals to you walking along the street, then you ask a friend from that street about her. If he says it's O.K., you ask him to speak with her, and if he comes back and tells you he's spoken with her successfully, you tell him to tell her to meet you at such and such a place at such and such a time. They are always different girls.

If she hasn't got a place of her own, we could go to a hotel. A room for a night is seven shillings, six pence. Some girls will go for nothing after having been given a few beers in a pub, while others will want some money and may be given five or ten shillings. We Africans see a pretty face and immediately we want to go to bed with that girl. We like a change.

My wives actually know I'm chasing, but they can't catch me red-handed at it. I don't think they could ever catch me, but if they did they would fight with the girl, not with me. Naturally, they would be jealous of someone interfering with their own property. They wouldn't much consider the waste of money involved.

Pam was also concerned about contracting venereal disease, and, in this regard, he showed consideration for the safety of his wives.

I had gotten gonorrhea once which a pharmacist friend of mine cured through injections and tablets. I don't know whether he had a license for giving injections. Since then I've had no trouble; I leave it to luck. Whenever I meet an outside girl, I'll stay away from my wives for a week so I can see if there'll be a reaction.

Pam's reasons for philandering should be accepted as valid, but they are by nature cultural rationalizations. There are additional reasons that lie on a different cultural level or dimension, and I will offer one. Pam is not alone in his behavior, although he is exceptionally successful at it. Adultery is a common practice among married men who live in urban areas and hold modern cultural orientations, although the degree to which persons indulge in it will vary considerably. In this respect, it is legitimate to regard such behavior as culturally expected, however much lip-service is given in favor of greater puritanism. I believe adultery is a carryover from some traditional values associated with polygyny; namely, power and wealth. Traditionally, a man indicated his possession of these desired qualities in the number of wives he had been able to acquire and the size of the household he was able to maintain. It is much less possible for a man to maintain a polygynous household under modern urban conditions, but a man who demonstrates his wealth in his ability to acquire women, and in his attractiveness to women (for whatever reasons), is envied and admired by his peers.

Pam Choji enjoyed people, especially the company of close friends, and people reciprocated this sentiment. I observed that no matter how convivial and gay a group might be, the appearance of Pam on the scene heightened the pleasure of everyone. For example, sitting with him, one could be sure of being amused by the flirtations that took place between him and the waitresses or other women who might be in the vicinity. Pam has many friends, extending over many tribes, and he could invariably be seen with them during the afternoon or evening, drinking at a pub or relaxing at the Recreation Club. Pam was usually with fellow employees and superior office holders of the Jos Native Authority. They would get together after working hours to "cool down" with beer; they sometimes added to their pleasure by munching peanuts, roast chicken, lamb, or goat meat. Because most of the staff of the Jos Native Authority consists of northerners, only a few of Pam's office friends are southerners. He meets most of his southern friends at the Saturday night dances, and at the Recreation Club. The members of this club, and that of the other athletic and social clubs in Jos and Bukuru, have been trying for years to persuade Pam to become a member, but he has been most reluctant to join them. He has joined one or two clubs that have small initiation fees and light dues, although he never attends formal membership meetings; but in other cases he has refused to join, always providing a variety of excuses such as momentary financial difficulties or inability to participate regularly.

It might appear that Pam has an aversion to joining formal organizations, for he rarely goes to church, and, as a civil servant, is prohibited from political party membership. With regard to his political sympathies, his career potentials as a northern civil servant would be nonexistent were these sentiments commonly known, although, I might add, they are more than merely suspected by the Northern People's Congress politicians in Jos and Kaduna. For these reasons, it served him better not to be too closely associated with modern elite African social clubs in Jos, which are recognized as dominated by southerners. However, there was one voluntary association to which Pam felt strongly committed: an organization that did not yet exist. He wanted to create a Birom tribal union, or at least to start an improvement union for Kwol people, working up gradually to a more inclusive body. With this aim in mind, he had obtained from a Yoruba friend a copy of the formal constitution and bylaws of a Yoruba tribal union, upon which he intended to model the constitution of his own envisioned ethnic organization. But because of the political strife and factionalism that had developed among the Birom over the past few years, Pam did not intend to move too rapidly in this plan.

Pam, then, seemed to want to preserve something of the past. I could not attempt to explain here the basis of his desire, nor what meanings this area of his life held for him, but he obviously had wistful feelings about old traditions. He once told me:

When I was District Head, every Sunday I used to gather the elders, buy them *sirin* [Birom for "native beer"], and they used to tell me ancient stories. From there one could pick up the traditions. Learning Birom custom is interwoven with juju practice, and Christians would object to that. We can only educate our children generally in Birom traditions, and the rest they will have to pick up from anthropology books. For instance, I can't now follow our practice of doing special things, such as secretly drawing water at night from a special place when my wife is about to give birth to her first child, or to bury my child's umbilical cord at a special *tsafi* [Hausa for "sacred"] area. My children haven't yet reached the age where they could understand these things, but they're now being taught the names of the family members, to know my father's name and my father's father's name and the names of all my ancestors back to the original founder of the homestead, which goes back eight or nine generations. The only thing we can do is to try to tell our children about how our fathers used to do things.

Chapter IX

SUMMARY AND DISCUSSION
OF THE INFORMANTS

T HIS chapter reviews the lives of the principal informants presented in Chapters IV–VII and attempts to place them analytically within the fabric of modern urban life in Jos, relating their
different patterns of adjustment to historical, social, and cultural
determinants. The fact that an individual was born at a particular
time and place, into a certain family and community, influences his
life chances, his career, occupation, religious and political affiliations, etc. Discussion of each informant's prior personal experiences, whether unique to himself or shared with other members of
his culture, should lead to an understanding of the significant influences on his manner of adjustment to urban life.

Because of its cool climate, extensive mining activities, and large
population of relatively permanent European residents, Jos contrasts with most West African urban centers and is reminiscent of
modern cities in East, Central, and South Africa. The number of
Europeans, who were first attracted to the area by the prospect of
tin ore mining, swelled when Jos became an administrative center
and a transportation and communications hub. The African population reflects the great ethnic diversity of Nigeria in rough approxi-
mation to their national proportions.

Although the large European population encouraged an early and generous development of social services and amenities, the colonial government's segregation policy based on race in the use of these facilities rankled Nigerian nationalists. The European bias in favor of Muslim northern Nigerians further aggravated the sensitivity of southerners, who formed the core of the educated, modern Nigerian elite, oriented toward Western culture, and did little to alleviate the traditional animosity between southerners and northerners. In 1945 these ethnic and religious antagonisms resulted in a riot in Jos; however, most often they found expression in local and national political activities. Economic competition formed part of the undercurrent of hostility, and political activities in turn had economic consequences. Southerners, who held favorable positions in the past because of the skills they obtained through Western education received earlier than northerners, were being effectively displaced by northerners, due to the Northernization Policy of the Northern Regional Government.

In Jos, as well as in other cities of the Northern Region, the southern "aliens" who were initially attracted to the area by its economic opportunities have become rooted over the years and now bitterly resent the current pressures placed upon them. While they frequently assert the wish to leave Jos, where they are not welcome, and to return to their tribal homelands, they sometimes also verbalize a reluctance to do so. The fact is that most cannot return to their tribal areas and expect to resume their economic or occupational pursuits easily, for economic developments in their home areas have not kept pace with the technical skills which many educated individuals now possess. But their investments in Jos are not merely economic, for it is here that they experience a rewarding social life which they do not want to interrupt.

To many southerners, Jos represented an advance toward the ideal of modernization and the bright future projected for an ethnically integrated Nigeria. The discrimination based on tribal origin and a forced return to the tribal area carry the implications of traditional parochialism and a reversion to the past. These polar ideas—

modern versus traditional—do not serve as foci sharply dividing the population, but are attributes held by everyone to varying degrees. The most ardent conservatives to some extent value the modernization of Nigeria, often expressed in the wish to have their children or grandchildren receive a substantial formal education. And Nigerians who are modern-oriented hold nostalgic sentiments for tribal traditions.

Just as past colonial policy and expatriate attitudes toward blacks heightened African nationalism and helped submerge tribal differences, so have such features as the Northernization Policy worked in the reverse by inhibiting the decline of ethnic loyalties and even encouraging the resumption of very parochial allegiances. Thus it is not surprising that individuals in Jos may hold office or be prominent members of modern Western institutions—school boards, traders associations, church congregations, political parties, trade unions, social culbs, and international fraternal orders—in which they interact with members of other tribes, while at the same time participating in tradition-oriented institutions such as tribal unions.

Isaac Olu Oyewumi

Isaac Olu Oyewumi, the 60-year-old Yoruba informant, was born in the old Yoruba city of Ogbomosho, and was raised there in the tradition of the Yoruba people. He came to Jos in his early twenties to seek his fortune, following a pattern typical of Ogbomosho men who traditionally traded far afield and who, just after the founding of Jos, became a part of the initial core of its African mercantile element. Olu's lack of formal education and his inability to speak English were no more of a handicap to him in achieving great wealth through trading than they had been to many of his illiterate Yoruba contemporaries and forefathers.

Olu considered his marriages and family life successful and emotionally rewarding, except his third marriage which produced no living children and ended in an early divorce. His other two marriages were stable and notably fruitful. Many of his children were married, had children of their own, and had been, on the whole, successful in their own careers.

That Olu chose a Baptist Christian religious affiliation is not remarkable when we realize that the vast majority of Christians in Ogbomosho are Baptists, constituting almost half the city's total population. Olu delayed making this personal decision until he had lived in Jos for a while, but he could have just as well still been living in Ogbomosho as far as conditioning influences are concerned, for the Ogbomosho community in Jos is large, localized, and has a stronger sense of corporate identity than do other ethnic groups in Jos. It is a tightly-knit community wherein one would expect that the applied social pressures designed to influence decisions of political and religious affiliations would be the same as those in Ogbomosho.

A core value held by Olu was maintaining the dignity and good reputation of his immediate lineage. This traditional Yoruba ideal, which he verbalized as keeping the family name spotless, could be upheld only by constant unreproachable conduct. This was a difficult burden, for a single thoughtless act by himself or any person under his charge could undo the results of generations of self-control and create a blemish that would be remembered and recalled in the future. Nor could he, as he put it, rest on his laurels. Therefore, Olu was civic-minded, participating actively in many community organizations, and at one time even serving as a Jos Town Council member. He was a prominent member of his traders' organization and the Baptist Church and a leader of various Yoruba tribal voluntary associations.

Elements in Olu's account suggest that he valued Yoruba tradition all the more because of his lack of a Western education and command of English, a lack which denied him a wider range of opportunities to exploit for the enhancement of his prestige. He could not direct more of his energies into Western-type or national institutions, such as assuming political party leadership, toward which, I suspect, his intelligence and drive inclined him.

Sensitive to his public image, he constantly validated his earned prestige by doing good works and maintaining the deportment of a socially prestigious figure. He was equally committed to his own integrity and ethic, so that he readily assumed the roles of mediator in the family disputes of friends, neighbors, and relatives, and of guardian of the welfare of other people's children. In brief, he tried to be, and to a large extent was, the traditionally good Yoruba man with overlays of Western culture and Christian morality.

Isaac Cookey-Jaja

The 43-year-old Ijaw informant, Isaac, was born and raised in the Niger Delta area where the Anglican Church and its influence were established early in colonialization. He attended mission-sponsored schools, eventually becoming a civil engineer and beginning his own contracting business in the Northern Region. He held Anglican Church membership and was an active member of a congregation in Jos. Most Opobo Ijaw men of Isaac's generation have similar life histories; if they are not engineers, they very likely have a professional or white-collar job.

Outwardly, Isaac Cookey-Jaja appeared highly Europeanized, but a closer inspection revealed his strong adherence to traditional Opobo Ijaw culture. For a better understanding of this and some of Isaac's other characteristics, it is necessary to understand something of Ijaw culture and history. Prior to European administration, the Ijaw lacked an integrated polity of the scope and complexity of the Yoruba or Edo, with whom they had cultural and economic contacts. Ijaw political, social, and economic organization somewhat resembled the Greek maritime city-states, each polity being independent of the other, and the traditional autonomy and mutual hostility of traditional Ijaw polities such as Brass, Bonny, and Opobo are reflected today in their inability to achieve a pan-Ijaw integration. Historically, the Ijaw were imperialistic, economically and politically, and dominated the Nigerian peoples in and around the Niger Delta area. Their slaves came from such groups as the Ibo and the Ibibio, but the Ijaw society did not have a caste rigidity; men of proven ability could rise to high political office and achieve great wealth, and even slaves of foreign birth could become Ijaw chiefs. The Ijaw selected only those items of the European cultural inventory which suited them: bronze cannons for their large war canoes, tailored clothing, prefabricated houses, European furniture, and Western education and training. They were practiced international diplomats, pragmatic and skilled military strategists, and clever businessmen. The traditional Ijaw man has been described as proud, confident, and aggressive, his haughtiness extending even over Europeans. Extremely ethnocentric, the Ijaw traditionally held himself superior to all other peoples (see Dike 1959:17).

Like other Opobo men, Isaac's sense of superiority and confidence and his entrepreneurial spirit contributed to his pioneering sense of enterprise and his choice of a professional occupation. His confidence left him convinced that he could achieve whatever he set out to do. When the evidence of reality contradicted his self-assurance, he attributed his failures to mystical causes, thereby maintaining confidence in his own technical abilities. He showed an orientation toward innovation and experimentation, and boasted of his avant-garde engineering practices. Perhaps more than other Africans, because he was an Ijaw, he bitterly resented European attitudes of superiority toward himself and other Africans. Much of his energy was therefore directed toward demonstrating his equality with, if not superiority to, Englishmen, who symbolized the European for him.

His anger at being rebuffed by Europeans who did not welcome him as an equal was chauvinistically channeled into the idealization of African cultural elements, such as traditional forms of divination and the glories of Opobo's past. This reaction was also expressed in his militant Nigerian nationalism. With regard to these polar cultural elements, European as against African, he was oscillating rather than ambivalent in belief and behavior, syncretic rather than synthetic. The diverse cultural elements were not merged but remained distinct, so that it was possible for Isaac to shift back and forth between traditional Westernized and African behavior. In public he always wore Western clothing in good taste, spoke English flawlessly, and took pride in these accomplishments. He was equally proud of his skills as an architect, engineer, and mechanic. In private he consulted native diviners, following their prescriptions in such details as propitiating spirits and having his children's faces scarred to "disguise" them from the malevolent supernatural being who sought their souls. Isaac's supernatural beliefs may be generally considered as an example of his traditional orientation, but the particular form these beliefs took was somewhat idiosyncratic.

His American car, trucks, and heavy construction equipment belied his actual near-bankruptcy. His loss of prosperity, occasioned by a combination of personal circumstances and the northern government's discrimination against southerners, Isaac partly attributed to supernatural sanctions, which he had incurred through neglect of his personal spiritual mentors. After residing in Jos for fifteen years, Isaac began making efforts to remove the remains of his business to the Eastern Region, where he felt conditions would be more favorable for its revival and success. If he could successfully accomplish this transfer and rehabilitation, he thought he would go into semi-retirement and, because he was close to his natal home, assume more responsibilities in traditional activities. This incorporation of Western and traditional native goals and forms of behavior, each held as distinct and appropriate for specific times and places, is perhaps the most significant aspect of modern African urbanization at the individual level.

Isaac, like his ancestors, had a good deal of the cosmopolite about him. In spite of the Ijaw sense of superiority as a people, he was not bound by particularistic and parochial attitudes in his personal relationships. He could appreciate valued qualities in persons not of his tribe, as indicated by the fact that all but one of his closest friends were not Ijaw. Along with a cosmopolitan outlook he could also be parochial, but it was not always clear under what conditions one principle superseded another. He avoided the exclusively Ibo congregation of the Anglican Church, while the members of his own congregation were of many backgrounds. In acquiring a lawyer, his first choice was an Ijaw, but when he sought the services of native magicians, he readily expressed appreciation for the mystical reputations of various tribes. His father's two wives (including Isaac's own mother) were Ibo (as was his best friend), but Isaac insisted that his children follow his own example in marrying only Opobo Ijaw. While he felt an affinity toward Ibo, especially those of the Niger Delta area, whence came his servant girls with whom he and his family established fictive kinship relations, he could also express contrasting hostility toward them, especially in his national political views. In his alternating praise and deprecation of national political figures, he again demonstrated the pervasive Ijaw qualities of flexibility and opportunism.

Isaac felt that his marriage had been blessed. He admired, respected, and loved his wife, whom he considered as perfectly suited to him, especially because she combined traditional with modern elite orientations. Both were leaders in the activities of the Anglican Church and their tribal unions. His children were developing according to his ideals and ambitions for them, which included the realistic possibility that they might be educated at overseas universities.

Like the Yoruba informant, Isaac was a leader within his tribal community in Jos and was often called upon to mediate in disputes between spouses, kinsmen, or unrelated persons. He was eminently eligible for membership in the modern Nigerian elite, where his propensity for civic prominence could have been implemented, but his precarious financial situation forced him to decline reluctantly the repeated invitations to membership. He maintained friendships with individual members of the modern elite, thereby keeping open the opportunity for his future full entrance to their group, but he concentrated his community voluntary activities within his church and the tribal organizations of his fellow countrymen.

Gande Ikowe

The Tiv informant was born at the turn of the century and reared according to custom at his lineage home in a small hamlet. Gande Ikowe and his brothers were forbidden by their father to attend the Protestant mission school which had been started during his early childhood. In his boyhood he witnessed the first appearance of Europeans in his area, but Western cultural influences remained negligible there for a long time. In his own estimation he was in his youth a progressive, in his old age a conservative. As a boy he played truant from his father's farm and surreptitiously attended the mission school, as an old man he regretted that he had not acquired more of the traditional native lore that his father had been willing to give him. As a youth he left home (against his deceased parents' wishes) and joined the army, whereas his contemporaries chose to remain home and farm. At the time of the study he most fervently wished to return home and live out his life on his farm in a traditional Tiv manner; in contrast, a younger generation of his tribesmen at home held aspirations of experiencing modern city life.

Whatever initially impelled Gande to act contrary to the pattern of his peers, little could be ascertained, but it is clear that he was premature and ill-prepared for entry into modern urban Nigerian life. Although his army experience gave him an understanding of the discipline desired by European employers and a rare command (when compared with other Tiv of his generation) of the Hausa lingua franca, these initial occupational advantages did not serve him for long, especially in Jos, and he eventually decided that life away from his homeland was unrewarding and unsatisfactory. As both his age and the labor force in Jos increased, his work continuum retrogressed from semi-skilled to unskilled and then from unemployed to a depressing dependence on the charity of friends and relatives.

Gande married five times. His first wife, now dead, left him an unmarried son and a married daughter living in Lagos. His second wife was living at his lineage home with married and unmarried sons. The third wife died without issue, and the fourth, also barren, deserted Gande after much marital difficulty. He considered his youthful fifth mate to be a good wife and mother by traditional standards. She had given him two daughters in quick succession. But by Tiv native law and custom his last wife and her offspring were not fully legally his for he had not paid the full bridewealth for her. In addition, since it was not entirely seemly for himself to have two wives while his mature son had none, he was under some parental obligation to acquire a wife for one of his sons at home, for which money was needed. Two of his sons-in-law were tardy in fulfilling their bridewealth obligations to him, and the money he had looked forward to upon the marriage of his older daughter was not forthcoming for she ran away from her husband soon after the marriage.

Gande's evaluation of himself as a prominent member of the Tiv community in Jos was based on traditional Tiv criteria that equated advanced age with power. During the period of study, a series of events made him aware that in the changing Nigerian world his age no longer assured him automatically an influential role in the community. He tried to assume the responsibility toward the Tiv community in Jos which he felt was incumbent upon him because of his age and knowledge of tradition. He was an elder in the main Tiv tribal union and had taken the initiative to found one of its segments. People had sometimes come to him with their disputes or problems or to seek native medical attention. But when he was drawn into a quarrel between his brother-in-law and a younger man, who was the son of the leader of another and larger Tiv segment in Jos, he found himself lacking support from the Tiv community. The situation forced Gande to question the reality of his presumed leadership. Because of his economic and social disappointments in Jos, he increasingly looked forward to returning to Tivland and to the traditional life he idealized.

From Gande's account we see that, while cultural changes had taken place, he and other Tiv living in Jos still viewed their intra-tribal relations on the model of their traditional localized segmentary lineage system. Alliances and factions were determined on this basis, as was expressed in the support withheld at his daughter's naming ceremony. Indeed, the traditional segmentary structure that provided for such segmentary fission and factionalism caused serious concern to those modern-oriented leaders of the Tiv community in Jos who sought to develop and maintain a sense of pan-Tiv solidarity and a strong Tiv tribal union.

In national politics, the same sort of parochial allegiances exhibited by the Yoruba informant (but not by the cosmopolitan Ijaw) were demonstrated by Gande. His party allegiance and ethnic allegiance were one and the same. In religious affiliation he claimed Christianity and saw little distinction between the different Protestant sects. Following his initial mission introduction to Christianity, he was disinclined toward Catholicism, and his peripheral position in the congregations which he sometimes attended may be related to the rather shallow religious impact the Protestant missions in his area made on him when he was a boy. It is interesting that Gande, unlike the other informants, verbalized conflicts in syncretizing traditional customs and religious beliefs with his adopted Christianity. He saw a conflict or contradiction in "having two Gods."

Many other good African Christians, including the Yoruba informant, were able to resolve what appears to Westerners as a conflict between traditional practices and Christian teachings. Many times I was asked where in the Bible it was stated that a man may not have more than one wife. Since a good many "*Christian* fathers of the Old Testament" were polygynists, many Africans found it reasonable to observe this precedent in spite of criticism from European missionaries. The Ijaw informant went so far as to insist that the traditional African spirits were manifestations of the one, true Christian God.

The contrast between Gande and other informants at first seemed anomalous, for the latter were far better versed in Christian knowledge and should, presumably, be more sensitive to Christian teachings and thus more aware of conflicts between Christianity and traditional beliefs and behavior. It occurred to me, however, that if I stood this conclusion on its head, the relationships might fall properly into place. It was because Gande lacked adequate knowledge of Christianity that he was thus unable to resolve a satisfactory synthesis. Although he could read a little Tiv, it was a struggle for him to do so, and the tracts on Christianity which he sometimes perused were of the simplest sort. He lacked the sophistication in Christian theology with which other Africans could make personal interpretations of dogma that were suitable to avoid conflicts with their cherished traditional beliefs.

Peter Ekong

The Efik informant, Peter Ekong, aged 55, was born and reared under Roman Catholic influence at his lineage home in the city of Calabar, and he remained Catholic in adulthood. Like most other Efik, Peter received sufficient formal education to assure him, until a brief period prior to my contact with him, of an income that provided a fair amount of comfort. Skilled mechanics were so rare in Nigeria during most of his adult life that even during the depression of the thirties he remained regularly employed at relatively high wages. After his formal retirement from the United Africa Company in 1954, he continued to work as a free lance mechanic and thereby earned enough to continue financing his children's education. Peter was not thrifty, however, and in 1961, when his major contract was not renewed, he was forced to seek steady employment. The only available job paying respectable wages was physically exhausting for a man of his age, and insecure because of the Northernization Policy.

Calabar's historic position as a trading port shows certain economic, cultural, and political parallels with Opobo and, thus, the Efik informant manifests certain characteristics shared with the Ijaw. These, however, must not be overstressed. The people of Calabar kept aloof from their neighbors, over whom they claimed a measure of superiority, and maintained distinction from their Ibibio cousins by calling themselves "Efik." They are indeed much more cosmopolitan than other Ibibio, and they also show greater Anglophilia than most Nigerians. Peter, in fact, signified his allegiance to European culture by claiming superiority for Efik because they were more acculturated than other Nigerians through longer European contact. This attraction to Western culture, coupled with the Efik sense of superiority over neighboring and related Nigerian peoples, may partially account for the Efik's lack of success in combining with Ibibio and other peoples from Calabar Province to form a strong tribal union in Jos (and other urban areas).[1] By themselves the Efik were too few in Jos to create a viable union. Characteristically, Peter expressed the attitude of being above political involvement, as if it were tainted because of party association with tribe, and hence uncivilized.

Peter's attempt to integrate his desire to be cosmopolitan and modern and his pride in traditional Efik culture appears to have been unsuccessful. The cosmopolitan and Western orientation impels Efik to associate with modern elite Nigerians, West Africans, and Europeans, and when they speak of the achievements of Efik men, it is usually within a Western institutional framework, so that examples often include outstanding doctors or athletes. Ambivalently, they sometimes express pride in the achievements of

1. For an extended discussion and analysis of historical influences on Calabar Efik social characteristics and contemporary values, see Morril (1963). For a contrasting interpretation of the same phenomena, see Henderson (1966).

their native magicians but counter this by deprecating such "uncivilized" customs of their forefathers as human sacrifice. The informant typically expressed these ambivalent sentiments and had difficulty in relating to traditional type institutions. His sense of Efik superiority would not allow him to accept a position of less than full leadership in the integrated tribal unions of his region.

Peter had once been a leader of his tribal organization in Jos, but a factional dispute split the Calabar community, and Peter was disinclined to join the new or other tribal unions for which he was an eligible member. At one time he had also been a member of a modern elite social club in Jos, but he had allowed his membership to lapse because of his financial difficulties, and since then he had received no encouragement to revive it. Nonetheless, his orientation to Western culture was so strong that he felt his life would not be satisfactorily complete without membership in the Royal Freemasons. Despite the Catholic Church's traditional opposition to it, he fixed his attention on this particular order because his father had belonged to it.

This informant's orientation to European culture was strengthened by his slight incorporation in his tribal group and its network of social relations in Jos. In the terminology of reference group theory, Peter may be described as the "non-member type" of person who is "dependently hostile" toward the group of his former membership—national, tribal, and kinship. These became for him negative reference groups when he, to varying degrees, alienated himself from them. He then sought closer affiliation with Westernized institutions (although he was uncertain of his eligibility for membership in some), and tried to adopt their associated norms and values (see Merton 1957:270).

On the whole, Peter seemed pleased enough with his wife, but the fruits of their marriage were largely disappointing. He was accustomed to her constant complaints of illness—he himself often did not feel well—and the death of a child, such as that of his grandson which occurred during the course of study, was also familiar to him; three of his own children died in infancy. These family troubles seemed not to concern him as much as those he experienced with his children in Jos and Kaduna, who had socially disappointed him, and with his kinsmen at Calabar. Only one of his children still seemed to hold a realistic possibility of living up to the goals he had established for them; the others had in one way or another behaved to his discredit. Peter's shame over their failures and his own financial plight he correctly viewed as severely limiting his prestige and his chances of being accepted as an equal by the modern Nigerian elite. These circumstances caused him to withdraw still further from community social life.

A good measure of his family problems originated in Calabar, where his eldest half-brother had squandered the father's wealth, where his full-brothers had exploited his properties to their own advantage, and where relatives had continually tapped him for money. The profits he had derived from the properties given him by his mother, and supervised by a brother, had been used to further his children's education, had helped start the building of his retirement house in Calabar, and, had they still been forthcoming, could have been used to help him out of his dire economic circumstances. Instead of aiding him, his brothers at home pocketed the money Peter regarded as rightfully intended for him. Under these circumstances he found it difficult to reconcile his declaration that Calabar, not Jos, was his true home, and his professed wish to live out his years of occupational retirement there. Ultimately, he had to admit that conditions at Calabar prevented him from returning there; he was stuck in Jos.

For all the informants, living in Jos meant living away from home—home being defined as that area of their tribal territory specifically associated with their ancestors. In Jos, each informant felt he was a member of an ethnic immigrant group where the dominant group (usually, but not always, subjectively ascribed to the Hausa-Fulani) was actively or potentially hostile. The Opobo Ijaw informant, Isaac Cookey-Jaja, felt himself especially persecuted in this respect. Each said he would rather live in his tribal homeland, with the exception of the Efik (Peter Ekong), who altered his initial expression of preference for Calabar over Jos. None was actually committed to living in Jos permanently. Nonetheless, all but the Tiv, Gande Ikowe, were able to make a suitable, if not totally successful, adaptation to urban living. He was the only one prone to complain about urban life—its unsatisfactory social nature, deceptive economic advantages, immorality, etc. While the others did so on occasion, he consistently compared the disadvantages of residence in Jos with the economic and social benefits available to those living and farming in his homeland. In this respect Gande was not necessarily typical of other Tiv living in Jos, most of who were very much younger than himself. His initially poor orientation toward western, urban culture was undermined further by his history of tenuous employment.

The three southerners, in marked contrast to the Tiv, had been accustomed early to urban life and were quite prepared to accept the necessity of spending most of their lives in cities. They had been raised in urban environments, and their cultures shared ideas of accommodation to life away from home. All four informants looked upon the economic advantages of living in an alien community as a means of gaining subsequent prestige at home. But while return to the homeland was an actual or ideal goal, living in Jos gave these immigrants positive satisfactions and moral and economic support from the company of their fellow tribesmen, with whom they shared similar circumstances and familiar traditions. The differences in their cultural backgrounds and in their emerging tribal communities in Jos had important consequences for their urban adjustments.

In addition to the traditional Ogbomosho Yoruba orientation to trade far afield, the Ogbomosho community in Jos was large, long-established, and its members were long accustomed to life in a large community. These factors served to facilitate the Ogbomosho immigrants' adjustment to Jos. On the other hand, the Opobo Ijaw and Calabar Efik had very small and highly transient ethnic populations in Jos, although the cosmopolitan ethos of their cultures permitted these immigrants to rely less on their own tribesmen for their social networks. That the Efik informant was not successful in his own adjustment was due to conditions peculiar to himself. Compared to the Calabar and Ijaw populations in Jos, the Tiv population was relatively large. Almost all of its members, however, had only recently arrived, and they had not yet developed into a community; they may more accurately be considered as a Tiv population rather than as a community. In the strange surroundings, Tiv traditional institutions had not adapted sufficiently to alien and urban conditions. Therefore, their tribal unions were not as yet able to serve as continuity bridges with the homeland. Lacking a traditional cosmopolitan ethos was an added disadvantage to Tiv immigrants, who tended to rely heavily on their tribesmen. This was even more true for older, less acculturated men, such as Gande.

Each informant believed that the ideal conclusion to life was retirement to the homeland. Although they all planned for this goal, each of them was obliged to modify his plans. Thus, because his wives wished to remain in Jos, Olu, the Yoruba, planned to marry again so that he might be surrounded by the proper entourage when he returned to Ogbomosho. Isaac, the Ijaw, shared with other southerners the increasingly uncertain business prospects in the Northern Region, and he considered relocating to the Eastern Region. Aba was Isaac's choice for relocating his business in preparation for his eventual retirement or semi-retirement for reasons of its advantageous location for business purposes, proximity to his hometown of Opobo, and its desirable modern amenities, which were lacking in his hometown. However, the undesirable political and economic developments in the Northern Region caused him to alter his original plans of remaining longer in the North and to advance the date of his resettlement. Gande, the Tiv informant, stayed on in Jos because he was unable to save enough money for even the semblance of an honorable return home. Peter, the Efik, was ambivalent about returning home. He lacked the armor of wealth and success with which he could combat his full brothers who had defrauded him, and against whom he was uncertain of finding allies of sufficient strength among his other relatives. The Tiv and Efik men provide examples of immigrants who may not easily return to their native land when economic opportunities in the employment centers cease to exist for them. Even when they were still committed to their eventual return home, the informants were also intensely concerned with gaining and holding a position of prestige in Jos, albeit within different evaluative criteria. Only the Yoruba could be said to have assuredly achieved his goals, and he alone among the informants was not faced with immediate problems of economic survival.

Forde (1956:43) has noted that a lack of clear-cut class divisions among Africans in urban settings is reflected in multiple and cross-cutting criteria for prestige. To enhance his social status, a person is not necessarily restricted to operating within a modern framework to the exclusion of a traditional one. The Ijaw informant, for example, was almost equally oriented to both types. Nonetheless, a person's chances of attaining recognition in one of the systems may be limited because he lacks the requisite qualifications, as with a person ignorant of the finer points of tribal custom, lore, and religion. For the Tiv informant, a knowledge of native cures was advantageous, but he realistically appraised his deficiencies with regard to Western institutions and oriented himself exclusively to traditional avenues of gaining prestige. Finally, we must not fail to realize that some individuals may be so disadvantageously situated that we could not realistically expect them to achieve or maintain leadership in either traditional or Western institutions. Peter, the Efik, had come to such a position.

Plural Reference Groups

From the extended description of the lives of the principal informants and the urban social setting in which they operate, it should be clear that these people recognized the plurality of the social and cultural worlds which Jos contains. Complex as Jos plurality might be, the participating actors knew the boundaries which defined appropriate institutional behavior. These boundaries contain different social and cultural fields, but the individuals, in most cases, knew that the different situations were to be understood by different frames of reference. When the informants did not understand all the norms for the institutions they participated in, they were sometimes troubled. If an individual is unaware of the characteristics that define culturally different institutions, and if he has not learned the full set of appropriate behaviors, he is either not fully enculturated, acculturated, educated, or socialized. But this is a condition common to all men, whether it is part of the socialization experience of the child or the learning of new and appropriate cultural habits of an adult immigrant to any alien area.

The following examples, taken from the accounts of the informants, illustrate the degree to which they were aware of what behaviors were appropriate within culturally different frames of reference and to what extent they were aware that their behaviors could be considered inconsistent.

For the Tiv informant, Gande, the social community forming his frame of reference in Jos was almost entirely that of his fellow tribesmen. Of all the informants, he was the most uncomfortable when it came to behaving outside his familiar and traditional cultural context. Insofar as he was able, he avoided contact or participation in non-Tiv institutions, and the main area of his outside participation was in the unavoidable economic and occupational institutions. Overly conscious as he was about his lack of sophistication in modern institutions, it was always clear to him where the boundaries lay. He knew what qualities employers desired, and he could behave accordingly when he worked for them. He could present rent receipts, the testimonials of former employers, and other documents that protected him in a culturally alien world; and, although he was functionally illiterate, he knew precisely what each document contained. He knew it was illegal for him to practice his native medicine, but (perhaps due to an excess of faith in the licensing powers of government) he falsely believed that one could obtain administrative permission to practice native magic. When he worked for the railways he knew what the penalty was for overstaying his leave, and thus anticipated a defense against this charge.

The Yoruba, Olu, like the Tiv, was most comfortable in familiar cultural surroundings. Yoruba music was sweetest to his ears, and he described his favorite Yoruba dishes with great relish. However, he also displayed some pride in his familiarity with the alien plural worlds of Jos. If we compare him with the Tiv, we may surmise that his greater confidence in relating to these plural conditions was based on a longer experience and a knowledgeability that the Tiv lacked. Olu claimed a modest acquaintance with Arabic, the Koran, and Islamic ritual, and he knew when to distribute gifts of food among his Muslim friends and neighbors. He was equally familiar with non-traditional institutions. Despite his illiteracy, when called on to make a civic donation, he knew how much to give and he knew how to write the check for the money. Perhaps the designation entrepreneur is not, strictly speaking, applicable to Olu, but he certainly possessed the qualities of adaptibility and flexibility associated with that term. When dealing with clerks in a Nigerian bureaucratic setting, he knew how to gain sympathy, and thereby preferred attention; he knew whom to bribe for what purpose, when to receive bribes, and what amounts were customary for particular circumstances. He entertained old Yoruba men in one fashion, and young Yoruba men, and sometimes Europeans, in another, in each case in accordance with the guests' respective standards of hospitality. His description of his hospitality stressed the necessity of relating behavior appropriately to varying social and cultural contexts. As if in anticipation of the present theoretical discussion, he pointed out to me incidents which would seem contradictory to the ideal of rational economic action held by both Europeans and Yoruba—his support of relatives and his charity to non-kinsmen, none of which would bring him any economic return. With a similar awareness of plural social conditions that are concomitant with rapid cultural change and divergent views between different generations of the same society, he commented that a traditional Yoruba man would not have been able to understand why he did not give his daughter in marriage to an old and wealthy friend, and that a European observer might have been dismayed when he refused to allow his son to help him carry a heavy load of cloths.

In addition to conducting his business and running his family successfully, Olu participated vigorously in the plural cultural worlds of which he felt a part. These worlds included his home town, his ethnic community in Jos, his church, his neighbors and his friends (who were not necessarily of his tribe, religion, or town) in and outside of Jos. In these areas of his life he was acting within institutional frameworks that existed either exclusively for his own ethnic group or that provided extra-tribal participation and interaction.

Peter, the Efik, was ingenious in making inconsistent statements, largely because of his attempt to live the life of a more socially prestigious man than he actually was. In some areas he was quite aware of contradictions in his behavior. He admitted that becoming a Freemason was not condoned by his religion, but he had calculated the advantages and disadvantages and deliberately chose to live with the discrepancy; his conscience was large enough to accommodate the ego-satisfaction of belonging to an elite social organization that went contrary to his religious tenets. It was this same quest for favorable community recognition that elicited from him a conservative Catholic viewpoint of his son's polygynous union with a Muslim girl.

Earlier I have discussed and analyzed the nature of Isaac's (the Ijaw informant) apparently contradictory and inconsistent behavior. It is sufficient to note here that for him, also, Jos presented plural communities to which he oriented his behavior. His world consisted of his own ethnic group and the inter-tribal modern Nigerian elite, within which he had achieved and maintained a small measure of recognition.

The Yoruba informant chose to acquire an elite status primarily by traditional criteria, to be climaxed by a successful retirement at home. The Ijaw, on the other hand, expressed his hope for inclusion in the modern elite by wishing for a house fine enough to entertain prominent national figures. Both men made use of existing institutions in Jos, creating a viable dual allegiance to Jos and to their tribal homes. The Tiv informant was totally committed to home, a man entirely alienated in the non-traditional arena of Jos. The Efik man, uncertain where his commitments should lie, was a misfit unable to operate effectively within any framework.

Chapter X

THEORETICAL CONCLUSIONS

IN Chapter I several questions indicating the theoretical intentions of this study were listed. In general these asked: what was the nature and pattern of individuals' adjustments to modern urban life as represented by conditions in Jos; whether prior experiences, personally unique to the immigrant or culturally shared, accounted for different modes of relating to the urban environment; whether modern African urban life was so disorganized as to be virtually "normless," as it has been frequently described; whether individual behavior reflected such disorganization; and the extent and nature of immigrants' commitment to urban life.

The nature of adjustments of individuals has been discussed in the preceding chapter, where the experiences of the four principal informants were reviewed and compared. It was shown that prior personal and culturally shared experiences significantly influence the manner of adjustment to urban life, in some cases accounting for poor, superficial, or negligible adjustment. The remaining questions may be succinctly answered as follows:

1. Urban life is complex but not disorganized as some sociologically oriented studies have suggested.

2. Urban behavior that may appear inconsistent and irrational to an outsider is logical and appropriate from the point of view of the individual concerned.

3. A "vicious cycle" prevents urban immigrants from achieving their desire of returning home upon occupational retirement.

1. *Urban life is complex but not disorganized.*

Jos, with its heterogeneous population and plural conditions, is neither a "sick" nor anomic community. Although much of its population is transient, its institutions—traditional, Western, or syncretic—are viable and durable, and serve to articulate and integrate the various ethnic components. While tribe and homeland appear to hold primary allegiances, people display a faith in the continuity of Jos urban life by their active participation in the existing institutions, by their economic investments, and by emotional involvement in their social networks. Despite the frequency with which the literature has implied or asserted the contrary for contemporary urban Africa, and however complex and diverse it may seem, Jos urban life is organized; social life there is systemic. Immigrants make pragmatic attempts to relate to the urban conditions which confront them as individuals, as members of ethnic communities, and as representatives of social categories such as religious or status groups. Let us take up these three analytical divisions in order.

Regardless of the strength of tribal loyalties and the depth of parochial village sentiments, even the most traditional men relate positively, as individuals, to Jos conditions. For example, the Yoruba informant could express both humaneness and friendship when asked to intercede and help settle the family disputes of his Hausa neighbors. The Tiv shared in the delightful pastime of African drafts with Yoruba men of his age, and had established a joking type of relationship with an old Hausa woman who lived across the street and who was friendly with his wife. The Ijaw informant's closest personal friends reflected a variety of ethnic backgrounds, and he also demonstrated civic responsibility when he occasionally gave (upon invitation) free professional advice to the Township Advisory Council and to his church congregation.

Social networks for most immigrants consist largely of intra-ethnic relationships. Generally, immigrants deal with the larger social and political environment of Jos corporately through their ethnic groups, particularly their respective tribal unions. In the past, tribal representatives were formally recognized on the Town Council, and today they are informally recognized. Tribal unions nominate assessors to the Alkali and Provincial Courts and frequently petition the local administration in their own behalf or the general civic interest. The unions also provide their members with a familiar cultural atmosphere, recreation, and various social and economic benefits: seeking employment for members, providing business loans, settling disputes, caring for the sick and destitute, and insuring proper funeral services. The tribal union assembly hall assumes symbolic importance, in part by reflecting the tribe's solidarity and political and economic strength, but perhaps more important as a sign of establishment and perpetuity. It is regarded as not only serving the present members in Jos but all those yet to come. It bespeaks of the immigrant tribe's intent to stay. The individual may be transient, but the tribal union is regarded as a permanent institution.

In relating to the wider community, ethnic groups attempt to project a favorable image. Since they intend to stay, they want to remain on good terms. They may donate their assembly hall for some civic purpose or rent it to other ethnic, social, business, or political groups. Through fines or other sanctions, they attempt to control their members' behavior so as not to damage the tribe's reputation in the community. Ethnic groups express pride in their traditions by holding public performances of plays, masquerades, and native dances. When they seek to raise money by staging formal dances, they may court community goodwill by inviting prominent individuals of other ethnic groups to serve as hosts and masters of ceremony.

It is sometimes difficult to distinguish concerted group action which represents ethnic behavior from that which represents behavior of status groups or other social categories. For example, in the previous example of ethnic groups relating to the wider community through their tribal unions, it is invariably the modern elite members of the tribal unions who initiate and carry out such programs. When the modern elite stage ballroom dances for their tribal unions they invite their status peers of other tribes to attend and help assume the ceremonial duties of hosts, and the latter do attend these occasions to express both their personal ties with those who have invited them and their non-parochial stance.

For another instance, we may turn to the efforts of the Jos clerks and artisans to found the Jos Government School in the 1920's, and the later similar success of the Hausa Muslim community in establishing the Native Authority School for northern children, as expressions of social categories that may or may not be ethnic. The artisans and clerks who wanted a school in Jos so that their children would not have to be sent to the southern provinces can be said to have represented a status group (an emerging modern African elite); but since they were so limited in the variety of their ethnic composition[1] their action could almost be equally viewed as the cooperative action of a few ethnic groups. Further, it can be seen from Table 6 that when mission schools were established in Jos, their composition of teachers and pupils reflected the tendency towards association of church denomination and ethnicity. In other words, the early modern African elite of different ethnic origin worked together to provide educational facilities for their children, but when their churches established schools in Jos they sent their children to the mission schools with which their ethnic groups were historically associated. And insofar as each church-school is dominated by a particular tribe, mission-sponsored schools may be considered equally as the action of religious groups or ethnic communities. Similar motives impelled the leaders of the Hausa community to have a school for their children that would include Arabic and Koranic studies. They, also, did not want their children to be sent away for an education. At first these persons were acting as Muslims, but they later appeared to be progressive northerners

---

1. These persons were Creoles from Sierra Leone, Ashanti, Fanti, and Ewe from the Gold Coast, and members of southern Nigerian ethnic groups such as Yoruba, Edo, Itsekri, Urhobo, Ijaw, Efik, and Ibo from Onitsha.

when enrollment was extended to all northern children, regardless of whether they were Muslim or of the core Muslim tribes (Fulani, Hausa, Kanuri, and Nupe), and when they demanded that adequate instruction in English be given. However, a similar shift occurred in this situation when Birom and other Christian Plateau tribes came to dominate the student enrollment of the Native Authority School, causing the Muslim community to establish three additional schools specifically oriented to Islamic studies.

What remains significant is the immigrants' concern to create for themselves in Jos as completely satisfactory an existence as they can. Establishing schools for their children makes possible an unbroken family life, and the relatively high proportion of schools in Jos can be directly attributed to immigrant efforts. Similarly, immigrants have established and maintained mosques, pagan religious institutions, and churches of all kinds.

The social institutions of status groups, such as those of the modern African elite, include international fraternal orders, social and recreation clubs, and literary societies. The ethic displayed by these groups regarding membership and recruitment is that neither ethnicity, race, nor religion is relevant. Finally, there are numerous voluntary associations of more or less clear purpose which also attempt to recruit on a non-tribal basis, e.g., business associations, trade unions, political parties, and athletic associations. Modern institutions, normally associated with Western European cities, are also well represented in Jos, and although modified, they have attained a stability and permanence alongside traditional institutions. All serve to make life for the immigrants, whether they be transient or relatively settled, more worthwhile, and indicate that Jos is an organized, on-going community.

2. *Behavior that may appear inconsistent or irrational to the onlooker is logical from the actor's point of view.*

The complexity of social life to be found in Jos stems from a combination of plural and rapidly changing conditions, and individuals reflect this flux and pluralism in their behavior. Similar conditions have been observed in Kampala by Southall and Gutkind (1957:91, 107, 112, 167), who point out that immigrants are especially conscious of alternative modes of behavior and multiple value systems, which they attempt to manipulate in order to provide themselves with maximum opportunities and satisfactions. Their observation is a refreshing departure from so much of the literature on this topic which stresses anomic (Mitchell 1956: 696) or "unpatterned" behavior (Balandier 1956: 495 ff.). What appears to have disturbed most observers is the neither consistent African nor consistent European behavior of the immigrants, a pattern which might appropriately be called *pluralistic behavior.*[2] Mitchell has noted that "it is quite possible for people to continue to follow tribal modes of behavior in some respects and participate in urban social relations in others" (1956: 695; see also Forde 1956: 37, and Hellmann 1948: 54, 117). It is not enough to say that my study has confirmed Mitchell's observation. What we, who study the social phenomena of modern African cities, seek to determine is precisely in what respects an individual behaves one way or the other—parochial and universal, tribal and Western—and one of the purposes of this study was to seek and define the determinants of such situational behavior.

We have come a long way from viewing the urban African scene as "the chaotic welter of transition" (Hellmann 1948: 116). My data show that while the complexity of the urban African setting cannot be minimized, patterns do emerge if we view the situation from the standpoint of the participating actors. What appear as individual contradictions and inconsistencies between professed beliefs and demonstrable behavior are usually attributable to the individual's changes of reference orientation; varying behavior and responses are reflections of his alternating definitions of situations. Rather than showing anomalous or inconsistent behavior, he is attempting to relate appropriately to the multiple frames of reference urban society presents.

2. American sociologists would call this *reference group behavior*; Gluckman and his associates would call it *situational selectivity*. At a general level, it is all the same.

Of course this pattern does not always hold, and we must not overlook the possibility that inconsistent behavior may be the result of the actor's distorted images or inaccurate evaluations. Southall appears to have come to the same general conclusion:

> Without introducing any idea of social disorganization, inconsistencies may be expected to appear in at least three different ways: as between different levels of generality from the universal to the particular in the statement of norms, between different social strata, and between different areas of the social life of the same individual [1961a: 15].

There indeed seems to be a convergence of opinion along those lines, even among anthropologists whose special areas of study are very different.[3]

3. A "vicious cycle" prevents urban immigrants from returning home.

Deeply emotional and often strong economic ties bind the immigrants in Jos to their native homelands. The immigrants express these ties by sending gifts and money to relatives at home and by planning to return to the tribal homeland with the onset of age and retirement.[4] They also look to their home communities and their kinsmen there as ever available sources of security which to fall back on when they can no longer find employment in the urban centers (Southall 1961a: 36). Forde (1956: 38) stresses indications which show these ties to be weakening, and Pons (1956: 669), commenting on Stanleyville, believes that many immigrants will fail to realize their ideal of returning to village life. This is my own view of immigrants in Jos despite the fact that tribal clashes in the North during 1966 drove many Eastern Nigerians to their natal regions. Had the national political situation not disturbed them, they would

3. See, for example, Eric Wolf (1959:142–43); Sofer also seems to have anticipated this view among urban Africanists (1956:590–91).

4. This has been reported for many parts of Africa. See Balandier (1956: 469); Doucy and Feldheim (1956: 677); McCulloch (1956: 160, 165); C. Sofer (1956: 603); and Southall (1961a: 36).

have remained in Jos. Pons's salient points and my data concur: while the home village is thought of nostalgically, especially for the abundance of good food, a return home would involve the immigrant in an intolerable situation. It is difficult to readjust to "uncivilized" ways after one has become accustomed to town amenities. "Furthermore, the village people are said to be distrustful and jealous of those who have 'followed the Europeans.' One may return home to visit . . . but to do so permanently is said to be courting disaster. 'They [the village people] like you to come back for a few months,' one man explained, 'but if you stay for good they will poison you.' " (Pons ibid.). This statement is almost word for word Peter's description of his prospects of returning home.

That Pons and I obtained such similar data and results is due, I am sure, to the similarity in our fieldwork methods. Initially, informants will give an idyllic view of their home area and, I confess, for a long time I believed that most of the people I knew in Jos would eventually return home to live out their lives—so prevalent was this sentiment. My investigation of this issue shows how primary or sole reliance on schedule and questionnaire surveys can yield distorted conclusions. Out of a sample of over one hundred men and women in the Copper Belt, Mitchell (1956) noted that 70 per cent expressed attitudes of temporary urbanization, while in Elizabethville, F. Grevisse found that "even those who have lived 20, 30, or 40 years in town . . . expect to return home when they retire, *although a number of factors*, including the bringing up of children, may prevent their doing so" (quoted in McCulloch 1956:160, 165, italics added). Had I not intensively interviewed my informants, I would have concluded that their return home was certain.

What are the factors that prevent the immigrants' return home, excluding those already mentioned? Immigrants are drawn to the city by the prospect of acquiring wealth and thereby becoming "big men" (Banton 1957:113). They feel bound not to return empty-handed to the envious stay-at-homes who desire to "eat bush money," i.e., to squeeze the returnee for all he is worth. The home community relentlessly maintains that emigrants are moral failures, and may not return with dignity unless they are economically successful and have shown primary loyalty to homeland and kinsmen by maintaining contact and fulfilling kinship obligations (usually expressed with personal appearances at family crises and ceremonies, with gifts and money to relatives, chiefs, and elders, as well as providing for the education of young male kinsmen). Ideally, natal loyalty should also be expressed in the eventual, even if stage-by-stage, erection of a European-type retirement house on lineage or home-town land. The successful migrant who forgets or neglects his native town and kinsmen is ostracized, and the unsuccessful native son is presumed to be more than lacking in ability, for the rural people, with their distorted view of the city as a place where money is abundant, believe he must be lazy, incompetent, or wasteful. A person who attempts to resettle at home does not find ready acceptance; he is often regarded suspiciously as one who may have rejected the old traditions and values. To those who constitute the traditional elite at home, the "newcomer" resembles a parvenu, an upstart whose manners challenge their traditional criteria for achievement, rank, and prestige. They will not generously give ground to welcome a returning competitor; and the very few successful returnees are likely to team up with the stay-at-homes to maintain a pressure of unwelcome for another new arrival, who they also see as a potential competitor.

As much as they may overtly profess a desire to return home, for all these reasons the immigrants are under pressure to remain away. Very likely the rationalizations employed to cover a delayed departure from Jos (such as the expressed preference for the cool climate) and the insistence that an ultimate return home is planned serve to keep open communications and commerce with kinsmen at home, and to pretend the wish is the reality. But it also allows the feeling that "home" is not in the alien city and thereby permits a psychological withdrawal from total urban commitments when the individual views his career in town as being less successful than he had imagined it would be. Thus, as in other cities, various pressures maintain the large immigrant population of Jos as an urban population, and ideological means act as safety valves for the release of personal pressures. This is part of the process that lends stability to the Jos population, as it does elsewhere. And aside from individual adjustment, the developed and developing social institutions supply organization, viability, durability, a measure of social security, and the satisfactions that allow urban life to be worthwhile to its inhabitants.

Appendix, Bibliography, Index

GENEALOGICAL CHARTS
FOR FOUR INFORMANTS

The Key to Genealogies pertaining to all charts
appears on that of the Yoruba informant.

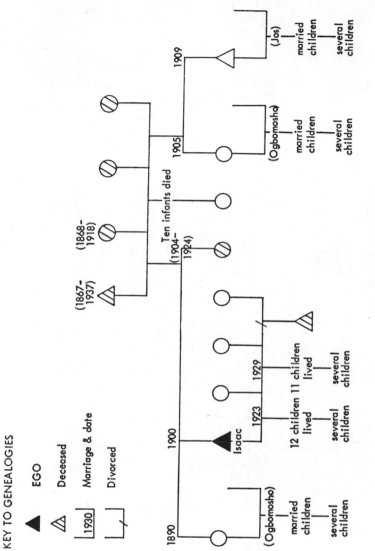

KEY TO GENEALOGIES

▲ EGO

△ Deceased

1930 Marriage & date

⌐ ⌐ Divorced

Isaac Olu Oyewumi (Yoruba)

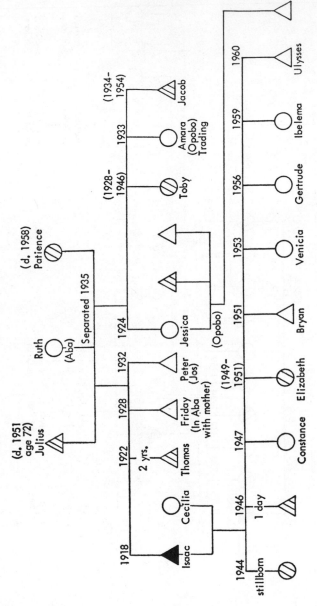

Isaac Cookey-Jaja (Ijaw)

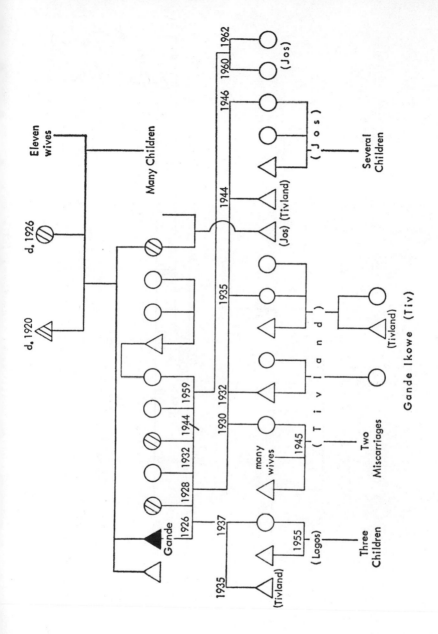

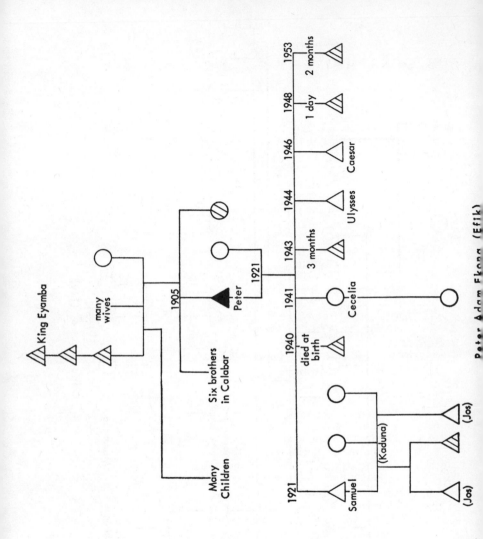

Peter Adam Ekong (Efik)

BIBLIOGRAPHY

Acquah (née Crabtree), I.
1958 Accra survey. London, London U. Press.
Adam, T. R.
1962 Government and politics in Africa south of the Sahara. New York, Random House.
Almond, G. and J. S. Coleman (eds.)
1960 The politics of the developing areas. Princeton, Princeton U. Press.
Ames, C. G.
1934 Gazetteer of the Plateau Province. Jos, published by the Jos Native Administration.
Balandier, G.
1955 Sociologies des Brazzaville noires. Paris.
1956 Urbanization in West and Central Africa: the scope and aims of research. In UNESCO, Social implications . . . , pp. 495–510.
Banton, M.
1957 West African city. London, Oxford U. Press for the International African Institute.
Banton, M., ed.
1966 The social anthropology of complex societies. New York, Praeger.
Bascom, W. R.
1955 Urbanization among the Yoruba. In World urbanism. American Journal of Sociology 60:446–54.
1962 Some aspects of Yoruba urbanism. American Anthropologist 64:699–709.
Bower, P. A.
1948 The mining industry. In Mining, commerce, and finance in Nigeria, vol. 2, Economics of a tropical dependency, M. Perham, ed. London, Faber & Faber.
Brooke, N. J.
1934 Census of Nigeria, 1931: village directory Northern Provinces, Nigeria, vol. 2A. Lagos, Government Printer.
Browne, G. St. J. O.
1941 Labour conditions in West Africa. London, HMSO.

Buchanan, K. M. and J. C. Pugh
1955 Land and people in Nigeria: the human geography of Nigeria and its environmental background. London, U. of London Press.

Busia, K. A.
1950 Social survey of Sekondi-Takoradi. Accra, Gold Coast Government.
1956 The present situation and aspirations of elites in the Gold Coast. International Social Science Bull. 8:424–30.

Calvert, A. F.
1910 Nigeria and its tin fields. London, Edward Stanford.

Church, R. J. H.
1959 West African urbanization: a geographical review. Sociological Rev. 7:15–28.

Coleman, James S.
1958 Nigeria: background to nationalism. Berkeley, U. of California Press.
1960 The politics of sub-Saharan Africa. In G. A. Almond and J. S. Coleman, eds., The politics of the developing areas. Princeton, Princeton U. Press.

Cook, A. N.
1943 British enterprises in Nigeria. Philadelphia, U. of Pennsylvania Press.

Davies, J. G.
1949 The Birom. Jos, unpublished ms.

Dike, K. O.
1956 Trade and politics in the Niger Delta: 1830–1885. Oxford, Clarendon Press.

Doucy, A. and P. Feldheim
1956 Some effects of industrialization in two districts of Equatoria province (Belgian Congo). In UNESCO, Social implications . . . , pp. 670–92.

Epstein, A. L.
1953 The role of African courts in urban communities of the Northern Rhodesia Copperbelt. Rhodes-Livingston Journal 13:1–16.
1956 An outline of the political structure of an African urban community on the Copperbelt of Northern Rhodesia. In UNESCO, Social implications . . . , pp. 711–24.
1958 Politics in an urban African community. Manchester, Manchester U. Press.
1961 The network and urban social organization. Human Problems in British Central Africa 29:28–62.

Fiawoo, D. K.
1959 Urbanisation and religion in Eastern Ghana. Sociological Rev. 7 (n.s.):83–98.
Forde, D.
1956 Social aspects of urbanization and industrialization in Africa south of the Sahara. *In* UNESCO, Social implications . . . , pp. 11–50.
Gluckman, M.
1960 Tribalism in modern British Central Africa. Cahiers d'études africaines 1:55–70.
Gulliver, P. H.
1957 Labour migration in a rural economy. Kampala, East African Studies, No. 6, East African Institute of Social Research.
1965 Anthropology. *In* Robert A. Lystad, ed., The African world: a survey of social research. London, Pall Mall Press.
Gunn, H. D.
1953 Peoples of the Plateau area of Northern Nigeria. London, International African Institute.
Gutkind, P. C. W.
1960 Congestion and overcrowding: an African urban problem. Human Organization 19:129–34.
1962 Accommodation and conflict in an African peri-urban area. Anthropologica 2:163–73.
Hailey, Lord
1951 Native administration in the British African territories, Pt. 3. London, HMSO.
Hance, W. A.
1960 The economic location and functions of tropical African cities. Human Organization 19:135–36.
Hellman, E.
1948 Rooiyard: a social survey of an urban slum area. Rhodes-Livingston Paper No. 13. Capetown: Oxford U. Press for the Rhodes-Livingston Institute.
1956 The development of social groupings among urban Africans in the Union of South Africa. *In* UNESCO, Social implications . . . , pp. 724–43.
Henderson, R. N.
1966 Generalized cultures and evolutionary adaptability: a comparison of urban Efik and Ibo in Nigeria. Ethnology 5:365–91.
Herskovits, M. J.
1962 The human factor in changing Africa. New York, Knopf.
INCIDI
1957 Ethnic and cultural pluralism in intertropical communities.

Report of the 30th meeting held in Lisbon. Brussels, International Institute of Differing Civilizations.

Laws, H. W.
1954   Some reminiscences. Nigerian Field 19:105–17.

Lewis, O.
1959   Five Families: Mexican case studies in the culture of poverty. New York, Basic Books.
1961   The children of Sanchez: an autobiography of a Mexican family. New York, Random House.

Little, K.
1957   The role of voluntary association in West African urbanization. American Anthropologist 59:579–96.
1959a Introduction to special number on urbanism in West Africa. Sociological Rev. 7(n.s.):5–14.
1959b Some urban patterns of marriage and domesticity in West Africa. Sociological Rev. 7 (n.s.):65–82.
1962   Some traditionally based forms of mutual aid in West African urbanization. Ethnology 1:197–211.

Mackay, R. A., R. Greenwood, and J. E. Rockingham
1949   The geology of the Plateau tinfields: resurvey 1945–48. Kaduna, Government Printer.

Mayer, P.
1961   Townsmen or tribesmen. Capetown, Oxford U. Press for Rhodes University Institute for Social and Economic Research.
1962   Africans in towns. American Anthropologist 64:576–92.

McCall, D. F.
1955   Dynamics of urbanization in Africa. The American Academy of Political and Social Science, Annals 298:151–60.

McCulloch, M.
1956   Survey of recent and current field studies in the social effects of economic development in inter-tropical Africa. *In* UNESCO, Social implications . . . , pp. 53–225.

Meek, C. R.
1925   The northern tribes of Nigeria. London, HMSO.

Merton, R. K.
1957   Social theory and social structure. Glencoe, Free Press.

Mitchell, J. C.
1956   Urbanization, detribalization and stabilization in Southern Africa: a problem of definition and measurement. *In* UNESCO, Social implications . . . , pp. 693–711.
1960   Tribalism and the plural society, an inaugural lecture given

in the University College of Rhodesia and Nyasaland. London, Oxford U. Press.
1966   Theoretical orientations in African urban studies. *In* M. Banton, ed., The social anthropology of complex societies. New York, Praeger.
Mitchell, J. C. and A. L. Epstein
1959   Occupational prestige and social status among urban Africans in Northern Rhodesia. Africa 29:22–40.
Morill, W. T.
1963   Immigrants and associations: the Ibo in twentieth century Calabar. Comparative studies in society and history 5:424–48.
Murdock, G. P.
1962   The traditional socio-political systems of Nigeria: an introductory survey. *In* R. O. Tilman and T. Cole, eds., The Nigerian political scene. Durham, N. C., Duke U. Press for the Duke U. Commonwealth–Studies Center.
Nigeria
1961   National directory of Nigeria: trades and professions 1960–1961. London, Unimex.
Orr, C. W.
1911   The making of Northern Nigeria. London, Macmillan.
Perham, M.
1937   Native administration in Nigeria. London, Oxford U. Press.
1948   Mining, commerce, and finance in Nigeria, vol. 2 of The economics of a tropical dependency. London, Faber & Faber.
Plotnicov, L.
1964   "Nativism" in contemporary Nigeria. Anthropological Qtly. 37:121–37.
1965   Going home again—Nigerians: the dream is unfulfilled. Trans-Action 3 (1): 18–22.
1967   The composition and role of the modern African elite in a middle-sized Nigerian city. *In* A. Tuden and L. Plotnicov, eds., Social stratification in Africa. New York, Free Press (in press).
Pons, V. G.
1956   The changing significance of ethnic affiliation and of westernization in the African settlement patterns in Stanleyville. *In* UNESCO, Social implications . . . , pp. 638–39.
Royal Institute of International Affairs
1960   Nigeria: the political and economic background. London, Oxford U. Press.

Rubin, V., ed.
  1960   Social and cultural pluralism in the Caribbean. The New York
         Academy of Sciences, Annals 83:761–918.

Schwab, W. B.
  1961   Social stratification in Gwelo. *In* A. Southall, ed., Social
         change in modern Africa. London, Oxford U. Press for the
         International African Institute.

Sklar, R. L.
  1963   Nigerian political parties: power in an emergent African na-
         tion. Princeton, Princeton U. Press.

Smith, M. F.
  1954   Baba of Karo: a woman of the Moslem Hausa. London, Faber
         & Faber.

Smith, M. G.
  1960   Social and cultural pluralism. *In* V. Rubin, ed., Social and
         cultural pluralism in the Caribbean. The New York Academy
         of Science, Annals 83:763–85.

Smith, R. T.
  1961   Review of social and cultural pluralism in the Caribbean.
         American Anthropologist 63:155–57.
  1963   Culture and social structure in the Caribbean: some recent
         work on family and kinship studies. Comparative studies in
         society and history 6:24–46.

Smythe, H. H.
  1960   Urbanization in Nigeria. Anthropological Qtly. 33:143–48.

Smythe, H. H. and M. M.
  1960   The new Nigerian elite. Stanford, Stanford U. Press.

Sofer, C.
  1956   Urban African social structure and working group behaviour
         at Jinja (Uganda). *In* UNESCO, Social implications . . . , pp.
         590–612.

Sofer, C. and R.
  1955   Jinja transformed. East African Studies No. 4. Kampala, East
         African Institute of Social Research.

Southall, A. W.
  1956   Determinants of the social structure of African urban popu-
         lations, with special reference to Kampala (Uganda). *In*
         UNESCO, Social implications . . . , pp. 557–78.
  1961a Introductory summary. *In* A. Southall, ed., Social change
         in modern Africa. London, Oxford U. Press for the Inter-
         national African Institute.
  1961b Kinship, friendship, and the network of relations in Kisenyi,

Kampala. *In* A. Southall, ed., Social change in modern Africa. London, Oxford U. Press for the International African Institute.

Southall, A. and P. C. W. Gutkind
1957 Townsmen in the making: Kampala and its suburbs. East African Studies No. 9. Kampala, East African Institute of Social Research.

Stapleton, G. B.
1958 The wealth of Nigeria. London, Oxford U. Press.

Tilman, R. O. and T. Cole, eds.
1962 The Nigerian political scene. Durham, N.C., Duke U. Press for the Duke U. Commonwealth Studies Center.

Uchendu, V. C.
1965 The Igbo of southeast Nigeria. New York, Holt, Rinehart & Winston.

UNESCO [for International African Institute]
1956 Social implications of industrialization and urbanization in Africa south of the Sahara. Paris.

Wellerstein, I.
1960 Ethnicity and national integration in West Africa. Cahiers d'études africaines No. 3.

Winter, E. H.
1959 Beyond the Mountains of the Moon. Urbana, U. of Illinois Press.

Wolf, E. R.
1959 Specific aspects of plantation systems in the New World: community sub-cultures and social classes. *In* V. Rubin, ed., Plantation systems of the New World. Washington, D.C., Pan American Union and Research Institute for the Study of Man, Social Science Monographs VII.

Government Documents

Annual Reports, Bauchi Province, 1902, 1905, 1906
Kaduna, Nigerian National Archives File S.N.P. 10/3
Annual Report, Central Provinces, 1912
Kaduna, Nigerian National Archives File 373/1912
Annual Reports, Northern Provinces 1900–1911
1914 Lagos, Government Printer.
Annual Reports, Plateau Province, 1930; 1932–34; 1951
Kaduna, Nigerian National Archives Files 3/–, 301/, 488/1934
CCTA/CSA
1961 Abidjan, Commission for Technical Co-operation in Africa South of the Sahara, Publication No. 75

Labour Conditions—Department of Labour Qtly. Rev., 1943–51.
Kaduna and Nigerian National Archives File 1709/S.1
Nigeria, The Economic Development of
    1954   Report of a mission organized by the International Bank for Reconstruction and Development at the requests of the governments of Nigeria and the United Kingdom. Lagos, Government Printer.
Population Census of the Northern Region of Nigeria, 1952
    1952–53   Lagos, Department of Statistics
Rowling, R. J.
    1946   Report on land tenure: Plateau Province. DCJ 1403. Kaduna, Government Printer

INDEX

Administration, urban, 40–49
African-European personal relations, 81–83
Alkali Courts, 43

Birom informant: ambitions of, 255; children of, 258, 261–62; education of, 254; employment history of, 252–55; extra-marital affairs of, 263–65; family background of, 252, 254; financial status of, 252, 263; language proficiency of, 254; marital history of, 257–60; modern elite orientation of, 253, 265; occupation of, 251; personal characteristics of, 253; politics, attitude toward, 252; polygyny, attitude toward, 257; property owned by, 263; religion of, 257; residence of, 262; social life of, 263, 266; social status of, 253; traditional orientation of, 253, 265, 267

Cassiterite mining, 32–35
Cities, tropical Africa: development of, 3–11
Columbite mining, 35

Efik informant: analysis of, 279–82; children of, 185–88; education, attitude toward, 186; employment difficulties of, 203–05; employment history of, 180–81; Europeans, attitude toward, 178, 195; family background of, 183; financial status of, 192, 199, 202, 203; intertribal relationships of, 190; marital history of, 184–85; modern elite orientation of, 178, 188–89, 190, 196, 197; occupational skills of, 193; native magic, attitude

toward, 198; personal characteristics of, 178; photograph collection of, 190; polygyny, attitude toward, 184, 189; religion of, 188, 197; repatriation to home village, 198, 201; residence of, 181; self-concept of, 179, 205; social aspirations of, 178, 182, 190, 192, 193; social life of, 191, 192; traditional orientation of, 178, 190–91, 198
Ethnic groups, 72–73, 292–94
Ethnic relations, 60–66, 269
Ethnic-religious affiliation, *table* 76
Ethnic representation in schools, *table* 78–79
European-African personal relations, 81–83

Field research methods: ego-oriented, 12–13, 16–17, 18–19, 20, 21–22; situational analysis (reference group theory), 10–12; sociological (statistical), 9–10, 17–18, 19, 20, 21; traditional village approach, 9

Hausa District Head, 44
Hausa informant: children of, 219; education of, 208, 209, 212; employment history of, 209–12; Europeans, attitude toward, 210–11; family background of, 208–09; financial status of, 208; kinship relations, 221; language proficiency of, 208; marital history of, 216–19; native magic, attitude toward, 215; political affiliation of, 221–22; polygyny, attitude toward, 219; religion of, 208, 213–15; repatriation to home village, 222; residence